MATRIX OF THE MIND

UFO ABDUCTIONS · MK-ULTRA
And Electronic Harassment Technology
Designed to Warp Your Brain

GLOBAL COMMUNICATIONS
EX LIBRIS

POST OFFICE BOX 753
NEW BRUNSWICK, NJ 08903

MATRIX OF THE MIND—UFO ABDUCTIONS · MK-ULTRA
And Electronic Harassment Technology
Designed to Warp Your Brain

Compiled by Commander X
and the Committee Of Twelve To Save The Earth

Additional Material Provided by Scott Corrales
The Journal of Hispanic UFOlogy
www.Inexplicata.blogspot.com

Additional Material Provided by Sean Casteel
www.seancasteel.com

Additional Material Provided by Tim R. Swartz

Revised Edition

ISBN 1606111361
EAN 9781606111369

Published by Timothy Green Beckley
Box 753 · New Brunswick, NJ 08903
Printed in the United States of America

Staff Members
Timothy G. Beckley, Publisher
Carol Ann Rodriguez, Assistant to the Publisher
Sean Casteel, Associate Editor
Tim R. Swartz, Editorial Consultant
William Kern, Layout, Typesetting and Art Consultant

Disclaimer:

The publication of any and all content, e.g., articles, reports, editorials, commentary, opinions, as well as graphics and or images in this publication does not constitute sanction or acquiescence of said content; it is solely for informational purposes. This publication may contain material of use of which may not be authorized by the U.S. government. We are making such material available in our efforts to advance understanding of environmental, political, human rights, economic, democratic, scientific, social justice, and religious issues, etc. We believe this constitutes a 'fair use' of any such material. The material in this publication is distributed to those who have expressed an interest in receiving the included information for research and educational purposes.

FREE MIND CONTROL DVD —

DEAR READER:

**This book comes with a bonus DVD on Mind Control.
To obtain your free copy simply send an e mail or write and mention
the title, where you purchased the book and give code 84.**

Respond to:

mrufo8@hotmail.com

**or write. . .
Tim Beckley/Conspiracy Journal
Box 753 · Dept 84
New Brunswick, NJ 08903**

**Sign up for a free copy of the Conspiracy Journal at
www.ConspiracyJournal.Com**

GLOBAL COMMUNICATIONS

EX LIBRIS

POST OFFICE BOX 753
NEW BRUNSWICK, NJ 08903

CONTENTS

MATRIX OF THE MIND

THERE IS MUCH TO FEAR! – ARE WE IN THE GRIP OF EARTHLY AND OTHERWORLDLY MIND CONTROLLERS?

By Timothy Green Beckley

If you are a whistleblower, an intelligence operative or more or less just an ordinary American citizen, you had better look behind your back because someone is probably "escorting" you about, trying to invade your mind and control your thoughts. What is their purpose? Well, it's an individuated scenario you will have to decide about for yourself.

Over the years, I have heard some pretty incredible stories about mind control. Hey, everyone knows that I was a pretty good friend of Candy Jones, the model and talk show hostess who says she was an unwilling carrier of classified information and a conduit for the CIA.

As a runway model, she traveled the globe and could inconspicuously gain entrance to places most members of the intelligence community could not. Briton Colin Bennett explained Candy's background this way in an article for the UK's *"Fortean Times"*:

"Candy, as Arlene (one of her multiple personalities), was sent to Taiwan at least twice on test missions, delivering envelopes. There, she was tortured with electric prods to see if she would crack; she did not. Deeply perverted sexuality appears to have been an implicit element in the covert agenda. In episodes which are disturbing to read, she was frequently stripped, put to bed, drugged, hypnotized and tortured by various parties, including Americans on American soil. She was put onto medical examination tables,

MATRIX OF THE MIND

suffered Gestapo-like interrogations, and was sexually toyed with by women against her will. Sexual approaches were made under hypnosis by (a doctor) Jensen, but Candy appears to have fought him off."

Being a part of the UFO community, I have also heard my share of "alien" encounter stories which include the ability of the Ultra-terrestrials to mesmerize earthlings; to cloud their perception; to put thoughts into the earthlings' heads; and to make them believe and imagine things that might just be a nightmarish "fantasy."

And we have to worry about electronic harassment of all sorts. Is someone watching us through our TV set? Is our phone bugged 24/7? Is that a mental stun gun in your pocket or have you just missed me? How about the unmarked black helicopter or the satellite that passes over at the same time twice a day?

Commander X knows a lot about mind control. He says he was a part of various programs that used a variety of brain-busting techniques. He even had his henchmen – the Committee of 12 – go through the patent files to see what mind control devices have actually been legitimately registered with the Patent Office. But think of how many have not!

Sean Casteel, a prolific writer and researcher of the paranormal, did a bit of fact checking on his own and found out that some UFO percipients might have been "used" by a strange, clandestine group known as MK Ultra. . .perhaps with the unearthly assistance of a group of ETs most commonly known as the Greys.

It's all too spooky!

All too strange to entertain!

But yet we must, as there is now ample evidence that we are the pawns in someone else's global – possibly cosmic – chess game.

So be alert. Be vigilant. And, above all else, lock the door, pull down the blinds and turn down the night light as you crack open the pages of "Matrix of the Mind."

Tim Beckley, Publisher
mrufo8@hotmail.com
Free weekly newsletter
www.ConspiracyJournal.Com

MATRIX OF THE MIND

THE DISTURBING WORLD OF ALIEN ABDUCTIONS
AND MIND CONTROL

By Sean Casteel

There are a few alternative explanations for the alien abduction phenomenon, the most prevalent being that the experience does not involve actual aliens at all but is instead a complex, human-driven tool used for purposes of mind control. It is said that the alien abduction approach is actually a cover story intended to conceal something even more disturbing than aliens, that being an encroachment on the very souls of those chosen to be victims of government and military experiments that seek to control the workings of the human brain itself for purposes of psychological warfare and for intelligence operations requiring a "zombie" type agent who has no idea he is carrying out a covert mission at all.

This idea is not exactly new. It entered into the pop culture zeitgeist as early as the 1962 thriller "The Manchurian Candidate," in which a team of soldiers fighting the Korean War are brainwashed by their Chinese captors into various heinous acts, with one victim in particular charged to assassinate a candidate for president. The assassin is merely responding to post-hypnotic suggestion as he goes through the motions of his role in some dark political intrigue indeed.

Things Get Scary In "Nightmare Alley"

Global Communications, the publisher of the book you are now reading, has also published other treatments of this subject. For example, the book *"Nightmare Alley: Fearsome Tales Of Alien Abduction"* begins with capsule histories of some of the better-known abduction cases, such as the 1961 Betty and Barney Hill encounter that became a kind of template for the thousands of cases that came later. The cases in the book were compiled by Beckley, his editorial and art consultant William Kern, and B.J. Booth, a researcher known for his website www.ufocasebook.com. The team has gathered cases that stretch from the Hills to Betty Andreasson Luca on to the 2004 Francis Family abduction and the Clayton and Donna Lee event of 2005. As an easily digestible overview of the abduction phenomenon, it has few peers in the field.

But in the later sections of the book, the alien factor is moved to a backburner and the all-too-human quest for control of the individual's mind is given an excellent schol-

MATRIX OF THE MIND

Shot in his "sporting days," publisher Tim ("Mr UFO") Beckley poses with UFO abductee Betty Hill and her personal unearthly "Intruder."

arly and detailed treatment by researcher and writer Martin Cannon. Cannon begins by attempting to shine a light on what alien abduction is said to be.

"Among ufologists," Cannon writes, "the term 'abduction' has come to refer to an infinitely confounding experience, or matrix of experiences, shared by a dizzying number of individuals, who claim that travelers from the stars have scooped them out of their beds, or snatched them from their cars, and subjected them to interrogations, quasi-medical examinations, and 'instruction' periods."

He goes on to say that these sessions are said to occur within alien spacecraft and include terrifying details "reminiscent of the tortures inflicted in Germany's death camps."

The abductees often, though not always, lose all memory of these events, and find themselves back in their beds or cars unable to account for "missing time." Hypnosis or some other trigger can bring back these "haunted hours" in an explosion of recollection, and the abductee often begins to recall a history of similar experiences stretching all the way back to childhood. Cannon also expresses amazement that abductees, in spite of their vividly-recalled agonies, claim to "love" their alien tormentors.

MATRIX OF THE MIND

What's Really Happening In An Abduction

Cannon quickly shifts gears and begins to offer his own theories about the abduction phenomenon.

"I posit that the abductees have been abducted," he writes. "Yet they are also spewing fantasy – or, more precisely, they have been given a set of lies to repeat and believe. If my hypothesis proves true, then we must accept the following: The kidnapping is real. The fear is real. The pain is real. The instruction is real. But the little grey men from Zeti Reticuli are not real; they are constructs, Halloween masks meant to disguise the real faces of the controllers. The abductors may not be visitors from Beyond; rather, they may be a symptom of the carcinoma which blackens our body politic. The fault lies not in our stars, but in ourselves."

There is substantial evidence, according to Cannon, that links members of this country's intelligence community, to include the CIA, the Defense Advanced Research Projects Agency and the Office of Naval Intelligence, with "the esoteric technology of mind control."

"For decades," Cannon continues, "'spy-chiatrists' working mostly behind the scenes – on college campuses, in CIA-sponsored institutes, and (most heinously) in prisons – have experimented with erasure of memory, hypnotic resistance to torture, truth serums, post-hypnotic suggestion, rapid induction of hypnosis, electronic stimulation of the brain, non-iodizing radiation, microwave induction of intra-cerebral 'voices,' and a host of even more disturbing technologies. Some of the projects exploring these areas were ARTICHOKE, BLUEBIRD, PANDORA, MKDELTA, MKSEARCH and the infamous MKULTRA."

Cannon said his research includes reading nearly every available book on the subject, as well as all the relevant congressional testimony, plus spending much time in university libraries reading relevant articles. He also conducted numerous interviews, and was allowed to see the files of John Marks, the author of "The Search For 'The Manchurian Candidate,'" which included some 20,000 pages of CIA and Defense Department documents, interviews, scientific articles, letters, etc.

Cannon has certainly done his homework, which leads him to conclude that striking advances have been made in the field of brainwashing despite false and perjured claims made before Congress that these efforts had met with little success and had been discontinued. He also restates his belief that UFO abduction may be a continuation of clandestine mind control operations.

The Actual Devices Of Mind Control

The next section of Cannon's report is a fascinating overview of the known technology so far and introduces the reader to the term "wavies," or people who claim to be victims of clandestine bombardment with non-ionizing radiation, or microwaves.

"They report sudden changes in psychological states, alteration of sleep patterns, intra-cerebral voices and other sounds, and physiological effects. Are these troubled

5

MATRIX OF THE MIND

individuals seeking an exterior rationale for their mental problems? Maybe. Indeed, I'm sure that such is the case in many instances. But the fact is that the literature on the behavioral effects of microwaves, extra-low-frequencies and ultra-sonics is such that we cannot blithely dismiss all such claims."

When did this research really begin? Cannon says that in the early years of the 20ᵗʰ century, Nikola Tesla seems to have stumbled upon certain of the behavioral effects of electromagnetic exposure, and Cannon also cites a report from the 1930s in which two scientists claimed to be able to electrically stimulate the human nervous system by remote control. Meanwhile, who knows what has been achieved over the last few decades or what is the current state-of-the-art in mind control technology?

Cannon returns to his basic thesis, writing, "The abduction enigma contains within it sub-mysteries that slide into the mind control scenario with surprising ease, even elegance. As we have seen, the MKULTRA thesis explains the reports of abductee intra-cerebral implants (particularly reports involving nosebleeds), unusual scars, 'telepathic' communication (i.e., externally induced intra-cerebral voices) concurrent with or following the abduction, allegations that some abductees hear unusual sound effects, haywire electronic devices in abductee homes, personality shifts, 'training films,' manipulation of religious imagery, and missing time. Needless to say, the thesis of clandestine government experimentation readily accounts for abductee claims of human beings 'working' with the aliens, and for the government harassment that plays so prominent a role in certain abductee reports."

Laurence Harvey co-starred with Frank Sinatra in The Manchurian Candidate, a dark thriller about the danger of extreme politics. A troop of American soldiers return from the Korean war to find they have been subjected to a bizarre and violent brainwashing plot.

MATRIX OF THE MIND

The Mind Stalkers Come To Call

Another book from Global Communications, *"Mind Stalkers: Mind Control Of The Masses,"* covers some similar ground. The authors, Commander X and Tim R. Swartz, also offer some interesting history of what is known about mind control technology as well as some scientific background on how the various devices actually work. Chapters on secret experiments with drugs, subliminal seduction, electronics, microwaves, implants and "mind machines" in general are stuffed with frightening information on the potential enslavement of the human mind to those who can covertly manipulate it. The drive to create a "super soldier" quickly devolves into the search for an iron grip on mass consciousness that has been sought by every totalitarian leader throughout human history, only now such a nightmarish possibility may be terrifyingly within reach, with the mere flick of an "on switch."

Swartz and Commander X also tackle the thorny subject of human mind control as the true origin of UFO abduction.

"UFO literature is filled with hundreds of cases," the two authors write, "in which observers have been subjected to continuous harassments following an encounter with a UFO. Some witnesses report strange, ghost-like phenomena in their homes. In other cases, weird, mechanical-sounding voices, purported to be 'messages' from extraterrestrials, begin emanating from their phones, radios and televisions."

The authors point out that scant research has been done into this view of the phenomenon, and investigators are loathe to touch the subject, believing that the witnesses who complain of such harassment are most likely mentally ill. It is a kind of Catch-22 that victims must suffer through: after a prolonged period of skilled mismanagement of their brains, they are hardly credible witnesses who can coherently PROVE their stories. But the authors say that cases of UFO mind control are almost always identical.

"The eyewitness goes through a period of anxiety," the authors explain, "during which he is unable to consciously remember certain aspects of the incident. Within months, the personality of the observer actually changes. Eventually, it may change to the point where he finds it impossible to get along with coworkers, friends or even family. Personal tragedy seems to strike many of those who have had UFO experiences."

The person may also develop certain "gifts" or abilities, such as powers of ESP, precognition or psycho-kinesis, as well as a heightened intelligence level or an unusual increase in physical strength. These abilities may manifest themselves shortly before a person is about to be controlled. Soon he may begin slipping into a kind of trance, and it will appear an alien intelligence has taken over his body and is using his brain.

Human Military Abductors

But nevertheless, we could still be dealing with human "controllers," the authors insist, as they cite the research of Dr. Helmut Lammer, who recounts the stories of how some UFO abductees have been kidnapped by military personnel and taken to hospitals and/or military facilities, some of which are described as being underground.

MATRIX OF THE MIND

"Especially disconcerting is the fact that abductees recall seeing military intelligence personnel together with alien beings," Commander X and Swartz write, "working side by side in these secret facilities. Researchers in the field of mind control suggest that these cases are evidence that the whole UFO abduction phenomenon is staged by the intelligence community as a cover for their illegal experiments."

The authors go on to say that Lammer's research suggests that abductees are often harassed by dark, unmarked helicopters that fly around their houses. The mysterious helicopter activity goes back to the late 1960s and early 1970s, when they showed an apparent interest in animal mutilations, but not, at the time, in alleged UFO abductees. Still, UFO researcher Raymond Fowler reported some helicopter activity in connection with UFO witnesses during the 1970s, so the phenomenon is not without an earlier precedent.

(Meanwhile, the idea that the black helicopters are sent to "spy" on UFO witnesses is called absurd by Martin Cannon, who says if the military were seeking information on abductees they would certainly go about it in a much more subtle manner. The late abduction researcher Budd Hopkins once similarly stated that if the intelligence community wanted to spy on abductees, they could probably stand two blocks away and "point a cufflink" at their intended targets, so far advanced was their espionage technology likely to be. In any case, the true mission of the black helicopters remains unknown.)

Abductee Debbie Jordan reported in her book "Abducted!" that she was at one point kidnapped, drugged and taken to a kind of military hospital where she was examined by a medical doctor. This doctor told her he was going to remove a "bug" from her ear and proceeded to take out an implant that resembled a BB. Also, some of author Katharina Wilson's experiences are reminiscent of reported mind control experiments. She writes of a flashback from her childhood in which she remembers being forced into what appeared to be a Skinner Box that may have been used for behavior modification purposes. In some military abduction cases, military doctors searched for implants and sometimes even implanted the abductee with what may have been a manmade implant.

"Mind Stalkers" also includes an "Index Of Secret Mind Control Projects" that provides a quick rundown of the often confusing military codenames and the "alphabet soup" by which some of the various programs came to be called.

The Story Of One Who's Been There

Some victims of the abduction/mind control process have come forward to tell their stories, and one must admire their courage in doing so.

Christa Tilton, for example, is well-known in the field of ufology for her brave decision to go public with an abduction story involving human participants.

In an article by Tilton called *"Going Underground,"* she relates an experience she had in July of 1987.

"I had about three hours of 'missing time,'" Tilton writes, "in which later, under hypnosis, I relived the most unusual night of my life. I did not go willingly to the craft.

MATRIX OF THE MIND

Two small aliens dragged me by my two arms on my back to the craft after they rendered me unconscious. The next thing I remember is waking up on a table inside some small type of craft. A 'guide' greeted me and gave me something to drink. I now believe it was a stimulant of some kind because I was not sleepy after I drank the substance."

Tilton was next taken out of the craft and found herself on top of a hill. When she was next directed to enter a lighted cavern door, she saw a man, a human, wearing a red jumpsuit like a pilot would wear. The alien leading Tilton and the man greeted one another, and she noticed the man was carrying an automatic weapon. Tilton realized that the cavern door had led them to walk right into the side of a large hill or mountain.

"I asked my guide," Tilton writes, "where we were going and why. He didn't say too much the whole time, except that he was to show me some things that I would need to know for future reference. He told me that we had just entered Level One of the 'facility.' I asked what kind of facility it was and he did not answer."

One Level Two, Tilton saw yet more human guards in colored jumpsuits who seemed oblivious to Tilton's presence, as though it were a common occurrence for her to be there. She also saw multiple offices and cubicles with human employees hard at work. There were grey aliens there as well, who seemed to be doing the menial jobs and also took no notice of Tilton.

What Happened On Level Five?

She was taken down to Level Five, where the human guards were a little less friendly and were apparently arguing amongst themselves as they stared at her. Tilton could think only of escape, but she had come so far underground that she knew escape would be impossible. Tilton was taken to a large laboratory where she saw a human man dressed like a doctor in a white lab coat. The human called in a grey alien for assistance and Tilton was startled to see the alien glaring into her face with large black eyes as some kind of internal medical procedure was carried out. After the procedure was over, she was told to put her clothes back on; her guide told her that the operation had been "necessary" and that she should forget all about it.

She asked her guide again to explain what this facility was all about.

"He told me it was a very sensitive place," she writes, "and I would be brought back again in the next few years. I again asked where I was and he told me I could not be told for my own safety."

Tilton was escorted back to the elevator up through the various levels of the "facility," then to the waiting alien craft, and returned to her home some three hours after her abduction experience had begun. She has provided us with one the most believable, coherent stories of aliens and humans working side by side in all of the abduction literature, but she is not alone in that regard.

"It Doesn't Happen"

In an online posting called "The UFO Trail," former self-described alien abductee Leah Haley has "revised her perspectives about her experiences of high-strangeness to conclude that no alien abductions ever took place in her life. She now completely attributes her remarkable perceptions to having been an involuntary research subject. Commenting on literal alien abduction, Haley stated, 'It doesn't happen.'"

Haley changed her opinion after years of investigation. She had long acknowledged that military personnel were involved in her experiences to some extent, but she fully reevaluated her understanding of what had happened to her after viewing select Freedom of Information Act and U.S. Patent Office documents. She also based her later conclusions on hundreds of interactions with researchers and fellow abductees. She is now thoroughly convinced that mind control experiments are responsible for what became known as the alien abduction phenomenon.

"I can really explain every alien abduction away using human technology," Haley said.

As to her opinion on what she called "legitimate" reports of abduction, she said, "I don't know for sure, but every case that I know very, very well – every single one of them – if I probe deeply enough, I'm going to find that there were humans here and there too. That tells me it was a human-instigated situation. I can't think of a single case, not a single one that I've really delved into, that didn't have humans in it, too, so I just don't think alien abductions are happening."

Offered As Evidence

Haley cited circumstances, the article continues, such as confirmed mind control operations and FOIA documents that substantiated details of black budget operations, as supporting evidence for her contention. She also felt that the public lacked an adequate understanding of relevant issues like conditioned behavior and subliminal programming and that abductees too often take what happened to them at face value.

She pointed to U.S. Patent Office documents that demonstrate that the evolution of electronic technology and non-lethal weapons closely parallels the timeline of alien abduction. Advances in technology during the 20th century included using electromagnetic frequencies to remotely entrain brain waves, induce altered states of consciousness and transfer an otherwise inaudible voice directly into the brain. Overexposure to electromagnetic frequencies has been documented to cause hallucinations, nausea, short-term amnesia (missing time) and reddened skin, circumstances which became staples of abductee testimonies.

Haley said that she has shared the story of her recanting of the idea of alien abduction in favor of a human mind control scenario out of compassion and a sense of responsibility.

"It disturbs me greatly," she said, "that there are people who are still being victimized by that system. I want mind control and other invasive experiments on unwitting U.S. citizens to be stopped. And I want the mind control perpetrators brought to justice!"

MATRIX OF THE MIND

Nikola Tesla holding in his hands balls of flame

Is it possible that electrical wizard Nikola Tesla stumbled upon the behavioral effects of electromagnetic exposure sometime in the early 20th Century?

MATRIX OF THE MIND

MATRIX OF THE MIND

MENTAL ARMAGEDDON: The Quest For Mind Control

Tim Swartz

*"The dream of every leader, whether a tyrannical despot or a
benign prophet, is to regulate the behavior of his people."*

Colin Blakemore

Candy Jones
aka Arlene Grant

Candy Jones was a woman who seemed to have it all. She was a successful model who owned her own modeling agency. She was a popular author who wrote such books as: *"Make Your Name in Modeling and Television"* and *"Candy Jones' Complete Book of Beauty and Fashion."* She was married to Long John Nebel, the country's most listened to late-night talk show host, who broadcast on New York radio station WOR. However, it soon became apparent to her new husband that Candy's world was far more complex than even she could ever imagine.

Nebel noticed that Candy was prone to insomnia and abrupt changes in her normally "congenial disposition." He offered to hypnotize her in hopes of helping her sleep. Candy had told Nebel that years before she had been approached by the FBI and asked if she would allow them to use her office as a mail drop. She had said yes and also agreed to deliver mail for the FBI when traveling on business because she thought it was her patriotic duty. She had no idea what she was getting into.

Nebel found that his wife easily fell into a hypnotic trance and began speaking in another voice that identified herself as Arlene Grant. This second personality revealed that Jones had once delivered a package for the FBI to Oakland, California, to a doctor she knew from her USO days. The doctor, known by the pseudonym of "Gilbert Jensen,"

MATRIX OF THE MIND

offered her money to allow him to hypnotize her, and she accepted since she was divorced and in need of money. Afterwards, Jensen told Jones that the hypnosis did not work, but the Arlene personality told Nebel that it had.

Under hypnosis, Jensen told Candy that she was to be a messenger for the CIA in a secret unit whose employees were not listed in headquarters' records. Jensen said she needed a passport under an assumed name, as she would sometimes have to travel abroad. The name she chose was Arlene Grant. In order to serve she needed to be in top health, and was given injections of vitamins. But rather than vitamins, Jones was given drugs designed to bring out and reinforce the Arlene personality.

When she assumed the Arlene identity, Jones would alter her dress, her walk, her tone, and even took to wearing a dark wig. Arlene was supposedly sent to training camps where she was trained to kill with her bare hands, a hat pin, or anything else that was handy. She was trained with poison lipstick, hiding code numbers under her fingernail polish.

The Arlene personality could be triggered by a telephone call with particular sounds, and after the mission was completed, the normal personality remembered nothing. These missions were elaborate, and frequently involved world travel to deliver messages. Jones was once even subjected to torture at a seminar at CIA headquarters, as a means of demonstrating the psychiatrist's control over his subjects.

Candy Jones' story sounds like the wild fabrications of a deranged mind. However, there is some evidence for this bizarre tale outside of her hypnotic regression. Candy told Joe Vergara, her editor at Harper and Row, that she sometimes worked for a government agency as a courier and might disappear occasionally. There was also a letter she wrote to her attorney, William Williams, to cover herself in case she died or disappeared suddenly or under unusual circumstances; she told him she was not at liberty to reveal exactly what she was involved in. Also, a passport was discovered among Jones possessions that had been issued under the name of Arlene Grant. The photo showed Jones wearing a dark wig. Freedom of Information Act requests have also revealed that the CIA does have a substantial file on Jones, but refuses to release any part of it.

Other cases with similarities to the Candy Jones story have been reported. The disturbing question is how many other innocent victims of hypnotic manipulation are unknowingly being used to further someone else's secret agenda?

The recordings of the Jones hypnotic sessions were published in a book, ***The Control of Candy Jones***, by researcher Donald Bain. In 1974, when Bain's book was published, tales of CIA mind control and brainwashing were considered to be merely fiction. However, since then, new revelations on mind control experiments have been uncovered showing that not only the CIA but intelligence agencies all over the world have been actively pursuing mind control programs and the ultimate control of the human mind.

MATRIX OF THE MIND

Cleansing of the Mind

Most of human history has been a series of efforts by some people to control what other people think. The notion that the human mind could be influenced by an outside source was popularized by Edward Hunter in his 1951 book: ***Brainwashing in Red China***. During the Korean War, American prisoners renounced their citizenship in radio broadcasts and many signed confessions against American interests, including charges, still debated today, that the United States was engaged in germ warfare with anthrax. For Americans to abandon their ideals the Communists must have devised some nefarious new means of thought control – or so it was thought.

Hunter suggested that a new process of indoctrination had been developed by the Chinese communists, and that "they had discovered an intense manipulative process that had insidious power to actually alter the mental outlook of those who fell victim to it."

Brainwashing was Hunter's version for a Chinese term "hsi-nao," loosely translated as "cleansing of the mind." Hunter wrote: "It is practically impossible to fight something until it has been given a name," saying that brainwashing had a more "flesh-and-blood" quality than a more clinical alternative, "menticide," which means murder of the mind.

At the end of the war it was determined that some of the primary methods used on American prisoners included sleep deprivation and other intense psychological manipulations designed to break down the autonomy of individuals. Even though the use of brainwashing on prisoners produced some propaganda benefits, its main use to the Chinese lay in the fact that it significantly increased the maximum number of prisoners that one guard could control, thus freeing other Chinese soldiers to go to the battlefield.

Careful investigation has uncovered evidence that modern research and experiments in the field of mind control go back as far (and probably farther) as World War II. Shortly after the attack on Pearl Harbor, George Estabrooks, chairman of the Department of Psychology at Colgate University, was called to Washington by the War Department. As one of the leading authorities on hypnosis, Estabrooks was asked to evaluate how it might be used by the enemy.

In his opinion, one in five adult humans is capable of being placed in a trance so deep that they will have no memory of it They could be hypnotized secretly by using a disguised technique and given a post-hypnotic suggestion. Estabrooks suggested that a dual personality could be created using hypnosis, thereby creating the perfect double agent with an unshakable cover.

In the April 1971 issue of ***Science Digest***, Estabrooks detailed how he "programmed" American spies with hypnosis. "One of the most fascinating but dangerous applications of hypnosis is its use in military intelligence. This is a field with which I am familiar through formulating guidelines for the techniques used by the United States in two world wars."

During World War II, Estabrooks hypnotized a Marine lieutenant named Jones and spilt his personality into Jones A and Jones B. Jones A, once a "normal" working Marine, became entirely different. He talked communist doctrine and meant it. He was welcomed enthusiastically by communist cells, was deliberately given a dishonorable discharge by the Corps (which was in on the plot) and became a card-carrying party member.

However, Jones B, while under hypnosis, had been carefully coached by suggestion. Jones B was the deeper personality and knew all the thoughts of Jones A. Jones B was a loyal American, and was imprinted to say nothing during conscious phases. All Estabrooks had to do was hypnotize the whole man, get in touch with Jones B, the loyal American, and there was a pipeline straight into the Communist camp.

The technique worked beautifully, according to Estabrooks. However, the method for using dual personalities was also being used by other countries, and several agents used by the Soviet Union were caught trying to infiltrate into the United States. This amazing admission by Estabrooks on the use of hypnosis to create the perfect spy or soldier shows that the human mind can be easily harnessed for the purpose of others. It is hard to believe that even more sophisticated techniques for hypnotic mind control have not been perfected in the years since those early experiments.

MKULTRA

In 1977, a Senate subcommittee on Health and Scientific Research, chaired by Senator Ted Kennedy, focused on the CIA's secret testing of LSD on unwitting citizens. Only a mere handful of people within the CIA knew about the scope and details of the program. Through the testimony of a Dr. Sidney Gottlieb, the Kennedy subcommittee learned about the CIA's top secret Operation MKULTRA. The purpose of the program, according to his testimony, was to "investigate whether and how it was possible to modify an individual's behavior by covert means."

Claiming the protection of the National Security Act, Dr. Gottlieb was unwilling to tell the Senate subcommittee what had been learned by these experiments. He did state, however, that the program was initially started by a concern that the Soviets and other enemies of the United States would get ahead of the U.S. in this field. Through the Freedom of Information Act, researchers were able to obtain documents detailing the MKULTRA program and other CIA behavior modification projects.

In 1953, CIA director Allen Dulles, speaking before a national meeting of Princeton alumni, distinguished two fronts in the then-current "battle for men's minds": a "first front" of mass indoctrination through censorship and propaganda, and a "second front" of individual "brainwashing" and "brain changing." The same year, at CIA deputy director Richard Helm's suggestion, Dulles approved the MKULTRA project, and exempted it from normal CIA financial controls in order to hide it from the normal congressional checks and balances.

MKULTRA had grown out of an earlier secret program known as Bluebird that had been created to counter Soviet advances in brainwashing. In reality, the CIA had other objectives. An earlier aim was to study methods in which control of an individual could

MATRIX OF THE MIND

be attained. The CIA was also interested in being able to manipulate foreign leaders with such techniques. The emphasis of experimentation was "narco-hypnosis," the blending of mind altering drugs with careful hypnotic programming.

Eventually project Bluebird was later renamed Project Artichoke. Artichoke was an offensive program of mind control that gathered together the intelligence divisions of the Army, Navy, Air Force and FBI. The scope of the project was outlined in a memorandum dated January, 1952, that asked: "Can we get control of an individual to the point where he will do our bidding against his will and even against fundamental laws of nature such as self preservation?"

Candy Jones then and now

A special CIA team was formed and their task was to test the new interrogation techniques and ensure that victims would not remember being interrogated and programmed. All manner of narcotics, from marijuana to LSD, heroin and sodium pentathol were regularly used.

When it was formed in 1947, the CIA was forbidden to have any domestic police or internal security powers and was authorized only to operate overseas. Nevertheless, from the very beginning, MKULTRA staff broke this Congressional rule and began testing on unsuspecting U.S. citizens.

Reviewing the experiments in 1958, one CIA auditor wrote: "Precautions must be taken not only to protect operations from exposure to enemy forces but also to conceal these activities from the American public in general. The knowledge that the agency is engaging in unethical and illicit activities would have serious repercussions in political and diplomatic circles."

Precisely how extensive illegal testing became will never be known. Shortly before leaving office in 1973, CIA Director and chief architect of the program Richard Helms ordered the destruction of all MKULTRA records. Despite these precautions some documents were misfiled and came to light in the late 1970s.

The most notorious MKULTRA experiments were the CIA's pioneering studies of the drug lysergic acid diethylamide, or LSD. The CIA was intrigued by LSD, and had hopes that it, or a similar drug, could be used to clandestinely disorient and manipulate targeted foreign leaders.

One secret drug project that took place in the early 1960s was run by Dr. Harris Isabel, Director of the Public Service Hospital in Lexington, Kentucky - a facility specializing in drug abuse. Under funding by the CIA, Dr. Isabel began experimenting on African-American inmates by feeding his subjects large doses of LSD, mescaline, marijuana, scopolamine and other substances on a daily basis. Brought before the Senate subcommittees in 1975, Isabel saw no contradiction in providing hard drugs to the very addicts

MATRIX OF THE MIND

he was employed to cure.

Word got out that the CIA had been using innocent citizens to test their drugs and, in order to avoid further bad publicity, the CIA announced it had ceased its mind manipulation programs. However, scientists working for the agency secretly continued the experiments.

One researcher was Dr. Ewen Cameron, working at McGill University in Montreal. Dr. Cameron used a variety of experimental techniques, including using drugs to keep subjects unconscious for months at a time, administering huge electroshocks and continual doses of LSD. Many of the subjects who suffered trauma had never agreed to participate in the experiments.

It has been reported that enough LSD was manufactured during this period to dose every citizen in the United States at least a dozen times. No one knows for sure if all the LSD was used strictly for experiments or if it was also used on so-called social troublemakers and other political dissidents. It has been alleged that LSD and other drugs were secretly released into the general community by the CIA in the 1960s to destabilize the growing anti-war movement on college campuses.

Under scrutiny, the agency was quick to downplay the success of MKULTRA - claiming no real advances were achieved. Miles Copeland, a long-serving CIA officer disputed this. Speaking to a reporter, Copeland revealed that "the congressional subcommittee which went into this sort of thing only got the barest glimpse." Another source within the intelligence community says that after 1963, CIA efforts increasingly focused on electronic methods of mind control as drug research had come to a dead end.

ELECTRONIC CONTROL

"We need a program of psychosurgery and political control of our society. The purpose is physical control of the mind. Everyone who deviates from the given norm can be surgically mutilated. Man does not have the right to develop his own mind. This kind of liberal orientation has great appeal. We must electrically control the brain. Some day armies and generals will be controlled by electrical stimulation of the brain."

Dr. Jose Delgado - MKULTRA Researcher

Doctors have long recognized that the human brain can be influenced by a myriad of outside influences. Yet few people realize that the brain can be manipulated by such things as bright, flashing lights, implants, microwaves and other "beamed" electronic sources. Because of this evidence, the stereotypical image of the mentally ill person who complains that the government is beaming messages into their brain might not be so far-fetched after all.

There were three scientists who pioneered the work of using an electromagnetic field to control human behavior. The three were Dr. Jose Delgado, psychology professor at Yale University. Dr. W. Ross Adey, a physiologist at the Brain Research Institute at UCLA, and Dr. Wilder Penfield, a Canadian.

Dr. Jose Delgado was a pioneer of the technology of Electrical Stimulation of the

18

MATRIX OF THE MIND

Brain (ESB). While giving a lecture on the brain in 1965, Dr. Delgado said, "Science has developed a new methodology for the study and control of cerebral function in animals and humans." Dr. Delgado was able to achieve a type of mind control with the assistance of a device he named a "stimoceiver," a miniature electrode capable of receiving and transmitting electronic signals by FM radio that could be placed within an individual's cranium. Once in place, an outside operator could manipulate the subject's responses. This electronic apparatus was the forerunner of the more sophisticated computerized devices that are used today.

Delgado demonstrated the potential of his stimoceivers by wiring a fully-grown bull. With the device in place, Delgado stepped into the ring with the bull. The animal charged towards the experimenter – and then suddenly stopped, just before it reached him. The powerful beast had been stopped with the simple action of pushing a button on a small box held in Delgado's hand.

In 1966, Delgado asserted that his experiments "support the distasteful conclusion that motion, emotion and behavior can be directed by electrical forces and that humans can be controlled like robots by push buttons."

The records on MKULTRA subproject 94, dated November 22, 1961, echo Delgado's statements: "Miniaturized stimulating electrode implants in specific brain center areas will be utilized. The feasibility of remote control of activities in several species of animals has been demonstrated. The present investigations are directed toward improvement of techniques and will provide precise mapping of the useful brain centers. The ultimate objective of this research is to provide an understanding of the mechanisms involved in the directional control of animals and to provide practical systems suitable for human application."

Following the successes of Delgado's work, the CIA set up their own research program in the field of electromagnetic behavior modification under the code name "Sleeping Beauty." With the guidance of Dr. Ivor Browning, a laboratory was set up in New Mexico, specializing in working with the hypothalamus or "sweet spot" of the brain. Here it was found that stimulating this area could produce intense euphoria in the human brain.

Since that time a number of people have come forward claiming that they are the victims of electronic mind control experiments; people such as Robert Naeslund, who says that during an operation in 1967, the Swedish Security Police implanted a radio-transmitter/receiver into the frontal lobe of his brain. What makes Naeslund's story stand out is his proof, which consists of a number of X-rays that clearly show the presence of "foreign objects" deep within his brain.

In his 198-page book *Cybergods*, Naeslund writes: "In Sweden, as far back as 1946, at Karolinska Hospital's general surgery, patients had their skull opened during operations without their knowledge to enable the implantation of electrodes in their brains. Thus could they be held hostage to a lifetime of brutal experimentation in which they were connected via radio frequencies to a central receiver which recorded their various cognitive processes and even neurological functions."

19

MATRIX OF THE MIND

Naeslund believes that he and other unwitting victims were implanted to test emerging mind control technology using two-way radio-communication or remote control. The implant, when placed in the brain, head or body, can then transmit a radio signal that connects the brain's neuro-activities to a computer that stores a person's physical and mental information within its database. Improvements in the implants could also allow for voice and other physical information, sensations, smells, tastes, to be broadcast directly into the brain.

VOICES IN YOUR HEAD

The use of electronic brain implants may now be a thing of the past as new technologies were developed that can allegedly influence the human brain by using electromagnetic frequencies alone. In 1961, Dr. Allen Frey, a freelance biophysicist and engineering psychologist, reported that a human can hear microwaves. Frey found that human subjects exposed to 1310 MHz and 2982 MHz microwaves perceived auditory sensations described as buzzing or knocking sounds (also described as clicks or chirps).

Two researchers by the names of Joseph Sharp and Mark Grove performed experiments in which audible voices were sent by microwaves directly to the brain. A recording of someone speaking the numbers one through ten was first used in the experiment. By radiating themselves with voice-modulated microwaves, Sharp and Grove were able to hear, identify, and distinguish the words. The sounds heard were similar to those emitted by persons with artificial larynxes.

In the mid-1970s, the United States was extremely interested in combining high-frequency radio waves with hypnosis. Plans were on file to develop these techniques through experiments on human volunteers. The spoken word of a hypnotist could be conveyed by modulated electromagnetic energy directly into the subconscious parts of the human brain. This could be done without the use of implants or allowing the victim to control the input of information consciously. However, it appears that the United States was not the only one interested in using electronics for mind control of the masses.

In September 1990, the **Washington Post** published an article dealing with the growing concern within the United States intelligence community over the Russians' progress in the development of long-range electronic mind control: "According to the communications of Russian defectors, the Russians have succeeded in influencing human behavior, changing human feelings and health conditions, incurring unconsciousness and even killing people."

One document from the Intelligence Service at the United States Department of Defense says that the Soviet experiments imposed on the recipient resulted in, "disquietude combined with short-windedness and the feeling of being hit on the head." Some Western observers of electronic extra-sensorial developments were alarmed by the possible effects of "subconscious influencing when used against the U.S. staff operating nuclear missiles."

In March, 1994, **The Village Voice** published an interview with Steve Killion, deputy chief of the FBI's technical services division. Killion claimed that in March, 1993, "Rus-

MATRIX OF THE MIND

sian scientists demonstrated to ten American military, intelligence and law-enforcement officials in Washington a device they claimed could subliminally implant thoughts in people's minds and thereby control their actions."

Killion stated that he was present at the demonstration and was shown how siege situations could be ended easily. "In the normal course of your negotiation with the individual by telephone you can impress a coded message," said Killion. "It is not realized consciously by the individual, but subconsciously, subliminally, they understand it."

Directed-energy weapons currently being deployed include, for example, a micro-wave weapon manufactured by Lockheed-Sanders and used for a process known as "Voice Synthesis," which is remote beaming of audio (i.e., voices or other audible signals) directly into the brain of any selected human target. Today, the ability to remotely transmit microwave voices into a target's head is known inside the Pentagon as "Synthetic Telepathy." According to Dr. Robert Becker, in his 1998 book *The Body Electric*, "Synthetic Telepathy has applications in covert operations designed to drive a target crazy with voices or deliver undetected instructions to a programmed assassin."

In 1996, the U.S. Air Force Scientific Advisory Board published a 14-volume study of future developments in weapons called "New World Vistas." Hidden away on page 89 of an ancillary 15th volume are some frightening insights into the future "coupling" of man and machine in a section dealing with "Biological Process Control." The author refers to an "explosion" of knowledge in the field of neuroscience, adding, ominously:

"One can envision the development of electromagnetic energy sources, the output of which can be pulsed, shaped, and focused, that can couple with the human body in a fashion that will allow one to prevent voluntary muscular movements, control emotions (and thus actions), produce sleep, transmit suggestions, interfere with both short-term and long-term memory, produce an experience set, and delete an experience set."

For what reason would any government, military or intelligence agency subject innocent people to clandestine mind control operations? If such a program is being conducted, then the overall cost must amount to billions of dollars yearly. For such a budget, the secret mind control operation must be extremely important to someone.

The quest for operational mind control has come a long way since the early days of Candy Jones and her handlers' attempts to create a dual-personality spy by using drugs and hypnosis. It is now probable that electronics, computers, microwaves and even, as some claim, satellites, are being used to control the minds of not just an experimental few, but possibly whole populations.

So the next time you read a rambling letter from someone claiming that the government is beaming "mind control" rays into their brains - you may want to reconsider making a snap judgment on the sanity of the unfortunate victim. After all, no one takes the time to research, design and develop a weapon, such as mind control machines, unless they intend to use it.

21

MATRIX OF THE MIND

MATRIX OF THE MIND

"Let me keep it simple. They don't have to come inside your house. The eavesdropper can simply use a gps tracking device to perform electronic harassment and view everything about your life while you are in your car, shopping, what restaurant you like to eat at, where ever you go; friends, family, it doesn't matter. It is all in full view for your enemies and their allies, complete with your telephone conversations. They have full view of the inside of your home or business office online and it doesn't matter if the lights are off or what room you are in. The cameras are infrared and/or xray so you literally have no place to hide, even—or especially—in your own home. There are a large number of gps devices, phone bugs, wireless cameras and other tracking devices, so don't waste your money on over-the-counter bugsweeps. They are a rip-off because most of them can't locate or identify the newer surveillance devices."

Former Intelligence Officer

THE HAZING OF STEVE LEE

By Sean Casteel

Colorado resident Steve Lee does a daily battle with extremely strange happenings around his house. Everything from laser-like shafts of light that shine through the walls and then tie themselves in knots to ghostly faces that peer back at him from his mirrors are part of everyday life for Lee and his family.

But unlike most people with similar stories to tell, Lee puts no stock in the notion that he's being visited by ghosts or aliens.

"I think this whole paranormal thing is just a front for what's going on," Lee said. "I'm just that kind of person. Maybe it's the way I was raised."

Lee has also taken hundreds of photographs of the "paranormal" events around his house, and even his own photographic evidence fails to convince him that something genuinely supernatural is going on.

"People say, 'How can you not believe in this stuff when you've got pictures of it?'" Lee said. "Well, I don't. I guess the way I see it—if you could photograph

MATRIX OF THE MIND

ghosts and aliens, then how come everybody else doesn't have these pictures? Why do just I have them? I think it's all a big hoax. But, it's not being hoaxed by me. I don't know who it is."

Lee said the whole eerie business began about five years ago when he and his wife and two children returned from a ten-day hunting trip. They discovered that their expensive log cabin in the exclusive Black Forest area outside Colorado Springs had been trifled with in their absence.

"When we came back," he said, "we noticed the furniture wasn't in the same place. The dishes and the carpets were different. So whatever was put in the house was done in those ten days."

But there was more amiss than just the household fixtures.

"We started seeing lights," he said, "laser light-looking beams. Then shortly after that, we started hearing voices in the house that shouldn't be there. During this time period, I was taking photos of the kids around the house—I take a lot of pictures—and things started showing up in them."

Lee's first reaction to the strange photos was to throw them away.

"I thought it was a problem with my camera or with the developing," he said. "Then I started getting clear images, like faces, in my pictures. And especially in the mirrors in the house. Even now, if you take pictures in my mirrors, you're definitely going to get some kind of face in there."

A couple of months after their return from the hunting trip, Lee and his family experienced the first of a long string of even weirder incidents.

"It was shortly after New Year's," Lee said. "I walked out onto the front porch to smoke a cigarette because I can't smoke in the house. I saw these three guys in snow-camouflage about fifty yards out in front of the house with rifles pointing at me. I went, 'What the hell?' So I went inside and got my rifle and I got my wife and she got the camera. I said, 'You see those guys?' She said 'Yeah.' I said 'You start taking pictures. I'm going to walk up to them.'

"So I started walking towards them," he continued, "looking through my scope. And I'm ready to shoot. I get fifteen feet from them and one of them says, 'Easy does it, buddy.' And bam, they just vanished. There was fresh snow on the

24

MATRIX OF THE MIND

ground, but there were no tracks or anything. But I did get pictures of them."

Another similar incident involving twelve disappearing soldiers happened a short time later. This time there were more witnesses than just Lee and his wife.

"I had some friends over one night," Lee said, "who worked at Martin-Marietta, the space engineers. They'd been trying to figure out what was really happening for a long time. So we were looking with infrared binoculars over towards a nearby house, and we started seeing these twelve guys in camouflage fatigues go into his damn doghouse! After about the third one, one guy said 'Hey, that many people can't fit in a doghouse.' So we walked right over to the fence. His doghouse was about ten feet on the other side of the fence.

"And these guys continued to walk in there," he went on, "and there's a guy on the outside guarding it. They're acting like we're not even there. We're talking to them and they won't even look at us. So afterward I was wondering, 'Did we really see that stuff or was it a hologram?'"

Lee soon made the decision to confront his neighbor, which resulted in his neighbor's slapping a series of restraining orders on him.

Lee said it all began one day when he saw an usual truck in his neighbor's front yard.

"I looked over there," he said, "and there was a wall-cutting company in his front yard called 'Zig-Zag Wall Cutting.' They had this circular saw over there that they cut walls out with. I set up my video camera there at the window and they sawed a damn ten-foot section out of the front of the house. Then they started pulling these gigantic pieces of equipment out of the basement. It was like the equipment was made in the basement and they couldn't get it out. Well, there were two Feds over there watching this whole thing. So I videotaped it, and I knew then that this guy had something to do with what was go- ing on.

"So I threatened him about it," he continued. "I said 'I'm going to whip your ass or you're going to tell me what's going on one way or the other.' Being stupid I did it in front of people, and the next thing they did is put a restraining order on me."

A couple of nights later, Lee claims the neighbor was shining a spotlight through his house.

"I went over the fence," Lee said, "and of course he wouldn't come near me. He always stays just about 30 or 40 feet away from me. And my wife says, 'He's just antagonizing you and trying to get you thrown in jail.' She was right. I pulled his fence down, called him some choice names, and the next thing I know, I'm under arrest. And a couple of months later, I did the same damn thing again—tried to

MATRIX OF THE MIND

jump him and got arrested again. But after that, I put a restraining order on him and it came to a stop. The guy is like immune from prosecution by the law."

Along with his problems with his neighbor, Lee also began to experience what he feels were incidents of harassment and even attempts to murder him and his family.

"There have been three attempts on my life," he said. "Chemical poison. Not only mine, but on my children's, too. Whoever these people are, they follow my father around down in Louisiana. They follow my friends. They break into my friends' houses. It goes on and on and on."

And this is the crux of the problem as Lee tells it. His enemies are not a group of aliens or poltergeists; they are indeed people.

"During this whole time period" he said, "I've been followed. My phone's been tapped. I've had numerous break-ins, but nothing's ever been taken. But I know ghosts and aliens don't drive Taurus' and Tempos and wear suits. So I have to wonder why the government's been watching me so close."

The government, then, is behind it all. Lee feels he and his family are being subjected to secret mind control experiments being conducted by the U.S. Government for whatever sinister reason you care to imagine.

Lee said he only recently found out that such programs even existed or that others had been subjected to the same kind of mistreatment.

"I didn't even know that there were other people in this world that this was going on with," he said, "until someone turned me on to a web site about it about a month ago. Since then, I've talked to a lot of people and all the stories are the same. Unfortunately, the thing about most people is that they don't have any proof. All you've got is their word to go on. And after someone jacks with your head for a long time, it doesn't make you very credible."

MATRIX OF THE MIND

Lee said he understands the logic of the government's need to pursue the field of mind control.

"I came up with this idea about four years ago," he said, "and everybody thought I was nuts. If we get in a war with someone, the best thing to do is to first start making them see things and then hit them with a few chemicals to really mess them up. Make them start seeing planes and ships and people coming in that aren't really there. After all that, they wouldn't put up much of a fight."

Lee therefore feels that all the paranormal activity that has been seen and photographed around his cabin is the result of sophisticated but decidedly human technology.

"Every bit of technology that's being used here," he said, "is used in mind control. But if someone had told me this story five years ago, I'd have told them they were nuts and needed to go see a doctor. I'm from Louisiana, and we're kind of redneck down there. And this kind of **** just doesn't happen. But when it happens to you ..."

Feeling threatened on all sides, first by the strange lights, voices and apparitions, then secondly by the government harassment that started soon after, Lee's solution was to go to the media. He contacted the popular program on the paranormal, Sightings, who were quick to arrive on the scene.

"They were out here the next week," he said. "And while they were here, they got stuff on their cameras, too, like faces in my mirror. They've been out here three times now, and all three times something's happened while they were here. Everybody who comes here gets something on their pictures."

In addition to Sightings, Lee and his family have been featured on Strange Universe and The Unexplained as well as on many local television news programs and in area newspapers. He's even signed a deal for the movie rights to his story.

Lee feels the decision to go public was a crucial one.

"Let me put it this way," he said. "Maybe it's kept me alive. If it was to happen now, whether it be accidental or whatever, it's going to some kind of stir."

Lee even has the backing of his Senator, Charles Duke. [Duke declined to be interviewed for this article, saying he is currently accepting no interviews on any subject.]

After Duke took some pictures of his own on Lee's property, which also turned up some anomalous photo images, he became publicly involved in Lee's search for the truth.

"He tried to get something done," Lee said, "and they wouldn't answer his phone calls or letters or anything else. In fact, about three months ago, someone broke into his house and ruffled through his stuff. But when Senator Duke got involved and it hit the media, I had people knocking at my damn door wanting to investigate. Of course, they did an investigation and said, 'We can find no evidence of wrongdoing going on.'

"The FBI says that until a federal law is broken," he went on, "they can't investigate. Well, I would say 75 break-ins in a five year period, stalking me, putting chemicals in my car and in my house—I would say that's federal law being broken. The people who are doing this, they can make **** happen. They can make it look like you died of a drug overdose or you had a wreck or there's a thousand different things they can do. If they wanted to kill me, I'd already be dead. But you know what people say, I'm a guinea pig in a goddamn cage."

In addition to receiving no help from the FBI, Lee said that his appeals to the local sheriff also went unheeded.

"The cops have labeled me as a nut and a drug addict," he said. "The first question they asked me was, 'Have you ever used drugs before?' Of course, 'Well, yeah, I have.' 'So there's your problem right there,' they said. 'You're just having flashbacks and hallucinations.' But they know something's going on, and they know who's doing it."

After receiving both local and national publicity, Lee said he and his family have become somewhat locally famous.

"Most people like me and stand behind me," he said. "There's a few of them who say I'm nuts and that there's nothing going on. But the majority of people in my town know me and know what kind of person I am and they know this is really going on."

That local fame also had a downside as well, though.

"When it first started" Lee said "I had to put in security equipment and get guard dogs posted on my property and you name it, to keep people from gawking. But what was I supposed to do? I mean, if the cops aren't going to do anything and you know what's going on and everybody else does too, then you know that your next place to go is the media."

Having established a protective shield of media scrutiny for himself and his family, Lee began to do some detective work that ultimately yielded up at least a partial theory about what's been going on around his home.

That theory involves a confusing tale of both illegal drug trafficking and some shady dealings by a federal agency.

MATRIX OF THE MIND

"I think they are making some drugs around here," Lee said. "Because a lot of people have smelled sulfur, ether, acetone, you name it. All chemicals used in making drugs." Lee said he and a local law enforcement agent traced a trail back to another drug bust that led them back to one particular group.

"These people were supposed to go to jail for many, many years," he said, "but they never went to jail at all. These were people that were very knowledgeable about holograms, lasers, eavesdropping equipment, this and that. They were making a hell of a lot of money and they were spending it on things like that, just to play around. And that's how I put two and two together, and they know I know this."

Lee said he confronted a government office up in Denver with what he knew, and their response was to take him very seriously.

"I was set up for this. I knew the people involved and I said 'I know what's going on. One of these days this stuff is going to come to light and you are all going to be in an embarrassing situation.' And they said, 'Well, I'll tell you what. How about if we put you in the Witness Protection Program and buy your house,' And I said, 'Why in the hell would I do that? I haven't done anything to belong in that. The Witness Protection Program is for people who go to court and testify against other people. Or after they turn someone in, they have to get them away to someplace safe.' I said, 'Why would I do that?' And I turned it down."

Lee said he instead pressed the agency to simply come clean about what was going on so that he and his family could get on with their lives.

"That seems like it would be easier to me," he said. "Doesn't it to you? Just solve this situation and we'll both be happy."

Lee claims he still has information on several individuals that could cause problems for the agency. He also maintains that some of the people arrested in the drug busts he alludes to were working for the government manufacturing drugs at the time of their arrest. The money obtained by the sale of drugs is then used to fund the mind control experi-

MATRIX OF THE MIND

ments that are the true cause of the voices and apparitions heard and seen around Lee's property. Some investigators have maintained in recent years that a sort of "Secret Government" truly does exist and is funding its various projects by selling illegal drugs and making it seem that there really is some sort of alien intervention taking place on this planet.

"You can put it together yourself," he said. "There is probably only one percent of the people who get busted who would have brains enough to do this. Well, these people do."

Meanwhile, Lee's primary concern continues to be the safety of his family.

"The thing about it is," he said "I've got children. And that's not right, to be screwing around with children. If you're messing with an adult, that's one thing. But where I'm from, when you mess with someone, you do it to their face. You don't do it in a cowardly way like this. But when you start dragging kids into this, and older people like my parents and my wife's parents, who are not in good health, that's not right. Our government is down on Iraq and Iran for human rights violations, but this is happening right here in America to people who haven't done anything.

"I was willing to go on with my life," he continued, "and to keep quiet about what I know, but I'm not going to sit here and let someone harass me and not do anything. If I knew who these people were, I would go to them. I'm that kind of person. But when they stay off in the shadows and you can't find them or get your hands on them, it's kind of frustrating."

But Lee remains determined to fight to keep his property as well as his family safe.

"I got to a point where I'm not going to rearrange my life for these idiots,' he said. "I'm not going to back down from them. And I'm not going to be manipulated in any way whatsoever. I get at least 20 to 30 death threats a day from voices inside this house. They tell me all the time, 'We fixing to kill you' or 'We're going to poison you' or 'We're going to kill your kids' or 'You're fixing to find out who we are. This thing isn't what you think it is."

And while he still has no irrefutable evidence he can take to court, Lee still has his photos and videotapes to bear witness for him.

"I've taken pictures into my mirrors in my bedroom," he said, "and I've got people who look like they're from the Civil War turn up in them when they're developed. I've had apparitions appear in my house that we've got on tape. I mean full-sized apparitions that you could walk right up to. Of course they're scaring everybody else, but I just walk up to them and stick my hands in them and say,

MATRIX OF THE MIND

'This is bull****.' When I stuck my hands into this thing, it would disappear. You couldn't see my arm when I stuck it in there."

But even "hands on" experience still hasn't convinced Lee that he's dealing with paranormal phenomena.

"Everyone who's been here and seen it has said, 'This is the best ghost house I've ever seen,'" Lee explained. "Well you know, to me it's a little bit too good for a ghost house. One or two pictures is something, but when you get something on every roll of film you have to wonder. I've said from the very first that this is a hoax, but it's not being perpetrated by me."

So one is indeed left to wonder who the real culprit is behind the strangeness witnessed by Steve Lee, his family, their State Senator and a host of others. Have they unknowingly made contact with mysterious beings from some other plane of reality, or are they instead being bedeviled by bizarre technology in the hands of our own government? According to Steve Lee, the true source of the events is a decidedly human one that could ultimately be more dangerous than any ghost or alien.

Lee and his family's home have been featured on the Sci-Fi network's investigative program Sightings several rimes, as well as in other magazines on the paranormal. The situation has also received a great deal of local television and newspaper coverage.

But if a real life counterpart to Agents Fox Mulder and Dana Scully of The X-Files exists somewhere out there, they have yet to make a visit to Steve Lee's home, which continues to be the scene of numerous events that border on the paranormal but which may also be of human origin. While that sounds like something right up the alley of the intrepid fictional agents, in the world of "normal reality," the FBI publicly maintains that they cannot intervene until a federal law has been broken, in spite of all the things going bump in the night and haunting the daylight hours as well.

"But I've also got letters stating that the FBI has done a full investigation and can find nothing going on," Lee countered. "So somebody's not telling the truth."

Which is the typical sort of run-around that adds enormously to the frustration of Lee and his family. While they can get no official help or action from the government, at least the visiting television crews never seem to leave disappointed.

"I don't think I've ever had one person come to my house," Lee said, "who hasn't seen something. Or heard something or smelled something or whatever. I've never had anybody come here who hasn't witnessed something. Not ever"

MATRIX OF THE MIND

Even a local contractor who was hired by Lee to do some remodeling on his home did not escape unscathed. Lee and his wife had gone into town to do some shopping one day and returned to find the contractor in a very agitated state.

"He heard someone keep calling his name," Lee said. "At first, he thought it was me, but he thought it was me, but when he went outside he couldn't find anyone. He said "I thought you were playing a trick on me or some damned thing.' It kind of spooked him a little bit."

The situation has escalated however, from simple disembodied voices to outright danger for the Lee family and their neighbors. In the past year, a mysterious illness has begun to afflict the neighborhood.

"There's a lot of other people out here who are getting sick," Lee said, "and having illnesses that no one can explain. We've got something going around and we've all had it. I have it a lot. You kind of feel lightheaded all the time and dizzy—like you're going to pass out or are on the verge of passing out. There's six people in the hospital from the Black Forest area right now, and they can't figure out what the hell's wrong with them."

Lee claims that the Center for Disease Control out of Atlanta, Georgia, was brought in to assess the situation and could not pinpoint the origin of the malady.

"They couldn't find anything in the victims' blood or anything else," Lee said.

[When we tried to get verification of Lee's report, the Center For Disease Control replied to our inquiry by saying they had no knowledge of the outbreak in Colorado Springs and referred us to the Colorado State Health Department, who in turn referred us to the El Paso County Health Department, which has jurisdiction over Colorado Springs. Again, at both the state and county level, officials maintained they had no knowledge of the alleged outbreak.]

Whatever the sickness is, it followed Lee and his family on their summer vacation to his parents' home in Louisiana. Throughout the entire trip, they suffered from diarrhea, headaches, vomiting and lightheadedness.

MATRIX OF THE MIND

When asked if he had sought medical attention for himself and his family, he said "I used to do that all the time. It didn't do any good at all. They check me out and there's nothing wrong. Nothing in the blood; nothing in the urine. I've been through it a thousand times. All it does is just waste time and money."

The sickness has also spread to the neighbors in the area, who remain reluctant to discuss the matter. Lee said he placed an ad in the local newspaper in May of 1998 that asked if others in the area were suffering similar problems.

"I had a lot of people call me," he said, "but many of them were scared to say anything. Because they've got kids and they don't want any trouble coming down on them."

There is also a half-mile stretch of road near Lee's home that seems to cause motorists in the area to experience similar strange symptoms.

"People will be going down that damn thing," he said, "and they almost pass out. They think they're going to have a heart attack. Their heart starts beating real fast."

Beyond the medical anomalies going on, there is also the constant attack from the mysterious disembodied voices that afflict both Lee and his neighbors.

"As soon as I get into the car, I hear 'We're going to kill you. We're going to kill your kids.' It just goes on and on," Lee said.

Lee said that he knew of two members of area families who were confined to a mental institution after hearing these same voices. He also told the story of an unfortunate Vietnam veteran who was diagnosed as being mentally ill after talking to someone about intruders he had repeatedly sighted near his home.

"This guy kept seeing these two men in military fatigues on his property," Lee said. "I've seen these same two guys on my property as well. I've shot at them, and the bullets go right through them, so I know they're holograms. Anyway, this guy had served in Vietnam, so they said,'Oh, well, there you go. He's having flashbacks.' And they put him away, too. Whoever is behind that one, I think that's pretty low."

In addition to unexplainable sickness, threatening voices, and phantoms in military garb, the Black Forest area has also experienced massive power surges to residents' homes.

"I've got a lady who lives right directly north of me," Lee said "who's been having 10,000 volt power surges. Some of them are so strong, they're blowing up the mirrors in her house. I mean shattering the mirrors and burning up appliances."

MATRIX OF THE MIND

Lee has also been told the strange events in the area have been going on for a long time.

"I've only lived out here six years," he said, "but they say there's always been strange things going on out here. Of course, every little town has its stories."

Lee suspects that the weird events follow him around very closely, even when he visits others in his neighborhood.

"I've got pictures of me in different houses out here," he said. "And when I go to someone's house, the same chain of events happens. They start smelling a gas-type smell. They'll call the gas company, who won't be able to detect anything. They'll start thinking someone's been coming into their house and that things have been moved but nothing's been taken. They start thinking their phone's been tapped and that there are people following them. Pretty much the same thing happens at every house I go to. I take pictures there and weird things come out in them."

But Lee adamantly refuses to accept any kind of supernatural explanation for what is going on.

"When you get calls left on your answering machine saying that 'We're going to kill you if you don't stop trying to figure this out,' that tends to make me believe this ain't no ghosts," he said. "Poltergeists don't drive cars and look just like me and you. I don't think so anyway.

"I just know this is not paranormal," Lee continued, "and doesn't have anything to do with it. But someone is spending a lot of time and money to make it look like it is. I have people come out to the house who are really into investigating and studying the para- normal, and after they're here for awhile, they see the same thing—that this has nothing to do with anything paranormal. I've had people see other people walking through my house that aren't there. They walk right through the walls. But if you lived in my shoes for the last six years, you would still say this has nothing to do with the paranormal. I guarantee you."

So discouragement gets piled on top of frustration, and the whole picture is complicated by an unshakable but nevertheless elusive sense of victimization.

After years of trying to bring the situation under control, Lee is beginning to develop an attitude of begrudging acceptance.

"Something happens to us at least two or three times a day," he said. "But it's normal to us now. It doesn't scare me at all. The first two years this was happening, I think that what they wanted to do is to keep me paranoid. Keep me looking over my shoulder all the time. Restrict what I do and what I don't do. But I do exactly what I want when want to do it. I'm just stubborn and a redneck."

So it's all a secret government mind control operation?

"What else could it be?" Lee replied. "There is nobody that could get away with this for this amount of time without getting caught. Whoever is doing this has no fear of law enforcement in any shape or form. So who else could it be?"

Lee conjectures that he may have come to the government's attention after a relative of his was arrested for trafficking in illegal drugs. Lee claims it was the government's own drug trafficking business that had employed his relative. Lee also claims that he himself was offered the help of the Federal Witness Protection Program because of his knowledge of what was going on, but that he turned them down and has since often wondered how the two situations are related. What is the connection between the drug bust and the supposedly manmade haunting he endures?

"To tell you the truth," he said "I really don't know. But that's about the only thing I can think of as a possible cause. It kind of makes you wonder."

Lee said that after having suffered these weird sorts of events, what he calls "mass mind control," the average person strains credibility when trying to talk about the experience. The stranger your tale, the less likely it is that you will be believed.

Enter Colorado Springs psychologist Dr. Michael Coots.

Coots said he had heard about the Lee family's problems through the local media and the Sightings appearances. Coots was also encouraged to seek Lee out by a friend in Denver.

"The first time I went out there," Coots said, "it was just like a normal visit between you and I or anyone else. There were no problems at all. As a psychologist and a forensic psycho-pathologist, I thought that maybe there were weird things going on here that might possibly have come from Steve himself.

"But the second time I visited his house," Coots continued, "there were maybe a half-dozen guys on the far side of the back part of his property. They had the whole nine yards, lights and everything. It looked like they were dressed in either dark blue or black jumpsuits, and they had their faces covered by ski masks. I had no idea who they were, and it actually sort of scared me."

Having seen the men and their lights, Coots asked Lee what was going on, and Lee replied that he didn't know. Coots then shined a light of his own in the direction of the men, who promptly shined lights back at him.

"And I'm like, 'Jesus Christ, Steve, am I going to get killed or something in your back yard?' I wanted to leave, and I did leave," Coots said.

Coots made still a third visit that was the most disturbing of all. After leaving Lee's home, he realized he was being followed and pulled into the parking lot of a convenience store in the area.

"I pulled in because these two guys in a brown Suburban had been behind me the entire way," he said. "I didn't know who they were or what they wanted. They pulled in next to me and the driver rolled down his window and said 'Good evening, Dr. Coots. How are you doing' I said 'Do I know you?' And he backed up and left."

Coots described the two men in the Suburban as having light hair cut very short, like military or police haircuts. Coots said that after this incident, he began to avoid visiting Lee's home and maintained contact by phone instead.

"This was too weird for me," he said. "I didn't know if this was law enforcement, if it was the government, or if it was something that Steve was doing."

Coots also experienced trouble with his telephone message service. He repeatedly received notification that new messages were waiting for him, but when he went to retrieve them, there was nothing there.

"I called the cellular phone company and they told me the messages had already been retrieved," he explained. "Well, I'm the only one who has the code. I'm the only one who can get the messages from my phone."

Apparently some unknown entity was retrieving Coots' messages using his personal code and leaving no clues behind. Interestingly enough, the phone message problem stopped after Coots quit making visits to Lee's home. Meanwhile, Coots went to the local sheriff's department in an attempt to learn more about what was going on.

"I was told by several members of the command structure of the El Paso County Sheriff's Department that there are some things going on there," Coots said. "They do not know what these things are, and they would just as soon leave it alone. They told me about these two deputies who went out there and were overcome by something. They're not sure what it was, but the two deputies had to go to the emergency room. But it would be hard to get them to say they believed it was something not manmade, though they may very well have those opinions on their own."

Coots also confirmed Lee's claims about the outbreak of a localized disease.

"I've talked to quite a few people," Coots said "and they've told me that there have been illnesses in the area, but they can't admit it publicly. Neither will the Center For Disease Control. When they came out, they could not find anything biological, medical, organic, or chemical."

It is perhaps easy to understand why the Center For Disease Control would prefer not to discuss an outbreak that they can neither diagnose nor understand. The avoidance of public panic may be part of their strategy as well. In any case, Coots has come away from the whole business a changed man.

"Above all," he said, "Steve and his wife truly believe it. It's real to them regardless of whether it's real to me and you. I was there with Steve. I saw him take pictures and I saw manifestations. I was in the room when he took the pictures and I was with him when the film was developed. I saw what came out on film and there obviously was something there.

"Now whether it's paranormal," he said, "or whether it's some elaborate, unexplainable hoax, I don't know. But I can say that I was there as a witness, as a doctor, as a psychologist, as an individual and an unbeliever. And I saw things that made me change my mind."

Meanwhile, Steve Lee continues to pursue other possible sources of help. He said he had sent over three hundred letters and e-mails to United States Attorney General Janet Reno asking for an investigation by the Justice Department and has received no response. Lee readily admits that many of his letters contained threats directed at the government.

"I've put in the letters that if something happens to my family, I'm going to come after you," he said. "Usually when you put something like that in a letter, they come knock on your door and say 'We're fixing to arrest you.' But they don't do it. They just ignore it.

"I'm not going to let someone harass me and do nothing about it," Lee continued. "If I knew who it was, it wouldn't be going on right now. If I knew a person who was directly involved in this, I would be in jail. And law enforcement knows that I've told them if I ever find out [who's behind this], you go ahead and get me a cell ready. I've told Ms. Reno that if something happens to my kids, I'm going to hop a plane and come up there.

"You make comments like that, then they knock on your door and arrest your ass. Now tell me why they're not doing it to me?"

Lee also claims to have three suitcases full of documents that would "rock them right out of office," including Ms. Reno.

"It's material that most definitely would sign my death warrant," he said 'but if I feel like they've poisoned me or I'm going to die anyway, I damn sure will let it out. I'll have nothing to lose. I've got that stuff on computer disks and I've got copies stored everywhere."

Lee quit his job as a truck driver a couple of years ago so that he could stay home and watch over his children, never knowing if the continual strife and strangeness would one day harm them. He also helps take care of his mother-in-law, who lives down the street from him and suffers from Alzheimer's. Lee's wife supports the family with a job that keeps her on the road a great deal of the time. In that context, his collection of potentially damaging documents may be just one more slender thread helping to hold the Lee family's fragile existence together.

Though he may someday manage to get the confrontation with his tormentors he so passionately wishes for, Steve Lee must struggle on in the meantime without hard answers to the questions that plague him continually and without ever knowing if today will be the day it all comes crashing down around him.

But his willingness to continue the daily battle will surely go on serving him well, whether his enemy is ultimately revealed as a human one or not.

(Visit Sean Casteel's "UFO Journalist" web site at: www.seancasteel.com)

MATRIX OF THE MIND

THE SHOCKING MENACE OF SATELLITE SURVEILLANCE
by John Fleming

Unknown to most of the world, satellites can perform astonishing and often menacing feats. This should come as no surprise when one reflects on the massive effort poured into satellite technology since the Soviet satellite Sputnik, launched in 1957, caused panic in the U.S. A spy satellite can monitor a person's every movement, even when the "target" is indoors or deep in the interior of a building or traveling rapidly down the highway in a car, in any kind of weather (cloudy, rainy, stormy). There is no place to hide on the face of the earth.

It takes just three satellites to blanket the world with detection capacity. Besides tracking a person's every action and relaying the data to a computer screen on earth, amazing powers of satellites include reading a person's mind, monitoring conversations, manipulating electronic instruments and physically assaulting someone with a laser beam. Remote reading of someone's mind through satellite technology is quite bizarre, yet it is being done; it is a reality at present, not a chimera from a futuristic dystopia! To those who might disbelieve my description of satellite surveillance, I'd simply cite a tried-and-true Roman proverb: Time reveals all things (tempus omnia revelat)...

As extraordinary as clandestine satellite powers are, nevertheless prosaic satellite technology is much evident in daily life. Satellite businesses reportedly earned $26 billion in 1998. We can watch transcontinental television broadcasts "via satellite," make long- distance phone calls relayed by satellite, be informed

of cloud cover and weather conditions through satellite images shown on television, and find our geographical bearings with the aid of satellites in the GPS (Global Positioning System). But behind the facade of useful satellite technology is a Pandora's box of surreptitious technology.

Spy satellites-- as opposed to satellites for broadcasting and exploration of space--have little or no civilian use--except, perhaps, to subject one's enemy or favorite malefactor to surveillance. With reference to detecting things from space, Ford Rowan, author of Techno Spies, wrote "some U.S. military satellites are equipped with infra-red sensors that can pick up the heat generated on earth by trucks, airplanes, missiles, and cars, so that even on cloudy days the sensors can penetrate beneath the clouds and reproduce the patterns of heat emission on a TV-type screen. During the Vietnam War sky high infra-red sensors were tested which detect individual enemy soldiers walking around on the ground." Using this reference, we can establish 1970 as the approximate date of the beginning of satellite surveillance- -and the end of the possibility of privacy for several people.

The government agency most heavily involved in satellite surveillance technology is the Advanced Research Projects Agency (ARPA), an arm of the Pentagon. NASA is concerned with civilian satellites, but there is no hard and fast line between civilian and military satellites. NASA launches all satellites, from either Cape Kennedy in Florida or Vandenberg Air Force Base in California, whether they are military- operated, CIA-operated, corporate-operated or NASA's own. Blasting satellites into orbit is a major expense. It is also difficult to make a quick distinction between government and private satellites; research by NASA is often applicable to all types of satellites. Neither the ARPA nor NASA makes satellites; instead, they underwrite the technology while various corporations produce the hardware.

Corporations involved in the satellite business include Lockheed, General Dynamics, RCA, General Electric, Westinghouse, Comsat, Boeing, Hughes Aircraft, Rockwell International, Grumman Corp., CAE Electronics, Trimble Navigation and TRW.

The World Satellite Directory, 14th edition (1992), lists about a thousand companies concerned with satellites in one way or another. Many are merely in the broadcasting business, but there are also product headings like "remote sensing imagery," which includes Earth Observation Satellite Co. of Lanham, Maryland, Downl Inc. of Denver, and Spot Image Corp. of Reston, Virginia. There are five product categories referring to transponders. Other product categories include earth stations (14 types), "military products and systems," "microwave equipment," "video processors," "spectrum analyzers." The category "remote sensors" lists eight companies, including ITM Systems Inc., in Grants Pass, Oregon, Yool

MATRIX OF THE MIND

Engineering of Phoenix, and Satellite Technology Management of Costa Mesa, California. Sixty-five satellite associations are listed from all around the world, such as Aerospace Industries Association, American Astronautical Society, Amsat and several others in the U.S.

Spy satellites were already functioning and violating people's right to privacy when President Reagan proposed his "Strategic Defense Initiative," or Star Wars, in the early 80s, long after the Cuban Missile Crisis of 1962 had demonstrated the military usefulness of satellites. Star Wars was supposed to shield the U.S. from nuclear missiles, but shooting down missiles with satellite lasers proved infeasible, and many scientists and politicians criticized the massive program. Nevertheless, Star Wars gave an enormous boost to surveillance technology and to what may be called "black bag" technology, such as mind reading and lasers that can assault someone, even someone indoors. Aviation Week & Space Technology mentioned in 1984 that "facets of the project [in the Star Wars program] that are being hurried along include the awarding of contracts to study...a surveillance satellite network." It was bound to be abused, yet no group is fighting to cut back or subject to democratic control this terrifying new technology. As one diplomat to the U.N. remarked, "`Star Wars' was not a means of creating heaven on earth, but it could result in hell on earth."

The typical American actually may have little to fear, since the chances of being subjected to satellite surveillance are rather remote. Why someone would want to subject someone else to satellite surveillance might seem unclear at first, but to answer the question you must realize that only the elite have access to such satellite resources. Only the rich and powerful could even begin to contemplate putting someone under satellite surveillance, whereas a middle- or working-class person would not even know where to begin. Although access to surveillance capability is thus largely a function of the willfulness of the powerful, nevertheless we should not conclude that only the powerless are subjected to it. Perhaps those under satellite surveillance are mainly the powerless, but wealthy and famous people make more interesting targets, as it were, so despite their power to resist an outrageous violation of their privacy, a few of them may be victims of satellite surveillance. Princess Diana may have been under satellite reconnaissance. No claim of being subject to satellite surveillance can be dismissed a priori.

It is difficult to estimate just how many Americans are being watched by satellites, but if there are 200 working surveillance satellites (a common number in the literature), and if each satellite can monitor 20 human targets, then as many as 4000 Americans may be under satellite surveillance. However, the capability of a satellite for multiple-target monitoring is even harder to estimate than the number of satellites; it may be connected to the number of transponders on each satellite, the transponder being a key device for both receiving and transmitting

41

information. A society in the grips of the National Security State is necessarily kept in the dark about such things. Obviously, though, if one satellite can monitor simultaneously 40 or 80 human targets, then the number of possible victims of satellite surveillance would be doubled or quadrupled.

A sampling of the literature provides insight into this fiendish space-age technology. One satellite firm reports that "one of the original concepts for the Brilliant Eyes surveillance satellite system involved a long-wavelength infrared detector focal plane that requires periodic operation near 10 Kelvin." A surveillance satellite exploits the fact that the human body emits infra-red radiation, or radiant heat; according to William E. Burrows, author of Deep Black, "the infrared imagery would pass through the scanner and register on the [charged-couple device] array to form a moving infrared picture, which would then be amplified, digitalized, encrypted and transmitted up to one of the [satellite data system] spacecraft...for downlink [to earth]." But opinion differs as to whether infrared radiation can be detected in cloudy conditions.

According to one investigator, there is a way around this potential obstacle: "Unlike sensors that passively observe visible-light and infra-red radiation, which are blocked by cloud cover and largely unavailable at night, radar sensors actively emit microwave pulses that can penetrate clouds and work at any hour." This same person reported in 1988 that "the practical limit on achievable resolution for a satellite-based sensor is a matter of some dispute, but is probably roughly ten to thirty centimeters. After that point, atmospheric irregularities become a problem." But even at the time she wrote that, satellite resolution, down to each subpixel, on the contrary, was much more precise, a matter of millimeters--a fact which is more comprehensible when we consider the enormous sophistication of satellites, as reflected in such tools as multi- spectral scanners, interferometers, visible infrared spin scan radiometers, cryocoolers and hydride sorption beds. Probably the most sinister aspect of satellite surveillance, certainly its most stunning, is mind-reading.

As early as 1981, G. Harry Stine (in his book Confrontation in Space), could write that Computers have "read" human minds by means of deciphering the outputs of electroencephalogra phs (EEGs). Early work in this area was reported by the Defense Advanced Research Projects Agency (DARPA) in 1978. EEG's are now known to be crude sensors of neural activity in the human brain, depending as they do upon induced electrical currents in the skin. Magnetoencephalogra phs (MEGs) have since been developed using highly sensitive electromagnetic sensors that can directly map brain neural activity even through the bones of the skull. The responses of the visual areas of the brain have now been mapped by Kaufman and others at Vanderbilt University. Work may already be under way in mapping the neural activity of other portions of the human brain using the new

MATRIX OF THE MIND

MEG techniques. It does not require a great deal of prognostication to forecast that the neural electromagnetic activity of the human brain will be totally mapped within a decade or so and that crystalline computers can be programmed to decipher the electromagnetic neural signals.

In 1992, Newsweek reported that "with powerful new devices that peer through the skull and see the brain at work, neuroscientists seek the wellsprings of thoughts and emotions, the genesis of intelligence and language. They hope, in short, to read your mind." In 1994, a scientist noted that "current imaging techniques can depict physiological events in the brain which accompany sensory perception and motor activity, as well as cognition and speech." In order to give a satellite mind-reading capability, it only remains to put some type of EEG-like-device on a satellite and link it with a computer that has a data bank of brain-mapping research. I believe that surveillance satellites began reading minds--or rather, began allowing the minds of targets to be read--sometime in the early 1990s. Some satellites in fact can read a person's mind from space.

Also part of satellite technology is the notorious, patented "Neurophone, " the ability of which to manipulate behavior defies description. In Brave New World, Huxley anticipated the Neurophone. In that novel, people hold onto a metal knob to get "feely effects" in a simulated orgy where "the facial errogenous zones of the six thousand spectators in the Alhambra tingled with almost intolerable galvanic pleasure." Though not yet applied to sex, the Neurophone-- or more precisely, a Neurophone-like- instrument- -has been adapted for use by satellites and can alter behavior in the manner of subliminal audio "broadcasting, " but works on a different principle.

After converting sound into electrical impulses, the Neurophone transmits radio waves into the skin, where they proceed to the brain, bypassing the ears and the usual cranial auditory nerve and causing the brain to recognize a neurological pattern as though it were an audible communication, though often on a subconscious level. A person stimulated with this device "hears" by a very different route. The Neurophone can cause the deaf to "hear" again. Ominously, when its inventor applied for a second patent on an improved Neurophone, the National Security Agency tried unsuccessfully to appropriate the device.

A surveillance satellite, in addition, can detect human speech. Burrows observed that satellites can "even eavesdrop on conversations taking place deep within the walls of the Kremlin." Walls, ceilings, and floors are no barrier to the monitoring of conversation from space. Even if you were in a highrise building with ten stories above you and ten stories below, a satellite's audio surveillance of your speech would still be unhampered. Inside or outside, in any weather, any-place on earth, at any time of day, a satellite "parked" in space in a geosynchronous orbit (whereby the satellite, because it moves in tandem with the rotation of the earth, seems to stand still) can detect the speech of a human target. Apparently, as with reconnaissance in general, only by taking cover deep within the bowels of a lead-shielding fortified building could you escape audio monitoring by a satellite.

There are various other satellite powers, such as manipulating electronic instruments and appliances like alarms, electronic watches and clocks, a television, radio, smoke detector and the electrical system of an automobile. For example, the digital alarm on a watch, tiny though it is, can be set off by a satellite from hundreds of miles up in space. And the light bulb of a lamp can be burned out with the burst of a laser from a satellite. In addition, street lights and porch lights can be turned on and off at will by someone at the controls of a satellite, the means being an electromagnetic beam which reverses the light's polarity. Or a lamp can be made to burn out in a burst of blue light when the switch is flicked. As with other satellite powers, it makes no difference if the light is under a roof or a ton of concrete--it can still be manipulated by a satellite laser. Types of satellite lasers include the free-electron laser, the x-ray laser, the neutral-particle- beam laser, the chemical- oxygen-iodine laser and the mid-infra-red advanced chemical laser.

Along with mind-reading, one of the most bizarre uses of a satellite is to physically assault someone. An electronic satellite beam--using far less energy than needed to blast nuclear missiles in flight-- can "slap" or bludgeon someone on earth. A satellite beam can also be locked onto a human target, with the victim being unable to evade the menace by running around or driving around, and can cause harm through application of pressure on, for example, one's head. How severe a beating can be administered from space is a matter of conjecture, but if the ability to actually murder someone this way has not yet been worked out, there can be no doubt that it will soon become a reality.

There is no mention in satellite literature of a murder having been committed through the agency of a satellite, but the very possibility should make the world take note.

There is yet another macabre power possessed by some satellites: manipulating a person's mind with an audio subliminal "message" (a sound too low for the ear to consciously detect but which affects the unconscious) . In trying thereby to get a person to do what you want him to do, it does not matter if the target is asleep or awake. A message could be used to compel a person to say something you would like him to say, in a manner so spontaneous that noone would be able to realize the words were contrived by someone else; there is no limit to the range of ideas an unsuspecting person can be made to voice. The human target might

MATRIX OF THE MIND

be compelled to use an obscenity, or persons around the target might be compelled to say things that insult the target. A sleeping person, on the other hand, is more vulnerable and can be made to do something, rather than merely say something. An action compelled by an audio subliminal message could be to roll off the bed and fall onto the floor, or to get up and walk around in a trance. However, the sleeping person can only be made to engage in such an action for only a minute or so, it seems, since he usually wakes up by then and the "spell" wears off.

It should be noted here that although the "hypnotism" of a psychoanalyst is bogus, unconscious or subconscious manipulation of behavior is genuine. But the brevity of a subliminal spell effected by a satellite might be overcome by more research. "The psychiatric community," reported Newsweek in 1994, "generally agrees that subliminal perception exists; a smaller fringe group believes it can be used to change the psyche." A Russian doctor, Igor Smirnov, whom the magazine labeled a "subliminal Dr. Strangelove, " is one scientist studying the possibilities: "Using electroencephalogra phs, he measures brain waves, then uses computers to create a map of the subconscious and various human impulses, such as anger or the sex drive. Then. through taped subliminal messages, he claims to physically alter that landscape with the power of suggestion."

Combining this research with satellite technology-- which has already been done in part--could give its masters the possibility for the perfect crime, since satellites operate with perfect discretion, perfect concealment. All these satellite powers can be abused with impunity. A satellite makes a "clean getaway," as it were. Even if a given victim became aware of how a crime was effected, noone would believe him, and he would be powerless to defend himself or fight back.

And this indeed is the overriding evil of satellite technology. It is not just that the technology is unrestrained by public agencies; it is not just that it is entirely undemocratic. The menace of surveillance satellites is irresistible; it overwhelms its powerless victims. As writer Sandra Hochman foresaw near the beginning of the satellite age, though seriously underestimating the sophistication of the technology involved: Omniscient and discrete, satellites peer down at us from their lofty orbit and keep watch every moment of our lives... From more than five-hundred miles above earth, a satellite can sight a tennis ball, photograph it, and send back to earth an image as clear as if it had been taken on the court at ground zero. Satellites photograph and record many things...and beam this information, this data, back to quiet places where it is used in ways we don't know. Privacy has died." This terror is in the here and now.

It is not located in the mind of an eccentric scientist or futurologist. Satellite surveillance is currently being abused. Thousands of Americans are under satellite surveillance and have been stripped of their privacy. And presently they would have little or no recourse in their struggle against the iniquity, since technology advances well ahead of social institutions.

The powers of satellites, as here described, especially lend themselves to harassment of someone. The victim could be a business or political rival, an ex-spouse, a political dissident, a disliked competitor, or anyone who for whatever reason provokes hatred or contempt. Once the target is a "signature," he can almost never escape a satellite's probing eyes. (As an article in Science explained, "tiny computers... check the incoming signals with computerized images, or `signatures,' of what the target should like.") As long as his tormentor or tormentors-- those with the resources to hire a satellite--desire, the victim will be subject to continuous scrutiny. His movements will be known, his conversations heard, his thoughts picked clean, and his whole life subjected to bogus moralizing, should his tormentor diabolically use the information gained. A sadist could harass his target with sound bites, or audio messages, directly broadcast into his room; with physical assault with a laser; with subliminal audio messages that disturb his sleep or manipulate persons around him into saying something that emotionally distresses him; with lasers that turn off street lights as he approaches them; with tampering with lamps so that they burn out when he hits the switch; and in general with the knowledge gained acquired through the omniscient eyes and ears of satellites. In short, a person with access to satellite technology could make his victim's life a living nightmare, a living hell.

How you could arrange to have someone subjected to satellite surveillance is secretive; it might even be a conspiracy. However, there seem to be two basic possibilities: surveillance by a government satellite or surveillance by a commercial satellite.

According to an article in Time magazine from 1997, "commercial satellites are coming online that are eagle-eyed enough to spot you-- and maybe a companion--in a hot tub." The Journal of Defense & Diplomacy stated in 1985 that "the cost of remote sensors is within the reach of [any country] with an interest, and high-performance remote sensors (or the sensor products) are readily available.

Advances in fourth-generation (and soon fifth-generation) computer capabilities, especially in terms of VHSIC (very-high-speed integrated circuits) and parallel processing, hold the key to rapid exploitation of space-derived data. Wideband, low-power data relay satellites are, at the same time, providing support for communication needs and for relay of remote sensor data, thus providing world-wide sensor coverage." In addition, The New York Times reported in 1997 that "commercial spy satellites are about to let anyone with a credit card peer down from the heavens into the compounds of dictators or the back yards of neighbors with high fences." "To date [the newspaper further noted] the Commerce

MATRIX OF THE MIND

Department has issued licenses to nine American companies, some with foreign partners, for 11 different classes of satellites, which have a range of reconnaissance powers." But this last article discussed photographic reconnaissance, in which satellites took pictures of various sites on earth and ejected a capsule containing film to be recovered and processed, whereas the state of the art in satellite technology is imaging, detection of targets on earth in real time. Currently, industry is hard at work miniaturizing surveillance satellites in order to save money and be in a position to fill the heavens with more satellites.

Yet no source of information on satellites indicate whether the abuse of satellite surveillance is mediated by the government or corporations or both. More telling is the following disclosure by the author of Satellite Surveillance (1991): "Release of information about spy satellites would reveal that they have been used against U.S. citizens. While most of the public supports their use against the enemies of the U.S., most voters would probably change their attitudes towards reconnaissance satellites if they knew how extensive the spying has been. It's better...that this explosive issue never surfaces." Few people are aware of the destruction of the rights of some Americans through satellite surveillance, and fewer still have any inclination to oppose it, but unless we do, 1984 looms ever closer. "With the development of television and the technical device to receive and transmit on the same instrument, private life came to an end."

John Fleming is the author of The War of All Against All

MATRIX OF THE MIND

Bio-electromagnetic Weapons:
The Ultimate Weapon
by Institute of Science in Society
Global Research, May 29, 2007
ISIS Press Release

A weapon system that operates at the speed of light, that can kill, torture, enslave and escape detection

Harlan Girard

The ultimate weapon

Electromagnetic weapons operate at the speed of light; they can kill, torture and enslave; but the public are largely unaware that they exist, because these weapons operate by stealth and leave no physical evidence. Electromagnetic weapons have been tested on human beings since 1976. By widely dispersing the involuntary human test-subjects, and vehemently attacking their credibility, it has been possible for the United States to proceed with these human experiments unhindered by discussions or criticisms, let alone opposition.

This ultimate weapon system is currently being deployed in Iraq. The US Air Force and the Marine Corps refer to it as " active denial technology", as if it were used purely for defense, but it is not.

The truth about "active denial technology"

There is only one electromagnetic spectrum. Nuclear weapons release a great deal of ionizing radiation in the high frequency range above visible light, where the energy of the radiation is capable of breaking chemical bonds. Ionizing radiation is generally acknowledged to cause cancer.

The US military has weaponized the non-ionizing radiation below the visible range, the microwaves and radio waves that are used in mobile phones and telecommunications. The US government has strenuously denied that there could

48

be health hazards from non-ionizing electromagnetic radiation, both as a defence of the involuntary human research it has been conducting for many years but has not yet acknowledged, and to dissuade other countries from developing similar weapons.

The only biological effect of non-ionizing radiation that the US government has acknowledged for many years is heating, and accordingly, it characterizes " active denial technology" as that which produces pain from sudden heating of the skin; but this is not how it really works.

Reading brain waves and mind control

In 1959, Saul B. Sells, a professor of social psychology at a minor US university submitted a proposal to the Central Intelligence Agency (CIA) to build for them the most sophisticated electroencephalography machine that would have an integral computational capacity to analyze and, hopefully, make sense of the brain waves it recorded. In other words, the professor proposed to make a machine that could tell the CIA what a person was thinking, whether or not the person wished to disclose that information.

The CIA approved the project in 1960, adding some library research with five objectives. The fifth objective of the research was, "Techniques for Activating the Human Organism by Remote Electronic Means". The entire assignment was thereafter known as MKULTRA subproject 119, MKULTRA being the CIA's notorious mind control programme. It was based on the erroneous notion that the Soviets already possessed the means to control minds and the US had to catch up as rapidly as possible.

The documents pertaining to MKULTRA subproject 119 are now held in the National Security Archives (a non-governmental organization) at George Washington University in Washington, D.C. [1]. John Marks, author of The Search for the Manchurian Candidate: The CIA and Mind Control, (Times Books, New York, 1979) donated the MKULTRA documents; his book was republished by W.W. Norton & Company, Inc., New York, 1991 and is still in print.

Project Bizarre followed MKULTRA subproject 119 in 1965. The purpose of Bizarre was to record and analyze the complex microwave signal allegedly being beamed at the American Embassy in Moscow by the Soviets from a building across the street. The interesting thing about Project Bizarre is that while the United States has denied to this very day that there could be adverse health effects from microwave radiation, it immediately suspected that "the Moscow signal" was producing a variety of health effects in Embassy personnel, particularly in the successive ambassadors at whose office it was claimed the signal was being beamed. At the

MATRIX OF THE MIND

same time that the State Department was testing embassy personnel for DNA breaks produced by the Moscow signal, it felt constrained from complaining to the Soviets because the power of their signal was a tiny fraction of what the US said was a safe, human exposure level. Journalist Barton Reppert has written the most authoritative account of the Moscow signal [2]. (Editor's note: DNA breaks from exposure to mobile phones have been confirmed in recent lab research [3, 4] (Science in Society 24).)

Converting sound to microwaves

In 1973, Joseph C. Sharp, an experimental psychologist at Walter Reed Army Institute of Research performed an experiment that was pivotal to the development of the torture equipment being shipped to Iraq today. He had James Lin set up equipment in his laboratory which converted the shape of sound waves into microwave radiation that enabled him to hear himself vocalize the names of the numbers from one to ten in his head, by-passing the mechanism of his own ears. This particular experiment was never published but is mentioned in Lin's book, Microwave Auditory Effects and Applications, published in 1978 [5].

The experiment has been confirmed in US Patent 6 587 729, "Apparatus for Audibly Communicating Speech Using the Radio Frequency Hearing Effect" [6]. This patent is for an improved version of the apparatus used in the 1973 laboratory experiment, issued on July 1, 2003 and assigned to the Secretary of the Air Force. It provides scientific evidence that it is possible to hear threatening voices in one's head without suffering from paranoid schizophrenia.

Why has this patent been published openly at a time when the US Government is practicing a degree of secrecy that rivals Stalin's Kremlin? I have no satisfactory answer, except to say that the apparatus in the patent has already been superseded by equipment that achieves the same effect by far more sophisticated means. It blocks the normal processes of memory and thought by remote electronic means, while at the same time supplying false, distorted and/or unpleasant memories and suggestions by means of a process called "synthetic telepathy". The equipment that produces synthetic telepathy is sometimes referred to as "influence technology".

While voices and visions, daydreams and nightmares are the most astonishing manifestations of this weapon system, it is also capable of crippling the human subject by limiting his/her normal range of movement, causing acute pain the equivalent of major organ failure or even death, and interfering with normal functioning of any of the human senses. In other words, any of the tortures with which the words Guantanamo Bay have become

MATRIX OF THE MIND

synonymous can be achieved by remote, electronic means.

Instruments of torture

Influence technology is also capable of persuading the subjects that their mind is being read, that their intellectual property is being plundered, and can even motivate suicide or the murder of family, friends, and co-workers. During the years of the so-called "War on Drugs" (which preceded the "War on Terrorism"), letters that the involuntary human subjects had written or were about to receive regularly vanished from the mail, as though the government had a huge covert operation through post offices across the country. When George Herbert Walker Bush became president (in1989), the incidence of co-worker killings in the post offices became so great that the expression "going postal" began to replace the commonly used expression of "going crazy". The killing of co-workers in other workplaces began to command more media attention too [7].

I estimate that the cost of imprisoning a human being in his/her own body and applying unremitting torture is US$5 000 000 to $10 000 000 a year (see below).

By "unremitting torture" I mean exactly that. Because there is no visible evidence left by this new torture equipment such as damage to the skin, it is possible to torture the involuntary human subjects for 24 hours a day, 365 days a year. This can be done and is being done even on Christmas and Easter [8].

I arrived at my estimate on the cost of testing/using electromagnetic weapons on a human subject by visiting a cable TV channel that specializes in the sale of goods over the air 24 hours a day. I questioned the number of technical staff required, their working hours and salary range; also the number of back-up personnel required to prepare the programming for broadcast. I did not inquire about the cost of electronics and the schedule by which it is depreciated. I have estimated a cost for depreciation that is included in my estimate of the cost of torturing one involuntary human subject for one year.

Torture is a labor-intensive business. What objective would justify this investment? Could it be something as insane as to rule the world by enslaving the democratic governments of the more populous countries? This objective is certainly consistent with the United States' disdain for, and hostility toward, the United Nations, the international conventions and covenants it has ratified in the past and customary international law [9].

On 1 March 2001, the Marine Corps announced a new non-lethal weapon, "active denial technology". It produces enormous pain by allegedly boiling the molecules of water in the human skin without damaging the skin itself. As described in an article published in New Scientist, it employs pulsed electromag-

MATRIX OF THE MIND

netic radiation at a frequency of 95 GHz with a range of about 600 meters [10]. There have been several new reports in the magazine in 2005, including one published in July [11], describing volunteers taking part in tests to determine how safe the Active Denial System (ADS) weapon would be if used in real crowd-control. The ADS weapon's beam was reported to cause pain within 2 to 3 seconds, and becomes "intolerable after less than 5 seconds".

Active denial technology is the cornerstone of the system employed to torture 2 000 persons in the privacy of their own homes, not only in the United States but around the world, wherever countries have signed Status of Forces Agreements with the United States [12]. Allegations of torture were first received from countries with which the United States has a special intelligence-sharing relationship i.e. the United Kingdom, Canada, Australia and New Zealand. Then reports began to arrive from the conquered countries where the United States still has large numbers of troops stationed, i.e. Germany and Japan. When France rejoined the military arm of NATO in the late 90s, we began to receive allegations of torture in France. Very recently we have begun to receive allegations of torture from India, where American companies have begun to outsource, not only help lines, but also programming [13].

And then there is the case of Russia, where the involuntary, human subjects of torture experiments appear to be both numerous and well organized. I have been told reliably that every Russian scientist who could speak English has now found a home in an American university or government laboratory. This is plausible, considering the frequently voiced American worry that Soviet era experts in nuclear weaponry and biological warfare might find employment in Iran. It is a fact that at the end of World War II the US Army swept through Germany in an operation called Project Paperclip, recruiting, in particular, Nazi rocket scientists and experts in aerospace medicine. Some other scientists were recruited simply to deprive the Soviet Union of this resource. So what has become of the Soviet scientists who didn't speak English? In time we will find out for certain, but for now it is a safe guess that at least some of them have been employed to study the Russian value system and decision making processes by torturing other Russians with American "influence technology" [14].

Two interesting and important articles on bioelectromagnetic weapons have recently appeared in the New Scientist: "Maximum pain is aim of new U.S. weapon" and "Police toy with 'less lethal' weapons", both written by David Hambling [15]. See also US. Patent 6 536 440 of March 25, 2003 [16].

Since completing this article in mid-June 2005, it has come to my attention that the Israelis are deploying a device called "The Scream", which sends out bursts of audible, but not loud sound at intervals of about 10 seconds. A photographer at the scene of a demonstration said that he continued to hear the sound ringing in his head even after he covered his ears. This suggests to me that the active agent is electromagnetic rather than acoustic. In other words, the Israelis have come up with a device that is far cleverer than our " active denial technology". It not only deters rioters, but also issues an audible warning that it has been turned on, which the US device does not, leaving it entirely to the enlisted men operating it to determine how much burning pain their adversaries receive. The margin for error with the US device is unconscionable. It may as well be called a lethal weapon because in practice it very frequently will be [17].

"(technology to produce sounds or simulated voices where one individual is targeted and the effect is produced only in that individual and no one else in the vicinity). As far as I can tell the technology he is describing is something that creates an auditory effect rather than altering any kind of neural physiology or affecting brain chemistry."

One method I have heard of is a 3D focused sound beam, I think this is being sold to the public as a privacy sound curtain. I bet stores will start using them to target you with advertisements as you walk by display cases.

It looks like some of the old technology that needed contact electrodes can be made to work as light pulses or radiowaves at a distance.

Here are some patents.

http://www.rense.com/general3/patent.htm

http://www.rexresearch.com/sublimin/sublimin.htm

http://www.wanttoknow.info/050331behaviormodificationtv

http://www.freepatentsonline.com/4858612.html

Now that most everything has a chip and is going digital, it pretty much eliminates privacy aspects. Years ago I was reading about smart agents inside your television set. They record every click of your tv remote and collect your viewing data. This is primarily for advertisers. The old analog systems could not track every single tv and phone nor have two way communication. With digital you do have that capability.

Your cable box can periodically send this info back through the cable. I don't know how many companies are running this system but it has been available for about 3 or 4 years.

I remember the first time I heard about some of these aspects was the new digital phones. They always sell this to you as a benefit. They said they were leaving large amounts of space on the chips so they could be upgraded over the phone

MATRIX OF THE MIND

line later. They said if you were willing to pay an additional fee you could turn on your digital phone without it ringing and listen in on any room conversations if you wanted to check up on the kids, while you were on vacation, or listen for burglars.

I was watching the news one night and a vice-president of some television company started to brag that they could upgrade the chips in your tv at night while it was off, thru over the air signals, at a megabyte a second.

Remember the old portable VCR+ units you could buy to program your vcr with? One day it struck me how does it know whats on, the tv cable is shielded, it can't be getting the data from your system. I looked in the manual, nothing. I took a new unit and walked a few hundred feet from any houses and put the batteries in and the channel guide downloaded. I finally decided it must be a radio receiver and the tv cable company broadcasts a separate channel guide signal.

Subliminal Behavior Modification Through TV Described in US Patent

"It is therefore possible to manipulate the nervous system of a subject by pulsing images displayed on a nearby computer monitor or TV set. For the latter, the image pulsing may be imbedded in the program material, or it may be overlaid by modulating a video stream, either as an RF signal or as a video signal."

-- US Patent and Trade Office, Patent #6,506,148, 2/14/03

March 31, 2005

Dear friends,

The arsenal of mind control technologies developed by the government is quite vast. A number of well researched books on the subject have been published revealing the complexity and variety of these technologies. We highly recommend Dr. Armen Victorian's Mind Controllers for an excellent overview of the subject.

MATRIX OF THE MIND

The below patent describes technology used for behavior manipulation through TV, video, and DVD programming. If you have a science background, I invite you to read the patent to see the high level of sophistication involved. The manipulation is not done through the insertion of single-frame anomalies, as has been done in the past, but rather by modulation of the feed or signal. It is unfortunate that very few people are aware of these capabilities. I doubt there are any laws at present to protect us from such manipulation. Like any tool, these technologies can be used for either the benefit or detriment of society. Let us spread this information so that we might work together to assure that these technologies are not used for harm, but rather only for the benefit of humankind.

With best wishes,

Fred Burks for the WantToKnow.info Team

http://patft.uspto.gov/netahtml/srchnum.htm - US Patent and Trademark Office Website Patent Search Page

As the patent is 16 pages long, only key excerpts are included below.

United States Patent 6,506,148

Loos January 14, 2003

Nervous system manipulation by electromagnetic fields from monitors

Abstract

Physiological effects have been observed in a human subject in response to stimulation of the skin with weak electromagnetic fields that are pulsed with certain frequencies near 1/2 Hz or 2.4 Hz, such as to excite a sensory resonance. Many computer monitors and TV tubes, when displaying pulsed images, emit pulsed electromagnetic fields of sufficient amplitudes to cause such excitation. It is therefore possible to manipulate the nervous system of a subject by pulsing images displayed on a nearby computer monitor or TV set. For the latter, the image pulsing may be imbedded in the program material, or it may be overlaid by modulating a video stream, either as an RF signal or as a video signal. The image displayed on a computer monitor may be pulsed effectively by a simple computer program. For certain monitors, pulsed electromagnetic fields capable of exciting sensory resonances in nearby subjects may be generated even as the displayed images are pulsed with subliminal intensity.

Inventors: Loos; Hendricus G. (3019 Cresta Way, Laguna Beach, CA 92651)

Appl. No.: 872528

Filed: June 1, 2001

MATRIX OF THE MIND

SUMMARY

Computer monitor and TV monitors can be made to emit weak low-frequency electromagnetic fields merely by pulsing the intensity of displayed images. Experiments have shown that the 1/2 Hz sensory resonance can be excited in this manner in a subject near the monitor. The 2.4 Hz sensory resonance can also be excited in this fashion. Hence, a TV monitor or computer monitor can be used to manipulate the nervous system of nearby people.

The implementations of the invention are adapted to the source of video stream that drives the monitor, be it a computer program, a TV broadcast, a video tape or a digital video disc (DVD).

For a computer monitor, the image pulses can be produced by a suitable computer program. The pulse frequency may be controlled through keyboard input, so that the subject can tune to an individual sensory resonance frequency. The pulse amplitude can be controlled as well in this manner. A program written in Visual Basic(R) is particularly suitable for use on computers that run the Windows 95(R) or Windows 98(R) operating system. The structure of such a program is described. Production of periodic pulses requires an accurate timing procedure. Such a procedure is constructed from the GetTimeCount function available in the Application Program Interface (API) of the Windows operating system, together with an extrapolation procedure that improves the timing accuracy.

Pulse variability can be introduced through software, for the purpose of thwarting habituation of the nervous system to the field stimulation, or when the precise resonance frequency is not known. The variability may be a pseudo-random variation within a narrow interval, or it can take the form of a frequency or amplitude sweep in time. The pulse variability may be under control of the subject.

The program that causes a monitor to display a pulsing image may be run on a remote computer that is connected to the user computer by a link; the latter may partly belong to a network, which may be the Internet.

For a TV monitor, the image pulsing may be inherent in the video stream as it flows from the video source, or else the stream may be modulated such as to overlay the pulsing. In the first case, a live TV broadcast can be arranged to have the feature imbedded simply by slightly pulsing the illumination of the scene that is being broadcast. This method can of course also be used in making movies and recording video tapes and DVDs.

MATRIX OF THE MIND

Video tapes can be edited such as to overlay the pulsing by means of modulating hardware. A simple modulator is discussed wherein the luminance signal of composite video is pulsed without affecting the chroma signal. The same effect may be introduced at the consumer end, by modulating the video stream that is produced by the video source. A DVD can be edited through software, by introducing pulse-like variations in the digital RGB signals. Image intensity pulses can be overlaid onto the analog component video output of a DVD player by modulating the luminance signal component. Before entering the TV set, a television signal can be modulated such as to cause pulsing of the image intensity by means of a variable delay line that is connected to a pulse generator.

Certain monitors can emit electromagnetic field pulses that excite a sensory resonance in a nearby subject, through image pulses that are so weak as to be subliminal. This is unfortunate since it opens a way for mischievous application of the invention, whereby people are exposed unknowingly to manipulation of their nervous systems for someone else's purposes. Such application would be unethical and is of course not advocated. It is mentioned here in order to alert the public to the possibility of covert abuse that may occur while being online, or while watching TV, a video, or a DVD.

The following paragraph is from page 205 of Dr. Victorian's Mind Controllers:

The latest development in the technology of induced fear and mind control is the cloning of the human EEG or brain waves of any targeted victim, or indeed groups. With the use of powerful computers, segments of human emotions which include anger, anxiety, sadness, fear, embarrassment, jealousy, resentment, shame, and terror, have been identified and isolated within the EEG signals as 'emotion signature clusters.' Their relevant frequencies and amplitudes have been measured. Then the very frequency/amplitude cluster is synthesized and stored on another computer. Each one of these negative emotions is properly and separately tagged. They are then placed on the Silent Sound carrier frequencies and could silently trigger the occurrence of the same basic emotion in another human being.

100 US Patent Abstracts:

USP # 6,506,148 (January 14, 2003)

Nervous System Manipulation by EM Fields from Monitors

Loos, Hendricus

Abstract --- Physiological effects have been observed in a human subject in

MATRIX OF THE MIND

response to stimulation of the skin with weak electromagnetic fields that are pulsed with certain frequencies near 1/2 Hz or 2.4 Hz, such as to excite a sensory resonance. Many computer monitors and TV tubes, when displaying pulsed images, emit pulsed electromagnetic fields of sufficient amplitudes to cause such excitation. It is therefore possible to manipulate the nervous system of a subject by pulsing images displayed on a nearby computer monitor or TV set. For the latter, the image pulsing may be imbedded in the program material, or it may be overlaid by modulating a video stream, either as an RF signal or as a video signal. The image displayed on a computer monitor may be pulsed effectively by a simple computer program. For certain monitors, pulsed electromagnetic fields capable of exciting sensory resonances in nearby subjects may be generated even as the displayed images are pulsed with subliminal intensity.

USP # 6,488,617 (December 3, 2002)

Method and Device for Producing a Desired Brain State

Katz, Bruce

Abstract --- A method and device for the production of a desired brain state in an individual contain means for monitoring and analyzing the brain state while a set of one or more magnets produce fields that alter this state. A computational system alters various parameters of the magnetic fields in order to close the gap between the actual and desired brain state. This feedback process operates continuously until the gap is minimized and/or removed.

USP # 6,487,531 (November 26, 2002)

Signal Injection Coupling into the Human Vocal Tract...

Tosaya, Carol

Abstract --- A means and method are provided for enhancing or replacing the natural excitation of the human vocal tract by artificial excitation means, wherein the artificially created acoustics present additional spectral, temporal, or phase data useful for (1) enhancing the machine recognition robustness of audible speech or (2) enabling more robust machine-recognition of relatively inaudible mouthed or whispered speech. The artificial excitation (a) may be arranged to be audible or inaudible, (b) may be designed to be non-interfering with another user's similar means, (c) may be used in one or both of a vocal content-enhancement mode or a complimentary vocal tract-probing mode, and/or (d) may be used for the recognition of audible or inaudible continuous speech or isolated spoken commands.

MATRIX OF THE MIND

USP # 6,430,443 (August 6, 2002)

Method and Apparatus for Treating Auditory Hallucinations

Karell, Manuel

Abstract --- Stimulating one or more vestibulocochlear nerves or cochlea or cochlear regions will treat, prevent and control auditory hallucinations.

USP # 6,426,919 (July 30, 2002)

Portable and Hand-Held Device for Making Humanly Audible Sounds...

Gerosa, William

Abstract --- A portable and hand-held device for making humanly audible sounds responsive to the detecting of ultrasonic sounds. The device includes a hand-held housing and circuitry that is contained in the housing. The circuitry includes a microphone that receives the ultrasonic sound, a first low voltage audio power amplifier that strengthens the signal from the microphone, a second low voltage audio power amplifier that further strengthens the signal from the first low voltage audio power amplifier, a 7-stage ripple carry binary counter that lowers the frequency of the signal from the second low voltage audio power amplifier so as to be humanly audible, a third low voltage audio power amplifier that strengthens the signal from the 7-stage ripple carry binary counter, and a speaker that generates a humanly audible sound from the third low voltage audio power amplifier.

USP # 6,292,688 (September 18, 2001)

Method and Apparatus for Analyzing Neurological Response to Emotion-Inducing Stimuli

Patton, Richard

Abstract --- A method of determining the extent of the emotional response of a test subject to stimului having a time-varying visual content, for example, an advertising presentation. The test subject is positioned to observe the presentation for a given duration, and a path of communication is established between the subject and a brain wave detector/analyzer. The intensity component of each of at least two different brain wave frequencies is measured during the exposure, and each frequency is associated with a particular emotion. While the subject views the presentation, periodic variations in the intensity component of the brain waves of each of the particular frequencies selected is measured. The change rates in the intensity at regular periods during the duration are also measured. The intensity change rates are then used to construct a graph of plural coordinate points, and these coordinate points graphically establish the composite emotional reaction of the subject as the presentation continues.

USP # 6,258,022 (July 10,2001)

Behavior Modification

Rose, John

Abstract --- Behavior modification of a human subject takes place under hypnosis, when the subject is in a relaxed state. A machine plays back a video or audio recording, during which the subject is instructed to activate a device to create a perceptible stimulation which is linked, through the hypnosis, with a visualization of enhanced or improved performance. After the hypnosis, the user can reactivate the device at will, whenever the improved performance, such as an improved sporting performance, is desired. This will again create the perceptible stimulation and thus induce the required visualization.

USP # 6,239,705 (May 29,2001)

Intra-Oral Electronic Tracking Device

Glen, Jeffrey

Abstract --- An improved stealthy, non-surgical, biocompatable electronic tracking device is provided in which a housing is placed intraorally. The housing contains microcircuitry. The microcircuitry comprises a receiver, a passive mode to active mode activator, a signal decoder for determining positional fix, a transmitter, an antenna, and a power supply. Optionally, an amplifier may be utilized to boost signal strength. The power supply energizes the receiver. Upon receiving a coded activating signal, the positional fix signal decoder is energized, determining a positional fix. The transmitter subsequently transmits through the antenna a position locating signal to be received by a remote locator. In another embodiment of the present invention, the microcircuitry comprises a receiver, a passive mode to active mode activator, a transmitter, an antenna and a power supply. Optionally, an amplifier may be utilized to boost signal strength. The power supply energizes the receiver. Upon receiving a coded activating signal, the transmitter is energized. The transmitter subsequently transmits through the antenna a homing signal to be received by a remote locator.

USP # 6,167,304 (December 26, 2000)

Pulse Variability in Electric Field Manipulation of Nervous Systems

Loos, Hendricus

Abstract --- Apparatus and method for manipulating the nervous system of a subject by applying to the skin a pulsing external electric field which, although too weak to cause classical nerve stimulation, modulates the normal spontaneous spiking patterns of certain kinds of afferent nerves. For certain pulse frequencies the electric field stimulation can excite in the nervous system resonances with observable physiological consequences. Pulse variability is introduced for the purpose of thwarting habituation of the nervous system to the repetitive stimulation, or to alleviate the need for precise tuning to a resonance frequency, or to control pathological oscillatory neural activities such as tremors or seizures. Pulse generators with stochastic and deterministic pulse variability are disclosed, and the output of an effective generator of the latter type is characterized.

USP # 6,135,944 (October 24, 2000)

Method of Inducing Harmonious States of Being

Bowman, Gerard D., et al.

Abstract --- A method of inducing harmonious states of being using vibrational stimuli, preferably sound, comprised of a multitude of frequencies expressing a specific pattern of relationship. Two base signals are modulated by a set of ratios to generate a plurality of harmonics. The harmonics are combined to form a "fractal" arrangement.

USP # 6,122,322 (September 19, 2000)

Subliminal Message Protection

Jandel, Magnus

Abstract --- The present invention relates to a method and to a system for detecting a first context change between two frames. When a second context change between a further two frames occurs within a predetermined time interval, the frames accommodated within the two context changes are defined as a subliminal message. An alarm is sent to an observer upon detection of a subliminal message.

USP # 6,091,994 (July 18, 2000)

Pulsative Manipulation of Nervous Systems

Loos, Hendricus

Abstract --- Method and apparatus for manipulating the nervous system by imparting subliminal pulsative cooling to the subject's skin at a frequency that is suitable for the excitation of a sensory resonance. At present, two major sensory resonances are known, with frequencies near 1/2 Hz and 2.4 Hz. The 1/2 Hz sensory resonance causes relaxation, sleepiness, ptosis of the eyelids, a tonic smile, a "knot" in the stomach, or sexual excitement, depending on the precise frequency used. The 2.4 Hz resonance causes the slowing of certain cortical activities, and is characterized by a large increase of the time needed to silently count backward

MATRIX OF THE MIND

from 100 to 60, with the eyes closed. The invention can be used by the general public for inducing relaxation, sleep, or sexual excitement, and clinically for the control and perhaps a treatment of tremors, seizures, and autonomic system disorders such as panic attacks. Embodiments shown are a pulsed fan to impart subliminal cooling pulses to the subject's skin, and a silent device which induces periodically varying flow past the subject's skin, the flow being induced by pulsative rising warm air plumes that are caused by a thin resistive wire which is periodically heated by electric current pulses.

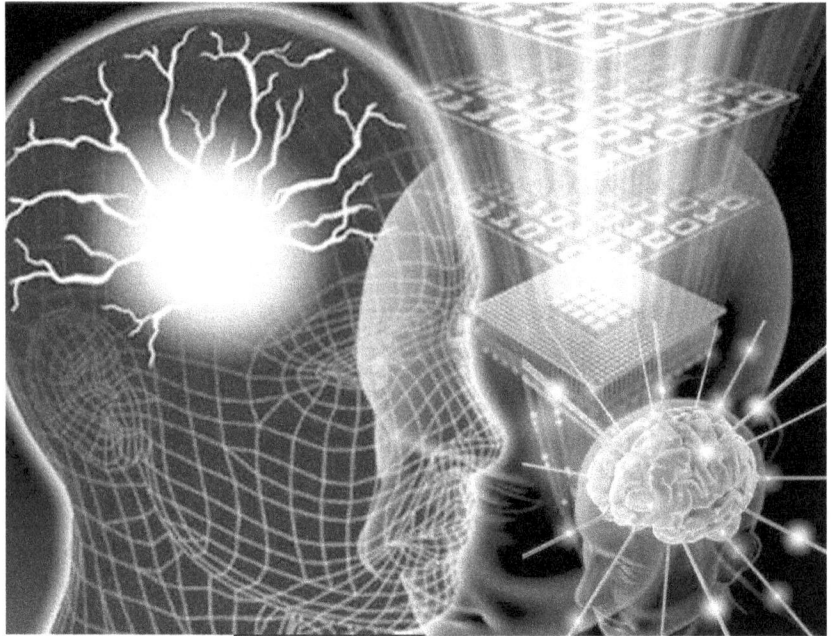

USP # 6,081,744 (June 27, 2000)

Electric Fringe Field Generator for Manipulating Nervous Systems

Loos, Hendricus

Abstract --- Apparatus and method for manipulating the nervous system of a subject through afferent nerves, modulated by externally applied weak fluctuating electric fields, tuned to certain frequencies such as to excite a resonance in neural circuits. Depending on the frequency chosen, excitation of such resonances causes in a human subject relaxation, sleepiness, sexual excitement, or the slowing of certain cortical processes. The electric field used for stimulation of the subject is induced by a pair of field electrodes charged to opposite polarity and placed such that the subject is entirely outside the space between the field electrodes. Such configuration allows for very compact devices where the field electrodes and a battery-powered voltage generator are contained in a small casing, such as a powder box. The stimulation by the weak external electric field relies on frequency modulation of spontaneous spiking patterns of afferent nerves. The method and apparatus can be used by the general public as an aid to relaxation, sleep, or arousal, and clinically for the control and perhaps the treatment of tremors and seizures, and disorders of the autonomic nervous system, such as panic attacks.

MATRIX OF THE MIND

USP # 6,052,336 (April 18, 2000)

Apparatus and Method of Broadcasting Audible Sound Using Ultrasonic Sound as a Carrier

Lowrey, Austin, III

Abstract --- An ultrasonic sound source broadcasts an ultrasonic signal which is amplitude and/or frequency modulated with an information input signal originating from an information input source. If the signals are amplitude modulated, a square root function of the information input signal is produced prior to modulation. The modulated signal, which may be amplified, is then broadcast via a projector unit, whereupon an individual or group of individuals located in the broadcast region detect the audible sound.

USP # 6,039,688 (March 21, 2000)

Therapeutic Behavior Modification Program, Compliance Monitoring and Feedback System

Douglas, Peter, et al.

Abstract --- A therapeutic behavior modification program, compliance monitoring and feedback system includes a server-based relational database and one or more microprocessors electronically coupled to the server. The system enables development of a therapeutic behavior modification program having a series of milestones for an individual to achieve lifestyle changes necessary to maintain his or her health or recover from ailments or medical procedures. The program may be modified by a physician or trained case advisor prior to implementation. The system monitors the individual's compliance with the program by prompting the individual to enter health-related data, correlating the individual's entered data with the milestones in the behavior modification program and generating compliance data indicative of the individual's progress toward achievement of the program milestones. The system also includes an integrated system of graphical system interfaces for motivating the individual to comply with the program. Through the interfaces, the individual can access the database to review the compliance data and obtain health information from a remote source such as selected sites on the Internet. The system also provides an electronic calendar integrated with the behavior modification program for signaling the individual to take action pursuant to the behavior modification program in which the calendar accesses the relational database and integrates requirements of the program with the individual's daily schedule, and an electronic journal for enabling the individual to enter personal health-related information into the system on a regular basis. In addition, the system includes an electronic meeting room for linking the individual to a plurality of other individuals having related behavior modification programs for facilitating group peer support sessions for compliance with the program. The system enables motivational media presentations to be made to the individuals in the electronic meeting room as part of the group support session to facilitate interactive group discussion about the presentations. The entire system is designed around a community of support motif including a graphical electronic navigator operable by the individual to control the microprocessor for accessing different parts of the system.

USP # 6,017,302 (January 25, 2000)

Subliminal Acoustic Manipulation of Nervous Systems

Loos, Hendricus

Abstract --- In human subjects, sensory resonances can be excited by subliminal atmospheric acoustic pulses that are tuned to the resonance frequency. The 1/2 Hz sensory resonance affects the autonomic nervous system and may cause relaxation, drowsiness, or sexual excitement, depending on the precise acoustic frequency near 1/2 Hz used. The effects of the 2.5 Hz resonance include slowing of certain cortical processes, sleepiness, and disorientation. For these effects to occur, the acoustic intensity must lie in a certain deeply subliminal range. Suitable apparatus consists of a portable battery-powered source of weak subaudio acoustic radiation. The method and apparatus can be used by the general public as an aid to relaxation, sleep, or sexual arousal, and clinically for the control and perhaps treatment of insomnia, tremors, epileptic seizures, and anxiety disorders. There is further application as a nonlethal weapon that can be used in law enforcement standoff situations, for causing drowsiness and disorientation in targeted subjects. It is then preferable to use venting acoustic monopoles in the form of a device that inhales and exhales air with subaudio frequency.

USP # 6,011,991 (January 4, 2000)

Communication System & Method Including Brain Wave Analysis...

Mardirossian, Aris

Abstract --- A system and method for enabling human beings to communicate by way of their monitored brain activity. The brain activity of an individual is monitored and transmitted to a remote location (e.g. by satellite). At the remote location, the monitored brain activity is compared with pre-recorded normalized brain activity curves, waveforms, or patterns to determine if a match or substantial match is found. If such a match is found, then the computer at the remote location determines that the individual was attempting to communicate the word, phrase, or thought corresponding to the matched stored normalized signal.

MATRIX OF THE MIND

USP # 6,006,188 (December 21, 1999)

Speech Signal Processing for Determining Psychological or Physiological Characteristics...

Bogdashevsky, Rostislav, et al.

Abstract --- A speech-based system for assessing the psychological, physiological, or other characteristics of a test subject is described. The system includes a knowledge base that stores one or more speech models, where each speech model corresponds to a characteristic of a group of reference subjects. Signal processing circuitry, which may be implemented in hardware, software and/or firmware, compares the test speech parameters of a test subject with the speech models. In one embodiment, each speech model is represented by a statistical time-ordered series of frequency representations of the speech of the reference subjects. The speech model is independent of a priori knowledge of style parameters associated with the voice or speech. The system includes speech parameterization circuitry for generating the test parameters in response to the test subject's speech. This circuitry includes speech acquisition circuitry, which may be located remotely from the knowledge base. The system further includes output circuitry for outputting at least one indicator of a characteristic in response to the comparison performed by the signal processing circuitry. The characteristic may be time-varying, in which case the output circuitry outputs the characteristic in a time-varying manner. The output circuitry also may output a ranking of each output characteristic. In one embodiment, one or more characteristics may indicate the degree of sincerity of the test subject, where the degree of sincerity may vary with time. The system may also be employed to determine the effectiveness of treatment for a psychological or physiological disorder by comparing psychological or physiological characteristics, respectively, before and after treatment.

USP # 5,954,630 (September 21, 1999)

FM Theta-Inducing Audible Sound...

Masaki, Kazumi, et al.

Abstract --- An audible sound of modulated wave where a very low-frequency wave of about 20 hertz or lower is superposed on an audio low-frequency wave effectively stimulates Fm theta in human brain waves to improve attention and concentration during mental tasks when auditorily administered. The audible sound is also effective in stimulation of human alpha wave when the very low-frequency wave lies within the range of about 2-10 hertz. Such audible sound is artificially obtainable by generating an electric signal which contains such a modulated wave, and transducing it into audible sound wave.

MATRIX OF THE MIND

USP # 5,954,629 (September 21, 1999)

Brain Wave Inducing System

Yanagidaira, Masatoshi, et al.

Abstract --- Sensors are provided for detecting brain waves of a user, and a band-pass filter is provided for extracting a particular brain waves including an .alpha. wave included in a detected brain wave. The band-pass filter comprises a first band-pass filter having a narrow pass band, and a second band-pass filter having a wide pass band. One of the first and second band-pass filters is selected, and a stimulation signal is produced in dependency on an .alpha. wave extracted by a selected band-pass filter. In accordance with the stimulation signal, a stimulation light is emitted to the user in order to induce the user to relax or sleeping state.

USP # 5,935,054 (August 10, 1999)

Magnetic Excitation of Sensory Resonances

Loos, H.

Abstract --- The invention pertains to influencing the nervous system of a subject by a weak externally applied magnetic field with a frequency near 1/2 Hz. In a range of amplitudes, such fields can excite the 1/2 sensory resonance, which is the physiological effect involved in "rocking the baby".

USP # 5,922,016 (July 13, 1999)

Apparatus for Electric Stimulation of Auditory Nerves of a Human Being

Wagner, Hermann

Abstract --- Apparatus for electric stimulation and diagnostics of auditory nerves of a human being, e.g. for determination of sensation level (SL), most conformable level (MCL) and uncomfortable level (UCL) audibility curves, includes a stimulator detachably secured to a human being for sending a signal into a human ear, and an electrode placed within the human ear and electrically connected to the stimulator by an electric conductor for conducting the signals from the stimulator into the ear. A control unit is operatively connected to the stimulator for instructing the stimulator as to characteristics of the generated signals being transmitted to the ear.

USP # 5,868,103 (February 9, 1999)

Method and Apparatus for Controlling an Animal

Boyd, Randal

MATRIX OF THE MIND

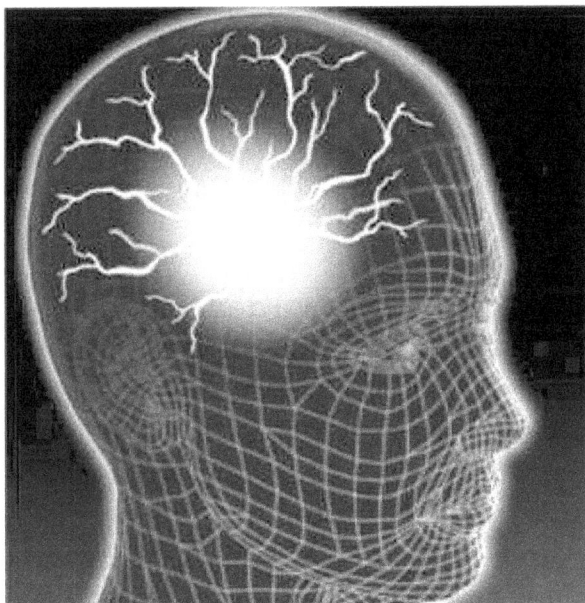

Abstract --- An apparatus for controlling an animal wherein the animal receives a control stimulus of the release of a substance having an adverse effect upon the animal as a corrective measure. The apparatus includes a transmitter for producing a transmitted field, and a releasable collar for attaching to the neck of the animal. The collar includes a receiver for receiving the transmitted field and for producing a received signal, a control circuit for determining when the received signal indicates that the animal requires a corrective measure and for producing a control signal, a container for containing the substance having an adverse effect upon the animal, and a mechanism for releasing the substance from the container into the presence of the animal upon the production of the control signal by the control circuit. In use, the transmitter is set to produce the transmitted field and the collar is attached to the neck of the animal. As the animal moves about, the receiver in the collar receives the transmitted field and produces a received signal. The control circuit determines when the received signal indicates that the animal requires a corrective measure. A control signal is produced by the control circuit when the determination is made that the animal requires a corrective measure. Upon the production of the control signal, the substance having an adverse effect upon the animal is released from the container and into the presence of the animal.

USP # 5,784,124 (July 21, 1998)

Supraliminal Method of Education...

D'Alitalia, Joseph A., et al.

Abstract   A method of behavior modification involves having a patient view supraliminal video messages superimposed upon an underlying video presentation. The video messages incorporate messages wherein at least some of the messages link a desired modified behavior to positive feelings of the patient. A supraliminal message generator and superimposer iteratively selects individual messages for display from the sequence of messages, decompressing the messages as required, and places the selected messages in a buffer memory of a video generation device. A processor of the supraliminal message generator and superimposer then fades the selected message from an invisible level to a visible level on the video display, and then fades the selected message from the visible level back to the invisible level.

USP # 5,649,061 (July 15, 1997)

Device and Method for Estimating a Mental Decision

Smyth, Christopher

Abstract --- A device and method for estimating a mental decision to select a visual cue from the viewer's eye fixation and corresponding single event evoked cerebral potential. The device comprises an eyetracker, an electronic biosignal processor and a digital computer. The eyetracker determines the instantaneous viewing direction from oculometric measurements and a head position and orientation sensor. The electronic processor continually estimates the cerebral electroencephalogramic potential from scalp surface measurements following corrections for electrooculogramic, electromyogramic and electrocardiogramic artifacts. The digital computer analyzes the viewing direction data for a fixation and then extracts the corresponding single event evoked cerebral potential. The fixation properties, such as duration, start and end pupil sizes, end state (saccade or blink) and gaze fixation count, and the parametric representation of the evoked potential are all inputs to an artificial neural network for outputting an estimate of the selection interest in the gaze point of regard. The artificial neural network is trained off-line prior to application to represent the mental decisions of the viewer. The device can be used to control computerized machinery from a video display by ocular gaze point of regard alone, by determining which visual cue the viewer is looking at and then using the estimation of the task-related selection as a selector switch.

USP # 5,644,363 (July 1, 1997)

Apparatus for Superimposing Visual Subliminal Instructions on a Video Signal

Mead, Talbert

Abstract --- A subliminal video instructional device comprises circuitry for receiving an underlying video signal and presenting this signal to horizontal and vertical synchronization detection circuits, circuitry for generating a subliminal video message synchronized to the underlying video signal, and circuitry for adding the subliminal video message to the underlying video signal to create a combination video signal.

USP # 5,586,967 (December 24, 1996)

Method & Recording for Producing Sounds and Messages to Achieve Alpha

MATRIX OF THE MIND

& Theta Brainwave States...

Davis, Mark E.

Abstract --- A method and recording for the use in achieving alpha and theta brainwave states and effecting positive emotional states in humans, is provided which includes a medium having a musical composition thereon with an initial tempo decreasing to a final tempo and verbal phrases recorded in synchrony with the decreasing tempo.

USP # 5,562,597 (October 8, 1996)

Method & Apparatus for Reducing Physiological Stress

Van Dick, Robert C.

Abstract --- Physiological stress in a human subject is treated by generating a weak electromagnetic field about a quartz crystal. The crystal is stimulated by applying electrical pulses of pulse widths between 0.1 and 50 microseconds each at a pulse repetition rate of between 0.5K and 10K pulses per second to a conductor positioned adjacent to the quartz crystal thereby generating a weak electromagnetic field. A subject is positioned within the weak electromagnetic field for a period of time sufficient to reduce stress.

USP # 5,551,879 (September 3, 1996)

Dream State Teaching Machine

Raynie, Arthur D.

Abstract --- A device for enhancing lucidity in the dream state of an individual. The device includes electronic circuitry incorporated into a headband for the user to wear while sleeping. The circuitry includes a detector for fitting adjacent to the eye of the sleeping individual, for detecting Rapid Eye Movement (REM), which occurs during the dream state. The detector emits a signal that is evaluated by additional circuitry to determine whether or not REM sleep is occurring. If REM sleep is occurring, a signal is generated to operate a recorded, which typically plays prerecorded messages through the headphones engaging the ear of the sleeping individual.

USP # 5,539,705 (July 23, 1996)

Ultrasonic Speech Translator and Communication System

M. A. Akerman, M., et al.

Abstract --- A wireless communication system, undetectable by radio-frequency methods, for converting audio signals, including human voice, to electronic signals in the ultrasonic frequency range, transmitting the ultrasonic signal

MATRIX OF THE MIND

by way of acoustic pressure waves across a carrier medium, including gases, liquids and solids, and reconverting the ultrasonic acoustic pressure waves back to the original audio signal. This invention was made with government support under Contract DE-ACO5-840R21400, awarded by the US Department of Energy to Martin Marietta Energy Systems, Inc.

USP # 5,507,291 (April 16, 1996)

Method & Apparatus for Remotely Determining Information as to Person's Emotional State ~

Stirbl, et al.

Abstract --- In a method for remotely determining information relating to a person's emotional state, an waveform energy having a predetermined frequency and a predetermined intensity is generated and wirelessly transmitted towards a remotely located subject. Waveform energy emitted from the subject is detected and automatically analyzed to derive information relating to the individual's emotional state. Physiological or physical parameters of blood pressure, pulse rate, pupil size, respiration rate and perspiration level are measured and compared with reference values to provide information utilizable in evaluating interviewee's responses or possibly criminal intent in security sensitive areas.

USP # 5,522,386 (June 4, 1996)

Apparatus for Determination of the Condition of the Vegetative Part of the Nervous System

Lerner, Eduard

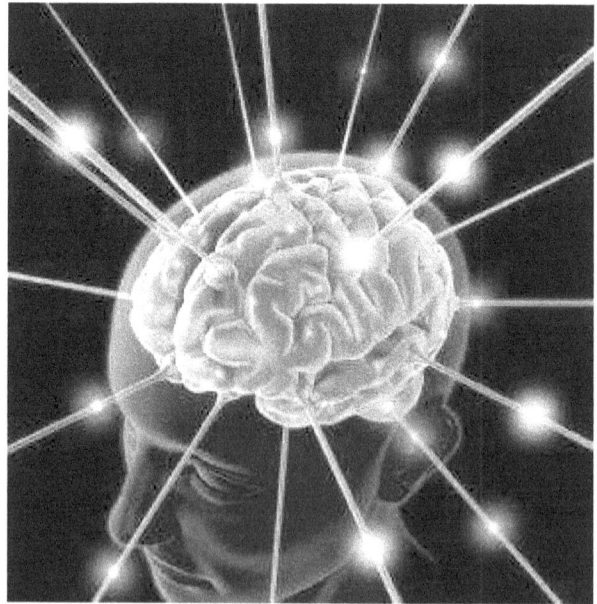

Abstract --- Apparatus for use in the determination of the condition of the vegetative part of the nervous system and/or of sensory functions of an organism, i.e. a human being or animal. The apparatus comprises devices for generating and supplying to said organism at least one sensory stimulus chosen from a group of sensory stimuli, such as visual, sound, olfactory, gustatory, tactile or pain stimuli, and devices for measuring the skin potential and the evoked response of the organism to a stimulus. The measured data are processed by processing devices for automatically controlling the supply of at least one stimulus for providing a non-rhythmical sequence of stimuli. Preferably, pairs of stimuli are supplied for developing a conditioned reflex.

MATRIX OF THE MIND

USP # 5,480,374 (January 2, 1996)

Method and Apparatus for Reducing Physiological Stress

Van Dick, Robert

Abstract --- Physiological stress in a human subject is treated by generating a weak electromagnetic field about a grounded electrode by the application of pulses of between 5 and 50 microseconds each at a pulse rate of between 0.5K and 10K pulses per second to a power electrode, the power electrode and grounded electrode being coupled to high voltage pulse generation means. A subject is positioned within the weak electromagnetic field for a period of time sufficient to cause an increase in his or her alpha or theta brain wave levels.

USP # 5,479,941 (January 2, 1996)

Device for Inducing Altered States of Consciousness

Harner, Michael

Abstract --- A rotating device for producing altered states of consciousness in a subject is provided. The subject's body rotates about a point in the center of the body support means at a speed between about 10 and about 60 revolutions per minute. In a preferred embodiment the direction of rotation is periodically reversed.

USP # 5,392,788 (February 28, 1995)

Method and Device for Interpreting Concepts and Conceptual Thought...

Hudspeth, William J.

Abstract --- A system for acquisition and decoding of EP and SP signals is provided which comprises a transducer for presenting stimuli to a subject, EEG transducers for recording brainwave signals from the subject, a computer for controlling and synchronizing stimuli presented to the subject and for concurrently recording brainwave signals, and either interpreting signals using a model for conceptual perceptional and emotional thought to correspond EEG signals to thought of the subject or comparing signals to normative EEG signals from a normative population to diagnose and locate the origin of brain dysfunctional underlying perception, conception, and emotion.

USP # 5,356,368 (October 18, 1994)

Method & Apparatus for Inducing Desired States of Consciousness

Monroe, Robert E.

Abstract --- Improved methods and apparatus for entraining human brain patterns, employing frequency following response (FFR) techniques, facilitate attainment of desired states of consciousness. In one embodiment, a plurality of electroencephalogram (EEG) waveforms, characteristic of a given state of consciousness, are combined to yield an EEG waveform to which subjects may be susceptible more readily. In another embodiment, sleep patterns are reproduced based on observed brain patterns during portions of a sleep cycle; entrainment principles are applied to induce sleep. In yet another embodiment, entrainment principles are applied in the work environment, to induce and maintain a desired level of consciousness. A portable device also is described.

USP # 5,352,181 (October 4, 1994)

Method & Recording for Producing Sounds and Messages...

Davis, Mark E.

Abstract --- A method and recording for use in achieving Alpha and Theta brain wave states and effecting positive emotional states in humans to enhance learning and self-improvement, is provided which includes a medium having a musical composition recorded thereon with an initial tempo decreasing to a final tempo and verbal phrases, comprising between approximately 4 and approximately 8 words, recorded in synchrony with the decreasing initial tempo.

USP # 5,330,414 (July 19, 1994)

Brain Wave Inducing Apparatus

Yasushi, Mitsuo

Abstract --- A random signal generator outputs a random noise signal to a band pass filter which selectively passes frequency components in the frequency range of a desired brain wave from a subject. The output of the band pass filter is supplied to an automatic level controller. The automatic level controller sets the output of band pass filter to a predetermined amplitude. Then, the output of the automatic level controller is fed to a stimulating light generator, which converts the output of the automatic level controller into a light signal for stimulating the subject in order to induce the desired brain wave from the subject. The light signal is then emitted into the subject's eyes.

USP # 5,289,438 (February 22, 1994)

Method & System for Altering Consciousness

Gall, James

Abstract --- A system for altering the states of human consciousness involves the simultaneous application of multiple stimuli, preferable sounds, having differing frequencies and wave forms. The relationship between the frequencies of

MATRIX OF THE MIND

the several stimuli is exhibited by the equation g = 2.sup.n/4 .multidot.f where: f = frequency of one stimulus; g = frequency of the other stimuli or stimulus; and n = a positive or negative integer which is different for each other stimulus.

USP # 5,245,666 (September 14, 1993)

Personal Subliminal Messaging System

Mikell, Bruce T.

Abstract --- A personal subliminal messaging system includes a wide range linear subliminal modulator (43), a digital audio recording or play device (46), a microphone (51) to pick up the sound at the ear, and an earpiece (50) to deliver the subliminal message. The sound level at the user's ear is detected and measured. After risetime and decay conditioning of the varying dc control signal, the wide range linear modulator (43) uses this signal to control the level of the message to the earpiece (50). The user adjusts the system for a liminal of a subliminal level. The psychoacoustic phenomena of Post Masking is used to increase the integrity of the message in subliminal messaging systems.

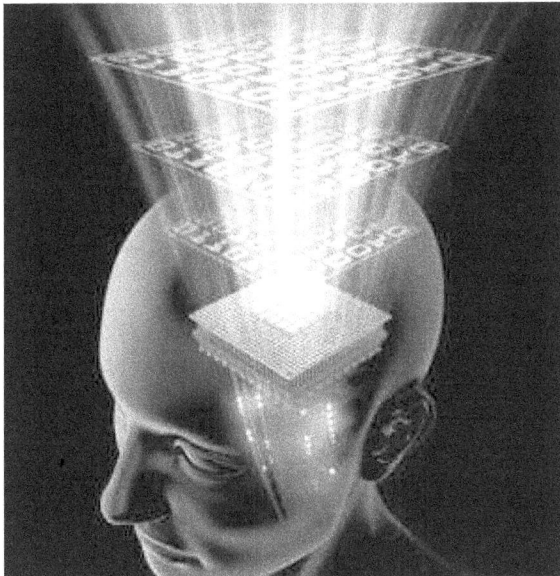

USP # 5,270,800 (December 14, 1993)

Subliminal Message Generator

Sweet. Robert L.

Abstract --- A combined subliminal and supraliminal message generator for use with a television receiver permits complete control of subliminal messages and their manner of presentation. A video synchronization detector enables a video display generator to generate a video message signal corresponding to a received alphanumeric text message in synchronism with a received television signal. A video mixer selects either the received video signal or tho video message signal for output. The messages produced by the video message generator are user selectable via a keyboard input. A message memory stores a plurality of alphanumeric text messages specified by user commands for use as subliminal messages. This message memory preferably includes a read only memory storing predetermined sets of alphanumeric text messages directed to differing topics. The sets of predetermined alphanumeric text messages preferably include several positive affirmations directed to the left brain and an equal number of positive affirmations directed to the right brain that are alternately presented subliminally. The left brain messages are presented in a linear text mode, while the right brain messages are presented in a three dimensional perspective mode. The user can control the length and spacing of the subliminal presentations to accommodate differing conscious thresholds. Alternative embodiments include a combined cable television converter and subliminal message generator, a combine television receiver and subliminal message generator and a computer capable of presenting subliminal messages.

USP # 5,224,864 (July 6, 1993)

Method of Recording and Reproducing Subliminal Signals that are 180 Degrees Out of Phase

Woith, Blake F.

Abstract --- A subliminal recording includes both subliminal message and mask signals applied to both tracks of a two track recording medium. The subliminal message signals are identical in content, and are recorded in an out-of-phase relationship. The mask signals are recorded in phase. The resulting recording may be utilized in the conventional manner for subliminal recordings. By combining the composite signals in an inverted relationship, the mask signals cancel while the subliminal message signals are additive, thus allowing the presence of the subliminal message signal to be confirmed on the recording.

USP # 5,221,962 (June 22, 1993)

Subliminal Device having Manual Adjustment of Perception Level of Subliminal Messages

Backus, Alan L., et al.

Abstract --- A method and apparatus for presenting subliminal visual and/or audio messages which allows user verification of message content and presence, as well as proper adjustment of message obviousness while accounting for ambient conditions and user sensitivities is disclosed. This method and apparatus also presents synchronized reinforced sensory input of subliminal messages. This is performed by simultaneously overlaying images received from a VCR over a plurality of television signals. This apparatus directs overlay images over RF television signals having both audio and video components

USP # 5,215,468 (June 1, 1993)

Method and Apparatus for Introducing Subliminal Changes to Audio Stimuli

Lauffer, Martha A., et al.

Abstract --- A method and apparatus for introducing gradual changes to an audio signal so that the changes are subliminal. The changes can involve tempo and volume, for example, and can take the form of a gentle gradient having ever increasing/decreasing ramp-like changes over a sufficient duration, or a more complex program involving several gentle gradients. In the preferred embodiment, an enhanced audio play-back device such as a portable audio cassette recorder can be programmed to subliminally alter the characteristics of a standard pre-recorded tape containing music, for example. As a motivational tool during walking, jogging or other repetitive exercise, the tempo is gradually increased over a period of time to encourage a corresponding gradual (and subliminal) increase in physical exertion by a user whose rate of movement is proportional to the tempo of the music. The tempo can be either manually changed in conjunction with a subliminal program, or by itself in an override mode, or by itself in a version of the present-inventive audio play-back device which allows only manual tempo alternation. In an alternate embodiment, a special pre-recorded tape contains subliminal changes in tempo, for example, for play-back on a standard audio cassette recorder (which operates at one speed, only) to cause the same effect as the preferred embodiment.

USP # 5,213,562 (May 25, 1993)

Method of Inducing Mental, Emotional and Physical States of Consciousness...

Monroe, Robert A.

Abstract --- A method having applicability in replication of desired consciousness states; in the training of an individual to replicate such a state of consciousness without further audio stimulation; and in the transferring of such states from one human being to another through the imposition of one individual's EEG, superimposed on desired stereo signals, on another individual, by inducement of a binaural beat phenomenon.

USP # 5,194,008 (March 16, 1993)

Subliminal Image Modulation Projection and Detection System and Method

Mohan, William L., et al.

Abstract --- Weapon training simulation system including a computer operated video display scene whereon is projected a plurality of visual targets. The computer controls the display scene and the targets, whether stationary or moving, and processes data of a point of aim sensor apparatus associated with a weapon operated by a trainee. The sensor apparatus is sensitive to non-visible or subliminal modulated areas having a controlled contrast of brightness between the target scene and the targets. The sensor apparatus locates a specific subliminal modulated area and the computer determines the location of a target image on the display scene with respect to the sensor apparatus

USP # 5,175,571 (December 29, 1992)

Glasses with Subliminal Message

Tanefsky, Faye, et al.

Abstract --- A pair of subliminal imaging spectacles is provided with a matched pair of visual subliminal images designed and placed so as to merge into one image due to the stereoscopic effect of human vision and thus to impart a subliminal message to the wearer.

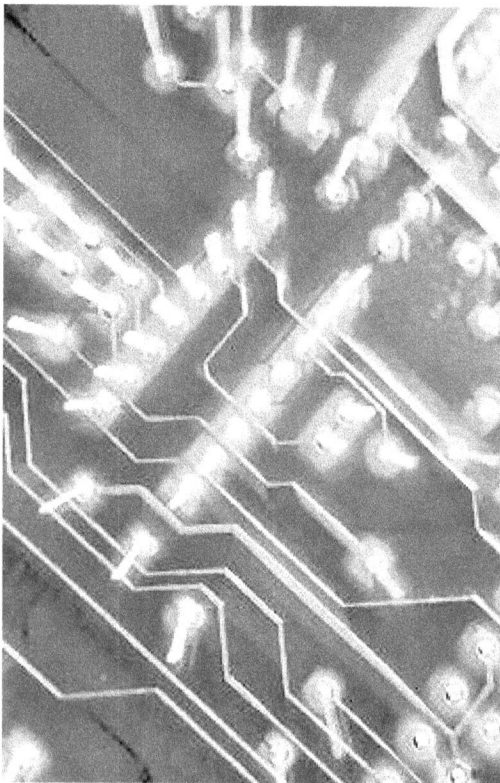

USP # 5,170,381 (December 8, 1992)

Method for Mixing Audio Subliminal Recordings

Taylor, Eldon, et al.

Abstract --- Audio subliminal recordings are made in which in addition to using a primary carrier, such as music, two audio channels are used to deliver subliminal messages to the brain. On one channel, accessing the left brain hemisphere, the message delivered is meaningfully spoken, forward-masked, permissive affirmations delivered in a round-robin manner by a male voice, a female voice and a child's voice. On the other channel, accessing the right brain, directive messages, in the same voices, are recorded in backward-masked (or meta-contrast). The three voices are recording in round-robin fashion with full echo reverberation. The audio tracks are mixed using a special processor which converts sound frequencies to electrical impulses and tracks the subliminal message to synchronize the subliminal message in stereo with the primary carrier. The processor maintains constant gain differential between the primary carrier and the subliminal verbiage and, with the subliminal verbiage being recorded with round-robin, full echo reverberation, ensures that none of a message is lost. The primary carrier should be continuous music without breaks or great differences in movements.

MATRIX OF THE MIND

USP # 5,159,703 (October 27, 1992)

Silent Subliminal Presentation System

Lowery, Oliver

Abstract --- A silent communications system in which nonaural carriers, in the very low or very high audio frequency range or in the adjacent ultrasonic frequency spectrum, are amplitude or frequency modulated with the desired intelligence and propagated acoustically or vibrationally, for inducement into the brain, typically through the use of loudspeakers, earphones or piezoelectric transducers.

USP # 5,151,080 (September 29, 1992)

Method & Apparatus for Inducing & Establishing a Changed State of Consciousness

Bick, Claus

Abstract --- An electroacoustic device includes a sound generator as well as a system for producing synthetic human speech, connected to a modulation stage for superimposing the output signals thereof. The superimposed output signals are applied via an amplifier stage to one of a headphone system or loudspeaker system.

USP # 5,135,468 (August 4, 1992)

Method & Apparatus of Varying the Brain State of a Person by Means of an Audio Signal

Meissner, Juergen P.

Abstract --- A method of varying the brain state of a person includes the steps of supplying the first audio signal to one ear of the person, supplying a second audio signal to the other ear of the person, and substantially continuously varying the frequency of at least one of the first and second audio signals to vary the brain state of the person.

USP # 5,134,484 (July 28, 1992)

Superimposing Method & Apparatus Useful for Subliminal Messages

Willson, Joseph

Abstract --- Data to be displayed is combined with a composite video signal. The data is stored in a memory in digital form. Each byte of the data is read out in sequential fashion to determine: the recurrence display rate of the data according to the frame sync pulses of the video signal; the location of the data within the video image according to the line sync pulses of the video signal; and the location of the data display within the video image according to the position information. Synchronization of the data with the video image is derived from the sync pulses of the composite video signal. A similar technique is employed to combine sound data with an audio signal. Data to be displayed may be presented as a subliminal message or may persist for a given time interval. The data may be derived from a variety of sources including a prerecorded or live video signal. The message may be a reminder message displayed upon a television screen to remind the viewer of an appointment. The data may be stored in a variety of different memory devices capable of high speed data retrieval. The data may be generated locally on-line or off-line and transferred to memory which stores the data necessary to create the message.

USP # 5,128,765 (July 7, 1992)

System for Implementing the Synchronized Superimposition of Subliminal Signals

Dingwall, Robert

Abstract --- An apparatus and system for the controlled delivery of a subliminal video and/or audio message on to a source signal from a video tape player or similar. The source signal is divided into audio and video portions. A video processor reads sychronization information from the source signal. A controller transmits a stored subliminal image at designated times to a mixer amplifier fully synchronized with the source signal. Concurrently, an audio subliminal message is applied to the source audio at a volume level regulated at some fraction to the source audio. The combined signals are transmitted to a monitor for undistracted viewing.

USP # 5,123,899 (June 23, 1992)

Method & System for Altering Consciousness

Gall, James

Abstract --- A system for altering the states of human consciousness involves the simultaneous application of multiple stimuli, preferable sounds, having differing frequencies and wave forms. The relationship between the frequencies of the several stimuli is exhibited by the equation $g = s.sup.n/4 .multidot.f$ where: $f =$ frequency of one stimulus; $g =$ frequency of the other stimuli of stimulus; and $n=a$ positive or negative integer which is different for each other stimulus.

MATRIX OF THE MIND

USP # 5,052,401 (October 1, 1991)

Sherwin, Gary

Product Detector for a Steady Visual Evoked Potential Stimulator and Product Detector

Abstract --- An automated visual testing system is disclosed which presents an alternating steady state visual stimulus to a patient through an optical system that modifies the stimulus image. As the image changes, the patient produces evoked potentials that change. The evoked potentials are detected by a product detector which produces the amplitude of the evoked potentials. The product detector includes filters which isolate the patient's evoked potentials, a modulator which detects the response using the stimulus source frequency and a demodulator that determines the amplitude of the response. The product detector detects the level of the steady state evoked potential signals even in the presence of substantial background noise and extraneous electroencephalograhic signals. These detectors can be used to monitor the evoked potential produced by visual, aural or somatic steady state stimuli. The components described above can be used to produce a system that can determine to which of several different displays an observer is paying attention by providing images that blink at different frequencies and product detectors for each of the stimulus frequencies. The product detector producing the highest output indicates the display upon which the observer is focused.

USP # 5,047,994 (September 10, 1991)

Supersonic Bone Conduction Hearing Aid and Method

Lenhardt, Martin, et al.

Abstract --- A supersonic bone conduction hearing aid that receives conventional audiometric frequencies and converts them to supersonic frequencies for connection to the human sensory system by vibration bone conduction. The hearing is believed to use channels of communications to the brain that are not normally used for hearing. These alternative channels do not deteriorate significantly with age as does the normal hearing channels. The supersonic bone conduction frequencies are discerned as frequencies in the audiometric range of frequencies.

USP # 5,036,858 (August 6, 1991)

Method & Apparatus for Changing Brain Wave Frequency

Carter, John L., et al.

Abstract --- A method for changing brain wave frequency to a desired frequency determines a current brain wave frequency of a user, generates two frequencies with a frequency difference of a magnitude between that of the current actual brain wave frequency and the desired frequency but always within a predetermined range of the current actual brain wave frequency, and produces an output to the user corresponding to the two frequencies. One apparatus to accomplish the method has a computer processor, a computer memory, EEG electrodes along with an amplifier, a programmable timing generator responsive to the computer processor for generating the two frequencies, audio amplifiers and a beat frequency generator driving a visual frequency amplifier.

USP # 5,027,208 (June 25,1991)

Therapeutic Subliminal Imaging System

Dwyer, Jr., Joseph, et al.

Abstract --- A therapeutic subliminal imaging system wherein a selected subliminal message is synchronized with and added to an existing video signal containing a supraliminal message. A television receiver or video recorder can be used to provide the supraliminal message and a video processing circuit varies the intensity of that perceptible message to incorporate one or more subliminal images.

USP # 5,017,143 (May 21, 1991)

Method and Apparatus for Producing Subliminal Images

Backus, Alan, et al.

Abstract --- A method and apparatus to produce more effective visual subliminal communications. Graphic and/or text images, presented for durations of less than a video frame, at organized rhythmic intervals, the rhythmic intervals intended to affect user receptivity, moods or behavior. Subliminal graphic images having translucent visual values locally dependent on background values in order to maintain desired levels of visual contrast.

USP # 4,958,638 (September 25, 1990)

Non-Contact Vital Signs Monitor

Sharpe, Steven, et al.

Abstract --- An apparatus for measuring simultaneous physiological parameters such as heart rate and respiration without physically connecting electrodes or other sensors to the body. A beam of frequency modulated continuous wave radio frequency energy is directed towards the body of a subject. The reflected signal contains phase information representing the movement of the surface of the body, from which respiration and heartbeat information can be obtained. The reflected phase modulated energy is received and demodulated by the apparatus using synchronous quadrature detection. The quadrature signals so obtained are then signal processed to obtain the heartbeat and respiratory information of interest.

USP # 4,924,744 (May 15, 1990)

Apparatus for Generating Sound through Low Frequency and Noise Modulation

Lenzen, Reiner

Abstract --- In an apparatus for generating sound, there are provided a plurality of channels for generating sounds. Each of the channels includes a memory for storing waveform data, and at least one of the channels includes a noise generator so that various kinds of sounds including rhythm sound-effects sound, effects sound-vibrato etc. are generated. There is further provided a controller by which voice sound signal is passed through the channels so that artificial sound, voice sound etc. are generated. There is still further provided a circuit for adjusting an amplitude level of a whole sound which is obtained by mixing output sounds of the channels so that far and near sound is produced. Further, each of the channels includes left and right attenuators which divide a channel sound into left and right channel sounds. Still further, the apparatus comprises a low frequency oscillator for controlling a depth of frequency modulation, and a controller for writing sampling data of a predetermined waveform into serial addresses of a memory.

USP # 4,889,526 (December 26, 1989)

Non-Invasive Method & Apparatus for Modulating Brain Signals...

Rauscher, Elizabeth A.

Abstract --- This invention incorporates the discovery of new principles which utilize magnetic and electric fields generated by time varying square wave currents of precise repetition, width, shape and magnitude to move through coils and cutaneously applied conductive eletrodes in order to stimulate the nervous system and reduce pain in humans. Timer means, adjustment means, and means to deliver current to the coils and conductive eletrodes are described, as well as a theoretical model of the process. The invention incorporates the concept of two cyclic expanding and collapsing magnetic fields which generate precise wave forms in conjunction with each other to create a beat frequency which in turn causes the ion flow in the nervous system of the human body to be efficiently moved along the nerve path where the locus of the pain exists to thereby reduce the pain. The wave forms are created either in one or more coils, one or more pairs of electrodes, or a combination of the two.

MATRIX OF THE MIND

USP # 4,883,067 (November 28, 1989)

Method & Apparatus for Translating the EEG into Music...

Knispel, Joel, et al.

Abstract --- A method and apparatus for applying a musical feedback signal to the human brain, or any other brain, to induce controllable psychological and physiological responses. A signal representing the ongoing electro-encephalographic (EEG) signal of a brain preferably is obtained from the electrode location on the scalp known as CZ or P3 in clinical notation. A signal processor converts the ongoing EEG into electrical signals which are converted into music by synthesizers. The music is acoustically fed back to the brain after a time delay calculated to shift the phase of the feedback in order to reinforce specific or desired ongoing EEG activity from the scalp position of interest. The music is comprised of at least one voice that follows the moment-by-moment contour of the EEG in real time to reinforce the desired EEG activity. The music drives the brain into resonance with the music to provide a closed loop or physiological feedback effect. Preferably, the musical feedback comprises additional voices that embody psychoacoustic principles as well as provide the content and direction normally supplied by the therapist in conventional biofeedback. The invention contemplates numerous applications for the results obtained.

USP # 4,877,027 (October 31, 1989)

Hearing System

Brunkan, Wayne B.

Abstract --- Sound is induced in the head of a person by radiating the head with microwaves in the range of 100 megahertz to 10,000 megahertz that are modulated with a particular waveform. The waveform consists of frequency modulated bursts. Each burst is made up of 10 to 20 uniformly spaced pulses grouped tightly together. The burst width is between 500 nanoseconds and 100 microseconds. The pulse width is in the range of 10 nanoseconds to 1 microsecond. The bursts are frequency modulated by the audio input to create the sensation of hearing in the person whose head is irradiated.

USP # 4,858,612 (August 22, 1989)

Hearing Device

Stocklin, Philip L.

Abstract --- A method and apparatus for stimulation of hearing in mammals by introduction of a plurality of microwaves into the region of the auditory cortex is shown and secribed. A microphone is used to transform sound signals into eletrical signals which are in turn analyzed and processed to provide controls for generating a plurality of microwave signals at different frequencies. the multifrequency microwaves are then applied to the brain in the region of the auditory cortex. By this method sounds are perceived by the mamal which are representative of the original sound received by the microphone.

USP # 4,834,701 (May 30, 1989)

Apparatus for Inducing Frequency Reduction in Brain Wave

Masaki, Kazumi

Abstract --- Frequency reduction in human brain wave is inducible by allowing human brain to perceive 4-16 hertz beat sound. Such beat sound can be easily produced with an apparatus, comprising at least one sound source generating a set of low-frequency signals different each other in frequency by 4-16 hertz. Electroencephalographic study revealed that the beat sound is effective to reduce beta-rhythm into alpha-rhythm, as well as to retain alpha-rhythm.

USP # 4,821,326 (April 11, 1989)

Non-Audible Speech Generation Method & Apparatus

MacLeod, Norman

Abstract --- A non-audible speech generation apparatus adn method for producing non-audible seech signals which includes an ultasonic transducer or vibrator for projecting a series of glottal shaped ultrasonic pulses to the vocal track of a speaker. The glottal pulses, in the approximate frequency spectrum extending from 15 kilohertz to 105 kilohertz, contains harmonics of approximately 30 times the grequency of the acoustical harmonicsgenerated by the vocal cords, but which may nevertheless be amplitude modulated to produce non-auduble speech by the speaker's silently mouthing of words. The ultrasonic speech is then received by an ultasonic transducer disposed outside of the speaker's mouth and electronically communicated to a translation device which down converts the ultrasonics signals to corresponding signals in the audible frquency range and synthesizes the signals into artificial speech.

USP # 4,777,529 (October 11, 1988)

Auditory Subliminal Programming System

Schultz, Richard M., et al.

Abstract --- An auditory subliminal programming system includes a subliminal message encoder that generates fixed frequency security tones and combines them with a subliminal message signal to produce an encoded subliminal message signal which is recorded on audio tape or the like. A corresponding subliminal decoder/mixer is connected as part of a user's conventional stereo system and receives as inputs an audio program selected by the user and the encoded subliminal message. The decoder/mixer filters the security tones, if present, from the subliminal message and combines the message signals with selected low frequency signals associated with enhanced relaxation and concentration to produce a composite auditory subliminal signal. The decoder/mixer combines the composite subliminal signal with the selected audio program signals to form composite signals only if it detects the presence of the security tones in the subliminal message signal. The decoder/mixer outputs the composite signal to the audio inputs of a conventional audio amplifier where it is amplified and broadcast by conventional audio speakers.

USP # 4,734,037 (March 29, 1988)

Message Screen

McClure, J. Patrick

Abstract --- A transparent sheet is disclosed having a message thereon. The sheet has a first side adapted to be attached facing a plate which is normally viewed by a viewer and a second side facing the viewer. The message is arranged to be readably intelligible from the second side but is not liminally visible to the viewer when viewed from a normal viewing distance from the second side under normal viewing conditions. The message has a subliminal effect upon the viewer when viewed from the normal viewing distance from the second side under normal viewing conditions. A viewer can electively subject him or herself to subliminal messages while viewing television at leisure.

USP # 4,717,343 (January 5, 1988)

Method of Changing a Person's Behavior

Densky, Alan B.

Abstract --- A method of conditioning a person's unconscious mind in order to effect a desired change in the person's behavior which does not require the services of a trained therapist. Instead the person to be treated views a program of video pictures appearing on a screen. The program as viewed by the person's unconscious mind acts to condition the person's thought patterns in a manner which alters that person's behavior in a positive way.

USP # 4,699,153 (October 13, 1987)

System for Assessing Verbal Psychobiological Correlates

Shevrin, Howard, et al.

Abstract --- A system for assessing psychobiological conditions of a subject utilizes a plurality of words which are selected to be in four categories as critical stimuli. The words are presented by a tachistoscope to the subject in subliminal and supraliminal modes of operation. Subliminal stimulation of the subject is achieved by presenting the selected words for an exposure period of approximately one millisecond. The supraliminal exposure time is approximately thirty milliseconds. Prior to stimulation, the subject is diagnosed in accordance with conventional psychoanalytical techniques to establish the presence and nature of a pathological condition. The words are selected and categorized in four groups: pleasant words, unpleasant words, words related to a diagnosed conscious pathological condition, and words related to a diagnosed unconscious pathological condition. The brain wave responses which are evoked by the stimulation are collected via electrodes and analyzed in accordance with a transinformation technique which is based on information signal theory for establishing a probabilistic value which corresponds to the information content of the evoked responses.

USP # 4,692,118 (September 8, 1987)

Video Subconscious Display Attachment

Mould, Richard E.

Abstract --- An apparatus and method for introducing messages to the subconscious mind is disclosed, which includes a panel positioned adjacent a television screen, with the panel having non-distractive messages imprinted thereon, such that as the subject consciously focuses his attention on the video screen, his subconscious mind records the message from the panel that is within his peripheral vision.

USP # 4,616,261 (October 7, 1986)

Method & Apparatus for Generating Subliminal Visual Messages

Crawford, James R., et al.

Abstract --- A system for generating a subliminal message during the display of a normal television program on a television receiver utilizes a personal computer to generate an RF carrier modulated with video signals encoding the subliminal message. The computer runs under the control of an application program which stores the subliminal message and also controls the computer to cause it to generate timing signals that are provided to a single pole double-throw switch. The source of the normal television program and the video output of the computer are connected to the two switch inputs and the switch output is connected to the television receiver antenna system. The timing signals cause the switch to normally display the conventional television program and to periodically switch to the computer output to generate the subliminal message. The video output of the computer includes horizontal and vertical synchronizing signals which are of substantially the same frequency as the synchronizing signals incorporated within the normal program source but of an arbitrary phase.

USP # 4,573,449 (March 4, 1986)

Method for Stimulating the Falling Asleep and/or Relaxing Behavior of a Person

Warnke, Egon F.

Abstract --- A method and apparatus is provided with which a person suffering from sleeplessness can be more easily relaxed and may more rapidly fall asleep. In particular, sound pulses are emitted by an electro-acoustic transducer, according to the cadence of which, the person seeking to fall asleep is induced to breathe in and out over a predetermined period of time. By suitably selecting the pulse sequence frequency, the pitch and the amplitude of the sound pulses may be adjusted thereby enhancing the process of falling asleep.

USP # 4,508,105 (April 2, 1985)

Shadow Generating Apparatus

Whitten, Glen, et al.

Abstract --- Disclosed is an apparatus for inducing various brain wave patterns through visual stimulation. The apparatus comprises a pair of spectacles or other viewing apparatus having a liquid crystal display embedded in each lens. By repetitively activating and deactivating the liquid crystals, shadows are generated which are perceived by the subject individual wearing the viewing apparatus. Responding to the frequency of shadow generation, the subject's brain is thereby induced to generate sympathetic brain wave frequencies. The apparatus finds particular utility in the generation of alpha waves. Because learning is enhanced when the brain is in the alpha state, activities such as listening to tapes or lectures and the like can be carried out with greater facility. Shadow generation is accomplished through the use of a timing mechanism for each liquid crystal display and the frequency for each is adjustable over a wide range, permitting synchronous or asynchronous timing.

USP # 4,395,600 (July 26, 1983)

Auditory Subliminal Message System & Method

Lundy, Rene R., et al.

Abstract --- Ambient audio signals from the customer shopping area within a store are sensed and fed to a signal processing circuit that produces a control signal which varies with variations in the amplitude of the sensed audio signals. A control circuit adjusts the amplitude of an auditory subliminal anti-shoplifting message to increase with increasing amplitudes of sensed audio signals and decrease with decreasing amplitudes of sensed audio signals. This amplitude controlled subliminal message may be mixed with background music and transmitted to the shopping area. To reduce distortion of the subliminal message, its amplitude is controlled to increase at a first rate slower than the rate of increase of the amplitude of ambient audio signals from the area. Also, the amplitude of the subliminal message is controlled to decrease at a second rate faster than the first rate with decreasing ambient audio signal amplitudes to minimize the possibility of the subliminal message becoming supraliminal upon rapid declines in ambient audio signal amplitudes in the area. A masking signal is provided with an amplitude which is also controlled in response to the amplitude of sensed ambient audio signals. This masking signal may be combined with the auditory subliminal message to provide a composite signal fed to, and controlled by, the control circuit.

USP # 4,388,918 (June 21, 1983)

Mental Harmonization Process

Filley, Charles C.

Abstract --- A state of relaxation or mental harmonization in a subject is created by exposing a color solely to one field of vision of a subject and the complement of that color solely to the other field of vision of the subject while simultaneously exposing an audible tone solely to one oar of the subject and a harmonious tone solely to the other ear of the subject. The color and tones employed are subjectively comfortable and compatible. Preferably, the frequency difference between the two audible tones is one-half the frequency of the audible tone having the lowest frequency.

MATRIX OF THE MIND

USP # 4,354,505 (October 19, 1982)

Method of and Apparatus for Testing and Indicating Relaxation State of a Human Subject

Shiga, Kazumasa

Abstract --- In a self-training biofeedback system, a physiological signal representing the state of relaxation of a person using the system is applied to a time counter to generate a binary count output representing the relaxation period. A visual indicator connected to the time counter provides the self trained person with a quick display of the measured time period so he can gauge the depth of his relaxation.

USP # 4,335,710 (June 22, 1982)

Device for the Induction of Specific Brain Wave Patterns

Williamson, John

Abstract --- Brain wave patterns associated with relaxd and meditative states in a subject are gradually induced without deleterious chemical or neurological side effects. A white noise generator (11) has the spectral noise density of its output signal modulated in a manner similar to the brain wave patterns by a switching transistor within a spetrum modulator and converted to an audio signal by acoustic transducer. Ramp generator gradually increases the voltage received by and resultant output frequency of voltage controlled oscillator whereby switching transistor periodically shunts the high frequency components of the white noise signal to ground.

USP # 4,315,501 (February 16, 1982)

Learning-Relaxation Device

Gorges, Denis E.

Abstract --- Disclosed is a device for relaxing, stimulating and/or driving brain wave form function in a human subject. The device comprises, in combination, an eye mask having independently controlled left and right eyepieces and a peripheral light array in each eyepiece, an audio headset having independently controlled left and right earpieces and a control panel which controls light and sound signals to the light arrays and earpieces, respectively. Various control functions allow simultaneous or alternating light and sound pulsations in the left and right light arrays and earpieces, as well as selective phasing between light and sound pulsations.

MATRIX OF THE MIND

USP # 4,227,516 (October 14, 1980)

Apparatus for Electrophysiological Stimulation

Meland, Bruce C., et al.

Abstract --- Apparatus for the electrophysiological stimulation of a patient is provided for creating an analgesic condition in the patient to induce sleep, treat psychosomatic disorders, and to aid in the induction of electrohypnosis and altered states of consciousness. The foregoing is achieved by repetitive stimuli in the patient for whom external influences, namely those of sight and sound, are intentionally excluded. The apparatus produces electrical stimulation of the patient in the form of a modulated wave which produces impulses in the delta, theta, alpha and beta regions of the brain's electrical activity, the electrical stimulation being accompanied by two sources of audio stimulation, one of which is a sinusoidal tone modulated by and synchronized with the electrical stimulation, and the other is derived from sound recordings.

USP # 4,191,175 (March 4, 1980)

Method & Apparatus for Repetitively Producing a Noise-like Audible Signal

Nagle, William L.

Abstract --- A digital pulse generator and shift register repetitively produce bursts of digital pulses at a first adjustable repetition frequency. The repetition frequency of the pulses in each burst is also adjustable. A pink noise filter accentuates the lower burst frequency components near 7 hz and substantially attenuates all frequency components of the bursts above a first cut-off point near 10 Khz. A tunable band pass amplifier having a center frequency adjustable over a preselected range of frequencies optimally detectable by the average human ear accentuates the pink noise filter output near 2.6 Khz. The tunable amplifier drives an audible signal source with noise-like pulses of varying amplitudes and frequency components. A low pass amplifier may be connected to the pink noise filter to generate a train of pulses having a repetition frequency near 7 hz which pulses a light source in synchronism with the audible noise-like signal.

MATRIX OF THE MIND

USP # 4,141,344 (February 27, 1979)

Sound Recording System

Barbara, Louis J.

Abstract --- In recording an audio program, such as music or voice, on a magnetic tape recorder an A.C. signal generator operating at a frequency below about 14 Hz provides an AC baseline for the audio program signal. This 14 Hz or lower AC signal is sensed by the listener's ear to create an Alpha or Theta state in his brain when the tape is played back.

USP # 4,082,918 (April 4, 1978)

Audio Analgesic Unit

Chang, Roland W., et al.

Abstract --- An audio analgesic unit for use in masking sounds and substituting another sound which includes earmuffs to be used by a dental patient in which speakers are arranged and connected to a patient operated remote control unit to control the sound levels and a master control unit to override the patient remote control unit and operated by an operator, such as a dentist. A beeper indicates operation mode change.

USP # 4,034,741 (July 12, 1977)

Noise Generator & Transmitter

Adams, Guy E., et al.

Abstract --- An analgesic noise generator employs a circuit that can be switched to provide a variable waveform from an active noise source out of an integrated circuit amplifier.

USP # 3,967,616 (July 6, 1976)

Multichannel System for & Multifactorial Method of Controlling the Nervous System of a Living Organism

Ross, Sidney A.

Abstract --- A novel method for controlling the nervous system of a living organism for therapeutic and research purposes, among other applications, and an electronic system utilized in, and enabling the practice of, the invented method. Bioelectrical signals generated in specific topological areas of the organism's nervous system, typically areas of the brain, are processed by the invented system so as to produce a sensory stimulus if the system detects the presence or absence, as the case may be, of certain characteristics in the waveform patterns of the bio-

MATRIX OF THE MIND

electrical signals being monitored. The coincidence of the same or different characteristics in two or more waveform patterns, or the non-coincidence thereof, may be correlated with a certain desired condition of the organism's nervous system; likewise, with respect to the coincidence or non-coincidence of different characteristics of a single waveform pattern. In any event, the sensory stimulus provided by the invented system, typically an audio or visual stimulus, or combination thereof, is fed back to the organism which associates its presence with the goal of achieving the desired condition of its nervous system. Responding to the stimulus, the organism can be trained to control the waveform patterns of the monitored bioelectrical signals and thereby, control its own nervous system. The results of the coincidence function permit results heretofore unobtainable.

USP # 3,951,134 (April 20, 1976)

Apparatus & Method for Remotely Monitoring & Altering Brain Waves

Malech, Robert G.

Abstract --- Apparatus for and method of sensing brain waves at a position remote from a subject whereby electromagnetic signals of different frequencies are simultaneously transmitted to the brain of the subject in which the signals interfere with one another to yield a waveform which is modulated by the subject's brain waves. The interference waveform which is representative of the brain wave activity is re-transmitted by the brain to a receiver where it is demodulated and amplified. The demodulated waveform is then displayed for visual viewing and routed to a computer for further processing and analysis. The demodulated waveform also can be used to produce a compensating signal which is transmitted back to the brain to effect a desired change in electrical activity therein.

USP # 3,884,218 (May 20, 1975)

Method of Inducing & Maintaining Various Stages of Sleep in the Human Being

Monroe, Robert A.

Abstract --- A method of inducing sleep in a human being wherein an audio signal is generated comprising a familiar pleasing repetitive sound modulated by an EEG sleep pattern. The volume of the audio signal is adjusted to overcome the ambient noise and a subject can select a familiar repetitive sound most pleasing to himself.

MATRIX OF THE MIND

USP # 3,837,331 (September 24, 1974)

System & Method for Controlling the Nervous System of a Living Organism

Ross, S.

Abstract --- A novel method for controlling the nervous system of a living organism for therapeutic and research purposes, among other applications, and an electronic system utilized in, and enabling the practice of the invented method. Bioelectrical signals generated in specific topological areas of the organism's nervous system, typically areas of the brain, are processed by the invented system so as to produce an output signal which is in some way an analog of selected characteristics detected in the bioelectrical signal. The output of the system, typically an audio or visual signal, is fed back to the organism as a stimulus. Responding to the stimulus, the organism can be trained to control the waveform pattern of the bioelectrical signal generated in its own nervous system.

USP # 3,835,833 (September 17, 1974)

Method for Obtaining Neurophysiological Effects

Limoge, A.

Abstract --- A method and apparatus for obtaining neurophysiological effects on the central and/or peripheral systems of a patient. Electrodes are suitably positioned on the body of the patient and a composite electric signal is applied at the electrodes. The composite signal is formed by the superpositioning of two signals: a first signal which is a rectified high-frequency carrier modulated in amplitude to about 100 percent by substantially square-shaped pulses whose duration, amplitude and frequency are chosen according to the neurophysiological effects desidered, and a second signal which has a relatively white noise spectrum. The mean value of the first electric signal has a predetermined sign which is opposite the sign of the mean value of the second electric signal.

USP # 3,773,049 (November 20, 1973)

Apparatus for Treatment of Neuropsychic & Somatic Diseases with Heat, Light, Sound & VHF Electromagnetic Radiation

L. Y. Rabichev, et al.

Abstract --- N/A

MATRIX OF THE MIND

USP # 3,766,331 (October 16, 1973)

Hearing Aid for Producing Sensations in the Brain

Zink, Henry R.

Abstract --- A pulsed oscillator or transmitter supplies energy to a pair of insulated electrodes mounted on a person's neck. The transmitter produces pulses of intensity greater than a predetermined threshold value and of a width and rate so as to produce the sensation of hearing without use of the auditory canal, thereby producing a hearing system enabling otherwise deaf people to hear.

USP # 3,727,616 (March 17, 1973)

Electronic System for Stimulation of Biological Systems

Lenskes, H.

Abstract --- A receiver totally implanted within a living body is inductively coupled by two associated receiving coils to a physically unattached external transmitter which transmits two signals of different frequencies to the receiver via two associated transmitting coils. One of the signals from the transmitter provides the implanted receiver with precise control or stimulating signals which are demodulated and processed in a signal processor network in the receiver and then used by the body for stimulation of a nerve, for example, while the other signal provides the receiver with a continuous wave power signal which is rectified in the receiver to provide a source of electrical operating power for the receiver circuitry without need for an implanted battery.

USP # 3,712,292 (January 23, 1973)

Method & Apparatus for Producing Swept FM Audio Signal Patterns for Inducing Sleep

Zentmeyer, J.

Abstract --- A method of producing sound signals for inducing sleep in a human being, and apparatus therefor together with REPRESENTATIONS thereof in recorded form, wherein an audio signal is generated representing a familiar, pleasing, repetitive sound, modulated by continuously sweeping frequencies in two selected frequency ranges having the dominant frequencies which occur in electrical wave patterns of the human brain during certain states of sleep. The volume of the audio signal is adjusted to mask the ambient noise and the subject can select any of several familiar, repetitive sounds most pleasing to him.

USP # 3,647,970 (March 7, 1972)

Method and System for Simplifying Speech Waveforms

Flanagan, G. Patrick

Abstract --- A complex speech waveform is simplified so that it can be transmitted directly through earth or water as a waveform and understood directly or after amplification.

USP # 3,629,521 (January 8, 1970)

Hearing Systems

Puharich, Henry K.

Abstract --- The present invention relates to the stimulation of the sensation of hearing in persons of impaired hearing abilities or in certain cases persons totally deaf utilizing RF energy. More particularly, the present invention relates to a method and apparatus for imparting synchronous AF or ""acoustic" signals and so-called "transdermal" or RF signals. Hearing and improved speech discrimination, in accordance with one aspect of the present invention, is stimulated by the application of an AF acoustical signal to the "ear system" conventional biomechanism of hearing, which is delivered to the brain through the "normal" channels of hearing and a separate transdermal RF electrical signal which is applied to the "facial nerve system" and is detectable as a sensation of hearing. Vastly improved and enhanced hearing may be achieved...

USP # 3,576,185 (April 27, 1971)

Sleep-Inducing Method & Arrangement using Modulated Sound & Light

Meseck, Oscar & Schulz, Hans R.

Abstract --- N/A

USP # 3,568,347 (February 23, 1971)

Psycho-Acoustic Projector

Flanders, Andrew

Abstract --- A system for producing aural psychological disturbances and partial deafness in the enemy during combat situations.

MATRIX OF THE MIND

USP # 3,393,279 (July 16, 1968)

Nervous System Excitation Device

Flanagan, Giles P.

Abstract --- A method of transmitting audio information via a radio frequency signal modulated with the audio info through electrodes placed on the subject's skin, causing the sensation of hearing the audio information in the brain.

USP # 3,170,993 (February 23, 1965)

Means for Aiding Hearing by Electrical Stimulation of the Facial Nerve System

Puharich, Henry & Lawrence, Joseph

Abstract --- N/A

USP # 3,156,787 (November 10, 1964)

Solid State Hearing System

Lawrence, Joseph & Puharich, Henry

Abstract --- N/A

USP # 2,995,633 (August 8, 1961)

Means for Aiding Hearing

Puharich, Henry & Lawrence, J.

Abstract --- Means for converting audible signals to electrical signals and conveying them to viable nerves of the facial system.

MATRIX OF THE MIND

Actual Patents Of Mind

Control And Behavior

Modification Technology

Compiled by Theresa de Veto

SURFING THE APOCALYPSE

http://www.surfingtheapocalypse.com

http://www.surfingtheapocalypse.com/intelligence2.html#patentscontrol

8-25-00

US PATENT --4,717,343 --METHOD OF CHANGING A PERSON'S BEHAVIOR--A method of conditioning a person's unconscious mind in order to effect a desired change in the person's behavior which does not require the services of a trained therapist. Instead the person to be treated views a program of video pictures appearing on a screen. The program as viewed by the person's unconscious mind acts to condition the person's thought patterns in a manner which alters that person's behavior in a positive way. SOURCE: Judy Wall, Mike Coyle and Jan Wiesemann. Paranoia Magazine Issue 24 Fall 2000 -Article -'Technology to Your Mind' - By Judy Wall

US PATENT 5,270,800 --SUBLIMINAL MESSAGE GENERATOR--A combined subliminal and supraliminal message generator for use with a television receiver permits complete control of subliminal messages and their manner of presentation. A video synchronization detector enables a video display generator to generate a video message signal corresponding to a received alphanumeric text message in synchronism with a received television signal. A video mixer selects either the received video signal or the video message signal for output. The messages produced by the video message generator are user selectable via a keyboard input. A message memory stores a plurality of alphanumeric text messages

MATRIX OF THE MIND

specified by user commands for use as subliminal messages. This message memory preferably includes a read only memory storing predetermined sets of alphanumeric text messages directed to differing topics. The sets of predetermined alphanumeric text messages preferably include several positive affirmations directed to the left brain and an equal number of positive affirmations directed to the right brain that are alternately presented subliminally. The left brain messages are presented in a linear text mode, while the right brain messages are presented in a three dimensional perspective mode. The user can control the length and spacing of the subliminal presentations to accommodate differing conscious thresholds. Alternative embodiments include a combined cable television converter and subliminal message generator, a combine television receiver and subliminal message generator and a computer capable of presenting subliminal messages. SOURCE: Judy Wall, Mike Coyle and Jan Wiesemann. Paranoia Magazine Issue 24 Fall 2000 -Article -'Technology to Your Mind' - By Judy Wall

US PATENT 5,123,899 --METHOD AND SYSTEM FOR ALTERING CONSCIOUSNESS--A system for altering the states of human consciousness involves the simultaneous application of multiple stimuli, preferable sounds, having differing frequencies and wave forms. The relationship between the frequencies of the several stimuli is exhibited by the equation $g = s.sup.n/4 .multidot.f$ where: f=frequency of one stimulus; g=frequency of the other stimuli of stimulus; and n=a positive or negative integer which is different for each other stimulus. ALSO SEE: US PATENT --5,289,438 --METHOD AND SYSTEM FOR ALTERING CONSCIOUSNESS SOURCE: Judy Wall, Mike Coyle and Jan Wiesemann. Paranoia Magazine Issue 24 Fall 2000 -Article -'Technology to Your Mind' - By Judy Wall

US PATENT 4,877,027--HEARING SYSTEM --Sound is induced in the head of a person by radiating the head with microwaves in the range of 100 megahertz to 10,000 megahertz that are modulated with a particular waveform. The waveform consists of frequency modulated bursts. Each burst is made up of ten to twenty uniformly spaced pulses grouped tightly together. The burst width is between 500 nanoseconds and 100 microseconds. The pulse width is in the range of 10 nanoseconds to 1 microsecond. The bursts are frequency modulated by the audio input to create the sensation of hearing in the person whose head is irradiated.

US PATENT 6,011,991--COMMUNICATION SYSTEM AND METHOD INCLUDING BRAIN WAVE ANALYSIS AND/OR USE OF BRAIN ACTIVITY--A system and method for enabling human beings to communicate by way of their monitored brain activity. The brain activity of an individual is monitored and transmitted to a remote location (e.g. by satellite). At the remote location, the monitored brain activity is compared with pre-recorded normalized brain activity curves, waveforms, or patterns to determine if a match or substantial match is found. If such a match is found, then the computer at the remote location determines that the individual was attempting to communicate the word, phrase, or thought corresponding to the matched stored normalized signal.

US PATENT 4,858,612 - HEARING DEVICE --A method and apparatus for simulation of hearing in mammals by introduction of a plurality of microwaves into the region of the auditory cortex is shown and described. A microphone is used to transform sound signals into electrical signals which are in turn analyzed and processed to provide controls for generating a plurality of microwave signals at different frequencies. The multifrequency microwaves are then applied to the brain in the region of the auditory cortex. By this method sounds are perceived by the mammal which are representative of the original sound received by the microphone.

US PATENT 3,951,134 - APPARATUS AND METHOD FOR REMOTELY MONITORING AND ALTERING BRAIN WAVES--Apparatus for and method of sensing brain waves at a position remote from a subject whereby electromagnetic signals of different frequencies are simultaneously transmitted to the brain of the subject in which the signals interfere with one another to yield a waveform which is modulated by the subject's brain waves. The interference waveform which is representative of the brain wave activity is re-transmitted by the brain to a receiver where it is demodulated and amplified. The demodulated waveform is then displayed for visual viewing and routed to a computer for further processing and analysis. The demodulated waveform also can be used to produce a compensating signal which is transmitted back to the brain to effect a desired change in electrical activity therein.

US PATENT 5,159,703 - SILENT SUBLIMINAL PRESENTATION SYSTEM --A silent communications system in which nonaural carriers, in the very low or very high audio frequency range or in the adjacent ultrasonic frequency spectrum, are amplitude or frequency modulated with the desired intelligence and propagated acoustically or vibrationally, for inducement into the brain, typically through the use of loudspeakers, earphones or piezoelectric transducers.

US PATENT 5,507,291- METHOD AND AN ASSOCIATED APPARATUS FOR REMOTELY DETERMINING INFORMATION AS TO A PERSON'S EMOTIONAL STATE

US PATENT: US5629678:IMPLANTABLE TRANSCEIVER-Apparatus for Tracking And Recovering Humans.

US PATENT FOR BARCODE TATTOO--Method for verifying human identity during electronic sale transactions. A method is presented for facilitating sales transactions by electronic media. A bar code or a design is tattooed on an individual. Before the sales transaction can be consummated, the tattoo is scanned with a scanner. Characteristics about the scanned tattoo are compared to charac-

MATRIX OF THE MIND

teristics about other tattoos stored on a computer database in order to verify the identity of the buyer. Once verified, the seller may be authorized to debit the buyer's electronic bank account in order to consummate the transaction. The seller's electronic bank account may be similarly updated.

US PATENT 5,539,705 - ULTRASONIC SPEECH TRANSLATOR AND COMMUNICATIONS SYSTEM--A wireless communication system undetectable by radio frequency methods for converting audio signals, including human voice, to electronic signals in the ultrasonic frequency range, transmitting the ultrasonic signal by way of acoustical pressure waves across a carrier medium, including gases, liquids, or solids, and reconverting the ultrasonic acoustical pressure waves back to the original audio signal. The ultrasonic speech translator and communication system (20) includes an ultrasonic transmitting device (100) and an ultrasonic receiving device (200). The ultrasonic transmitting device (100) accepts as input (115) an audio signal such as human voice input from a microphone (114) or tape deck.

US PATENT 5,629,678 - PERSONAL TRACKING AND RECOVERY SYSTEM-- Apparatus for tracking and recovering humans utilizes an implantable transceiver incorporating a power supply and actuation system allowing the unit to remain implanted and functional for years without maintenance. The implanted transmitter may be remotely actuated, or actuated by the implantee. Power for the remote-activated receiver is generated electromechanically through the movement of body muscle. The device is small enough to be implanted in a child, facilitating use as a safeguard against kidnapping, and has a transmission range which also makes it suitable for wilderness sporting activities. A novel biological monitoring feature allows the device to be used to facilitate prompt medical dispatch in the event of heart attack or similar medical emergency. A novel sensation-feedback feature allows the implantee to control and actuate the device with certainty.

US PATENT 5,760,692 - INTRA-ORAL TRACKING DEVICE-An intra-oral tracking device adapted for use in association with a tooth having a buccal surface and a lingual surface, the apparatus comprises a tooth mounting member having an inner surface and an outer surface, the inner surface including adhesive material.

MATRIX OF THE MIND

US PATENT 5,868,100 - FENCELESS ANIMAL CONTROL SYSTEM USING GPS LOCATION INFORMATION--A fenceless animal confinement system comprising portable units attached to the animal and including means for receiving GPS signals and for providing stimulation to the animal. The GPS signals are processed to provide location information which is compared to the desired boundary parameters. If the animal has moved outside the desired area, the stimulation means is activated. The signal processing circuitry may be included either within the portable unit or within a separate fixed station.

US PATENT 5,905,461 - GLOBAL POSITIONING SATELLITE TRACKING DEVICE--A global positioning and tracking system for locating one of a person and item of property. The global positioning and tracking system comprises at least one tracking device for connection to the one of the person and item of property including a processing device for determining a location of the tracking device and generating a position signal and a transmitter for transmitting said position signal.

US PATENT 5,935,054 - MAGNETIC EXCITATION OF SENSORY RESONANCES--The invention pertains to influencing the nervous system of a subject by a weak externally applied magnetic field with a frequency near 1/2 Hz. In a range of amplitudes, such fields can excite the 1/2 sensory resonance, which is the physiological effect involved in "rocking the baby".

US PATENT 5,952,600 -ENGINE DISABLING WEAPON-- A non-lethal weapon for disabling an engine such as that of a fleeing car by means of a high voltage discharge that perturbs or destroys the electrical circuits.

US PATENT 6,006,188 - SPEECH SIGNAL PROCESSING FOR DETERMINING PSYCHOLOGICAL OR PHYSIOLOGICAL CHARACTERISTICS USING A KNOWLEDGE BASE

US PATENT 6,014,080 - BODY WORN ACTIVE AND PASSIVE TRACKING DEVICE --Tamper resistant body-worn tracking device to be worn by offenders or potential victims for use in a wireless communication system receiving signals from a global positioning system (GPS).

US PATENT 6,017,302 - SUBLIMINAL ACOUSTIC MANIPULATION OF NERVOUS SYSTEMS --In human subjects, sensory resonances can be excited by subliminal atmospheric acoustic pulses that are tuned to the resonance frequency. The 1/2 Hz sensory resonance affects the autonomic nervous system and may cause relaxation, drowsiness, or sexual excitement, depending on the precise acoustic frequency near 1/2 Hz used. The effects of the 2.5 Hz resonance include slowing of certain cortical processes, sleepiness, and disorientation. For these effects to occur, the acoustic intensity must lie in a certain deeply subliminal range. Suitable apparatus consists of a portable battery-powered source of weak subaudio acoustic radiation. The method and apparatus can be used by the general public as an aid to relaxation, sleep, or sexual arousal, and clinically for the control and perhaps treatment of insomnia, tremors, epileptic seizures, and anxiety disorders. There is further application as a nonlethal weapon that can be used in law enforcement standoff situations, for causing drowsiness and disorientation in targeted subjects. It is then preferable to use venting acoustic monopoles in the form of a device that inhales and exhales air with subaudio frequency.

US PATENT 6,051,594 - METHODS AND FORMULATIONS FOR MODULATING THE HUMAN SEXUAL RESPONSE--The invention is directed to improved methods for modulating the human sexual response by orally administering a formulation of the vasodilator phentolamine to the blood circulation and thereby modulating the sexual response on demand.

US PATENT 6,052,336 - APPARATUS AND METHOD OF BROADCASTING AUDIBLE SOUND USING ULTRASONIC SOUND AS A CARRIER--An ultrasonic sound source broadcasts an ultrasonic signal which is amplitude and/or frequency modulated with an information input signal originating from an information input source. If the signals are amplitude modulated, a square root function of the information input signal is produced prior to modulation. The modulated signal, which may be amplified, is then broadcast via a projector unit, whereupon an individual or group of individuals located in the broadcast region detect the audible sound.

MATRIX OF THE MIND

Chip Surveillance

http://www.broadcastingcable.com/article/CA601520.html

Some of the largest U.S. cable operators are quietly testing a service in nearly 2 million homes that may offer the first real competitor or complement to Nielsen ratings. The technology can record every click of the remote control by every digital subscriber. And it offers an instant census of millions of homes that dwarfs Nielsen's current universe of thousands.

Cable operators have already begun tracking digital-cable viewership on a massive scale, without Nielsen. Comcast is collecting viewer data from 1.2 million homes in Philadelphia, for example, while Time Warner's Oceanic Cable is crunching viewing patterns in 200,000 households in Hawaii.

At the moment, Nielsen Media Research has teamed up with selected cable partners to experiment with new technology. The ratings giant is negotiating with cable giants Comcast and Time Warner Cable on ways to access and use the data to monitor viewing in non-Nielsen households. And it has gone further with Time Warner, developing software to track channel changes in Nielsen homes within Time Warner's subscriber universe.

Nielsen concedes that data from digital-cable set-top boxes could greatly enhance its offerings and expand the accuracy of current ratings, particularly for small networks. "Set-top data can have value if it's linked to existing Nielsen metered points," says Scott Brown, Nielsen Media Research senior VP, strategic relationships, marketing and technology.

http://www.whitedot.org/issue/iss_story.asp?slug=shortSpyTV

MATRIX OF THE MIND

A Guide to Interactive TV
Become an Early Rejector!
by David Burke

The average person in Britain or America spends a quarter of his waking life in front of the TV set, perhaps saying "it's like having someone in the room." Meanwhile, because of television, we are less involved with other people. We have fewer conversations, and fewer people who know us intimately.

But a new type of television is being developed. Millions of dollars are being spent to create a device that really is someone in the room with you. Matthew Timms, head of programming at Two Way TV in London describes this digital revolution you have heard so much about:

"..somehow they feel they're sitting there, it's just them and the television - even though the reality is it's got a wire leading straight back to somebody's computer. So it actually gets sort of interesting information back."

Timms is talking about his customers, the people who pay him money each month. Perhaps they were attracted to his company's subscriber list by its promises of Choice, Fun, Convenience, and Empowerment. Control - that's what interactive television offers. Sitting on your couch, you will soon be able to have almost any product or service you desire, delivered at the touch of a button.

But what if you prefer to monitor people in their homes, any time, day or night? What if you want to build up, over years, psychological profiles of individuals from a distance - what motivates them, what makes them anxious, what makes them jump? What if you want to use that knowledge to manipulate what they know, how they feel and, finally, what they do?

Interactive television can deliver that as well. It can provide all this control, to any company or government that is able to pay the money. "We can build up profiles of people," says Two Way TV Managing Director Simon Cornwell, "based on what they say and on their actual behavior. Eventually the product will target

MATRIX OF THE MIND

itself to individual customers and what one customer sees will be very different from what another customer sees."

Interactive television will be used to invade viewers' privacy. Contrary to what you might have heard, this is important, because privacy was never about information; it's about power - the individual's bargaining power with the rest of the world. If you have nothing left to hide, then your negotiating position is impossibly weak. Your free will is exposed to tampering, and you may have much to fear.

If asked, people who work in interactive television will admit that this technology creates experimental conditions in the home. The machines that control your TV set will show you something, check to see how you react, and then show you something different. That's not just convenient. It is a loop of stimulus, response and measurement as carefully designed as those boxes where rats hit buttons to get food and avoid electric shocks.

And if you want to know more about those rat boxes - what year they were first used and whose theories they were built to test - ask someone who has passed his or her Chartered Institute of Marketing exam. The people who sell it call interactive television "a convergence". And it is, of so many things: marketing, child-psychology, sociology, advertising, public relations and politics. Not to mention complex adaptive systems software.

But how will it affect your life? You are about to accept a powerful new device into your home, and interact with it every day for an average of four hours. That is half the time you are not sleeping or working, for the rest of your life. What is this machine designed to do? Look inside your digital set top box, and you will see much more than a TV tuner. It is actually a computer worth hundreds of dollars. Just like a PC, it contains, or will soon contain, all these components:

- Memory - processes data and runs programs. As with any computer, the functionality is not built into the hardware. The box will do whatever it is told by the software.

- Storage - flash ROM at the moment, but within a couple of years it will be replaced with something more powerful, perhaps a hard drive. This will allow the box to store software and data, even when turned off.

- Modem - or a network card, which allows data to be sent back and forth over a public network. Some boxes use a phone line. The more powerful ones use coaxial cable.

That is a lot of power. Best of all, you get it cheap, or for nothing. The digital TV companies have offered to subsidize or outright buy these computers for you.

104

MATRIX OF THE MIND

Profits crashed a Rupert Murdoch's BskyB Corporation, and shareholders had their dividends frozen when the company decided to pay $315 million to give each of its current subscribers a free box. That was just the beginning. Now it must also buy a box for every new customer. Why are they doing this? Why would somebody just give you all that hardware for nothing?

Here's a hint: You have no control over what it does. Unlike a normal PC, you have no say over the hardware or software. You can't add or take out bits and pieces, you can't start, stop, install or uninstall new programs. And, in the case of Sky Digital, if you choose not to plug your modem in, you'll lose your "Interactive Discount" and have to pay them up to $248. That makes interactive TV a service you pay not to have.

It is hard to find out the truth about this machine, and decide whether to accept it. The only people who know anything, and are doing all the talking, are the companies trying to sell it. And they haven't been telling the whole truth, not in their television commercials, glossy booklets or their carefully worded contracts.

So we wrote the book Spy TV to present some of the missing facts. It describes the engine of this two-way television, following data "straight back to someone's computer" and then back into individual living rooms. It lays out those analytic techniques that will be used to extract "sort of interesting information" and attempts to foresee how the use of such information will change us.

What Is Interactive Television?

Interactive TV (iTV) is any television with what is called a "return path". Information flows not only from broadcaster to viewer, but also back from viewer to broadcaster. Another feature common to all iTV systems is the ability to offer each TV set, or each viewer who uses that TV set, a different choice of content.

There are different hardware configurations and it is possible to build a crude interactive service using analog systems. But the type of systems now being offered, that will dramatically change how viewers live, are digital—either cable or satellite.

People are talking about interactive television for three main reasons:

* T-commerce: You will be able to buy a pizza without dialing a phone.

MATRIX OF THE MIND

* Interactive Goodies: You will be able to pause live TV or record shows. You will be able to click on advertisements to "find out more".

* Click stream Analysis ("telegraphics")

What Was That Last One?

Viewers will be told a great deal about the first two uses for interactive TV. If you are not seeing them already, prepare for a blizzard of advertisements showing happy families ordering gifts through their TV sets, choosing camera angles while watching their favorite sporting events and sending email to friends. Expect to hear words such as "control" and "empowerment".

But it is time that viewers and reporters and legislators started asking about that third use for iTV. Go to any trade show of interactive service providers and you will notice it there, lurking below most conversations. The issue no one likes to talk about.

Interactive Television Spies on Viewers

With interactive television every click of your remote control goes into a database. This is called your TV set's "click stream", and it can be analyzed to create a surprisingly sophisticated picture of who you are and what motivates you (sometimes called "telegraphics"). Such profiles of households or individuals can then be used to target consumers with direct marketing techniques, through their television, in the mail or over the phone. Your television will be able to show you something, monitor how you respond, and then show you something else, working on you over time until it you exhibit the desired behavior.

Even if you never do order a pizza through your TV set or click or help your child play with an interactive commercial, your iTV set will be 'interactive' all the same. What matters is your "click stream" and the people you have never met who will soon be studying it. Such observation and manipulation is not marginal or accidental. From the beginning, it has been built into the designs of interactive systems and the revenue columns of these companies' business plans.

White Dot Blows the Whistle

White Dot has been investigating this new technology for three years. Our book Get A Life! (David Burke and Jean Lotus, Bloomsbury Publishing - 1998) first raised these issues of privacy and interactive television. Our second book, Spy TV (David Burke, Slab-O-Concrete - 2000) was written specifically to expose what the industry had in development, and where it plans to go.

Spy TV was written as a concise viewer's guide to the hardware, the software, and the privacy issues of this new medium. Based on dozens of interviews with interactive television developers in Britain and America, Spy TV cuts through the hype of this "digital revolution" to found just who is being overthrown.

Who is Making Digital Interactive Television?

If you wish to understand interactive television, and plan to start asking questions, these are the types of people whom you will want to call:

* Box Makers Companies like Motorola, Scientific Atlantic, Pace and Microsoft are making set top boxes that run interactive television.

These manufacturers are incorporating into their set top boxes support for the kinds of data collection they think will drive sales to the service operators. They announce with fanfare their partnerships with companies that plan to gather and analyze viewer data. Motorola, for instance, is a major investor in SpotOn, a targeted advertising system.

Bob Evans, SpotOn's West Coast Head of Sales was justifiably proud when he pointed to one of his boxes at a trade show and told me:

"See that box? That box can hold 64,000 pieces of information about you!"

Each digital set top box, from any manufacturer, has an individual IP address, making it uniquely identifiable. Some boxes provide memory to hold a viewer's data until it can be sent out of the house by telephone call, known as "store and forward". Others provide software applications with information about other devices connected to the set top box-printers or a computer network.

Many people in the industry predict that the set top box will eventually become the network gateway into the home. All electronic devices, and soon even appliances, will be linked to your television. It will be able to record not just every click of your TV remote, but every time you go to the refrigerator.

* Multiple Service Operators (MSO) Like an internet service provider (ISP) an MSO offers access to content. But unlike the internet, where the content comes from anywhere, interactive television is gathered together buying and bundling.

Service Operators like Cox and AT&T are now buying from, or just buying up, smaller companies that produce the new data collection applications.

* Network Operators—These are the companies that own the cabling or satellites that carry the signal. They will usually offer their own services such as interactive television and broadband internet access, but there is no technical reason why they cannot carry other company's services.

* Operating System Providers—These are software companies such as Microsoft, Liberate and OpenTV that provide software operating systems that run on set top boxes. They are the equivalent of the Windows or Linux operating sys-

tems that run on PCs. In fact, both those operating systems are making the migration to the set top box.

 * Middleware and Development Tool Providers—Set top box middleware, offered by OpenTV, WorldGate and others, simplifies life for application developers, by offering easy access to various system functions. Also, by offering the same middleware interface on top of multiple operating systems, middleware providers hope to encourage developers to use their development tools to create a large body of cross-platform applications.

 * Application Providers—These can be software houses that have their own operating systems and tools, such as Microsoft, or they can be small, niche companies that specialize in some business need that interactive TV might fill. Their software will be used to produce iTV programming and advertising, or run interactive services over the networks.

These companies have done much of the innovation, thinking up new ways to gather, analyze and use information. Their products are now being taken up by the MSOs, networks and box makers who will put them in people's homes.

 * Program Content Producers—These people make television programs and advertisements that contain interactive elements. They will be commissioned by advertising agencies, television broadcasters and MSO's.

 * Advertisers and Manufacturers—Commission new interactive content, as they always have done. But with interactive television, they also benefit from or co-ordinate the use of data taken from viewers' living rooms.

Advertisers and manufacturers are being wooed by the people making iTV. Some companies, like Proctor & Gamble, Ford Motors, Domino pizza and some advertising agencies, like JWT and Starcom Worldwide have been enthusiastic participants.

 —Data Analysts—There are a number of companies that specialize in holding and analyzing consumer data. Some are huge data warehouses, some are small consulting firms that just do analysis. These companies have experience with direct marketing, and are now moving that experience into a world of faster turnaround, where cycles of offer, response and new offer will happen in a matter of hours instead of months.

Notable among these companies is Nielsen, which has been counting viewers for decades. Knowing that set-top boxes could turn every single household into a "Nielsen Family", they have sought to do deals with almost every company doing interactive television.

MATRIX OF THE MIND

Scott Coralles
The Journal of Hispanic UFOlogy
www.Inexplicata.blogspot.com

http://www.katherinealbrecht.com/

http://www.spychips.com/

http://www.nocards.org/faq/index.shtml

TECHNOTRONICS:
Making the Unreal Real
By Scott Coralles

A very strange case became known in August 2002, involving possible use of a holographic projection in the midst of a cattle mutilation and UFO wave in the Argentinean Pampas. The Institute of Hispanic Ufology received a number of e-mails from researchers and followers of the UFO scene suggesting that the events surrounding the mutilations and sightings could have been related to the use of highly advanced holographic projectors. The events surrounding the experiences of a young woman named Gabriela Lencinas,15, were investigated by the team of Francisco Villagrán, Eduardo López, Omar Vallejos and UFO reseacher/broadcaster Pablo Omastott.

In an interview with Ms. Lencinas, she was riding back to the town of Paso Lovera (20 km distant from Corrientes) on her bicycle after having spent the morning in San Luis del Palmar, four kilometers distant, with a friend. The day had been a warm and sunny Saturday in the early January 2002 (specifically the second saturday of the month, according to Ms. Lencinas) and as both young women pedaled back to their hometown, they came in contact with the unexplained.

The young woman and her unnamed friend saw what they described as a "giant figure", standing perhaps a few dozen meters. The strange giant was allegedly wearing what appeared to be a "ski outfit" whose details could not be precisely made out. They were unable to make out its face, but noted that "its hair seemed to be standing on end", as though from static electricity, and it stood with outstretched arms, as though beckoning them toward it. Ms. Lencinas and her friend did not think this was a friendly gesture: "it was as if [the image] was trying to scare us." At no point did they see the strange figure's eyes or teeth, according to the report.

The girls, paralyzed with fright, noticed that a car drove past them along the same stretch of road, only to screech to a halt as it came to the towering figure. According to the witness, the driver "got out of the car, took a good look at the figure, got back in his vehicle and kept driving" until it passed right under the giant's towering legs.

As they continued pedaling their bikes toward the figure, the image reportedly "began to rise" into the air some five meters. After that, both returned to their homes to inform their parents of the event. When asked if they thought that the giant could have been objectively real, or a "vapor image", Ms. Lencinas replied" "It wasn't real because..." and allowed her voice to trail off.

Pablo Omastott, the interviewer, seemed to elicit better replies from the older of the pair, nineteen year-old Griselda Olivera. "We were riding along and suddenly, we saw a black thing, that later looked like an ape...something really gigantic with spiky hair. My companion (Gabriela) asked me if I had seen what she'd seen, and I said yes."

"It later disappeared," Ms. Olivera went on, "and we saw nothing more than black smoke." She also admitted to feeling afraid of the strange image.

In estimating image's height, Ms. Olivera pointed out that it was larger than a 5 meter tall tree that stood nearby—more like a 10 meter tall eucalyptus tree.

Additional research has disclosed that the two cyclists weren't the only ones to see the apparition. "According to other sources," writes Omastott in his report, "the caretakers of a nearby ranch had already seen the same apparition in more than one occasion from nearby fields."

A female odontologist who preferred anonymity also told researchers that a year and a half prior to the event, while driving at night toward the city of Corrientes from San Luis del Palmar, she became aware of a person waving at her from the side of the road, urging her to stop. Upon getting closer, she realized that this figure's height ranged anywhere between two and half and three meters. This caused the driver to speed away.

Projected Out of Nowhere

As bizarre as the simian "image" of Paso Lovera may have been, it could not hold a candle to the events which played out on the shores of the South Atlantic Ocean in late July 2000, when a semi-solid figure known to the locals only as "The Shroud" began appearing the Ciudad Atlántida neighborhood of the city of Punta Alta—a scant 27 kilometers south of the notorious UFO hotspot of Bahía Blanca.

MATRIX OF THE MIND

The area where the nearly hallucinatory image manifested itself was an area filled with small sand dunes leading to the Arroyo Pareja Municipal Beach, which faces Ciudad Atlántida and is separated from the Puerto Belgrano Naval Base by a wire fence.

Reports received from Christian Quintero and Oscar Adolfo Mario of the Proyecto Condor-CEUFO organization state that the apparitions were witnessed by a considerable segment of local society, including residents, members of the provincial constabulary and naval personnel on duty at the Port Belgrano Naval Facility. The police has been summoned on many occasions to substantiate the sightings made by the locals, and patrols have increased in frequency, not so much out of concern for the resident's safety, but for that of the Naval Officer's Club on bordering on the area.

"These manifestations," states the report from Proyecto Condor-CEUFO, "which always occur in the early morning hours, have become so common that in recent days several neighbors have stayed up late to see them, and it is thus that they were able to confirm the simultaneous presence of up to 2 such beings, as well as red lights flying over the area. All of the witnesses, whether individuals or in a group, agree that the entities are nebulous ("as if made of tulle") and glowing, with a pair of red eyes being clearly identifiable, and glassy faces ("as though transparent"). Their movements are smooth and they always appear from behind the sand dunes, as though "coming from the [Naval] Base". Most witnesses agree that they show a great interest in the water tanks located above the roofs, and that they did not flee upon detecting the presence of local residents—rather, they stared at them fixedly for some minutes. Deep silence was perceived during the observations and "the air appears to become still" and neither heat nor cold can be felt—only a sensation of warmth, as though [the beings] emanated heat. Witnesses also state that things appear to be darker when "the shroud" appears, as though ambient lighting were dimmed. Another curious fact is the large number of cats and dogs who report to the place where the sightings occur and sit down to observe it in silence, in a state resembling a trance."

One researchor, an engineer who visited the site suggested that the apparition perhaps generates some sort of radiation that causes film to become exposed, relating it to the "heat" felt by witnesses when the figure approaches. It is not altogether unreasonable to suppose that such experimentation may extend to testing it out on the general population, and the proximity of the phenomenon to a major naval facility makes it even more suspect.

The Cuban Scenario Revisited

"Modern warfare requires that the population be conditioned to accept military engagements enthusiastically. Hitler understood this very well," wrote Jacques

MATRIX OF THE MIND

Bergier in his book The Secret War of the Occult. What better way to cause a wave of enthusiasm to wash over an apathetic or disheartened population than to suggest divine inspiration or support for such an adventure, one in which young men and women are sure to lose their lives.

It has been possible to manufacture heavenly supernatural images for quite some time, and these can be employed to manipulate people into believing certain ideas or others, and perhaps more importantly, to reinforce loyalties.

One such case dates back to April 1982, when hundreds of Cubans, taking their nightly walk along the seaside promenade known as the Malecón witnessed a sudden flash over Havana Bay,which immediately made them suspect they were under attack. But bombs did not rain out of the sky; instead, there was an overwhelming brightness which gradually coalesced into an image of the Blessed Virgin; more specifically, Cuba's patroness, la Caridad del Cobre—extending her arms toward the startled masses on the promenade, as she remained suspended in the night sky. Unlike traditional images of the Blessed Virgin, this one did not bear the Christ-child in arms, nor were there any other religious items (crosses, etc.) associated with it. The divine protector appeared to be wearing a snow white mantle which contrasted even more so against the prevailing darkness.

According to the late Andreas Faber Kaiser, who chronicled the incident in his landmark book Las Nubes del Engaño ("The Clouds of Deceit"), Cuban authorities did their best to suppress the story, but word of it was spread by Miami-based broadcasters WRHC and WQBA. There are further reports indicating that the divine image was seen again only days later at port of Mariel, where it was taken to be Our Lady of Regla. Such was the consternation created during this second sighting that soldiers opened machine gun fire against the image, and at least one of them required psychiatric treatment. Reports of similar responses were received from the cities of Guanabo and Trinidad as well.

Faber Kaiser would later suggest that it was a U.S. Navy submarine that projected an advanced holographic image as part of psychological warfare operations against the Cuban government. Hard though it may be to believe in both the sophistication of such techniques and the fact that their use would ever be authorized, the fact remains that it would be one—albeit the most spectacular—ever employed against that island's socialist regime. On February 2, 1962, the Pentagon authorized a number of psychological warfare techniques which ranged from bombarding the city of Havana with free plane tickets for destinations such as Mexico and Venezuela as well as photographs showing Fidel Castro entertaining foreign women in expensive restaurants.

In a planet as small as our own, it isn't surprising to find information regarding a given part of the world on the opposite side of the globe: when interviewed

MATRIX OF THE MIND

THE COMMUNIST AGENDA FOR GLOBAL DOMINANCE
'Man does not have the right to develop his own mind. This kind of liberal orientation has great appeal. We must electrically control the brain. Some day armies and generals will be controlled by electric stimulation of the brain.'

- U.S. government mind manipulator, Dr. Jose Delgado, Congressional Record, No. 262E, Vol. 118, 1974.

---

by Spanish researcher Manuel Carballal, who happened to be in Mongolia at the time on an unrelated assignment, General Battsagan Tsiiregzen provided new information on the Havana psy-ops event of 1982. The Mongolian had been part of his country's diplomatic mission to the Cuba at the time, and offered new insight into the mind-bending operation. A policeman had indeed unholstered his sidearm and fired at the apparition, being so unnerved by the event that he was hospitalized and given psychiatric treatment. A Russian sailor, informed the general, had a similar experience, due to his inability to fit what he was seeing within the Marxist-Leninist framework of his upbringing. The Mongolian attaché was also able to confirm another story—that a scuba diver who had been in the water in the vicinity of the apparition had lost consciousness and had been brought to an emergency room. According to the story, whenever the hapless diver opened his eyes, he would goggle as though witnessing a vision, and would then lose consciousness again.

In the city of Trinidad, southwest of Havana, strange phenomena apparently played out while the divine patroness cast her beatific gaze over the bewildered townspeople. There were reports of strange odors in the air and smoke issuing from the floors of every dwelling.

The amazing account by the Mongolian diplomat was included in Carballal's own book, Los Expedientes Secretos (Planeta,2001), and he adds the highly intriguing detail that the U.S. intelligence community is believed to have planned a follow-up to its successful

1982 demonstration: to spread the belief among Cubans that Fidel Castro was the Antichrist foretold in the Book of Revelation, projecting a holographic image of Christ over the skies. It was believed that this "miraculous" event would unleash a rebellion that would overthrow the government.

UFO lecturer and author Dr. Virgilio Sanchez Ocejo, while remaining unconvinced that a "hologram" was projected over the area, nonetheless accepts that something truly unusual occurred there. He recalls that on the first day after the "apparition", Havana's malecón became filled with people and the government police did its best to disperse the crowds, only to find that word of the apparition had already spread throughout the city ad its surrounding region: people

113

MATRIX OF THE MIND

from Havana province, Matanzas and Western Pinar del Río were pouring to the city to see the spectacular manifestation of the divine patroness.

Officials declared that whatever was being seen was not the Blessed Virgin, and local militiamen (the brigadas de contacto) were called up to assist the police in dealing with the 100,000 plus crowd. This armed force, writes Dr. Sánchez-Ocejo, "opened automatic fire against the unknown quantity in a show of force. Bullets, according to eyewitnesses, splashed harmlessly in the water around the phenomenon. At times, the machine gun blasts could be seen to pass right through the phenomenon."

Some readers may wonder why any government would invest so much time, effort and valuable resources like experimental holography to upset the citizenry of a Caribbean island-nation. The answer, obviously, lies in forty-year political battle to dislodge Cuba's revolutionary government from power, but the full extent to which the U.S. was willing to pursue such an objective is only being learned now: James Banford, author of Body of Secrets (Doubleday, 2001), reports that the Joint Chiefs of Staff (JCS) had approved an initiative known as Operation Northwoods in the early 1960s, which would unleash terrorism on American cities and villages—supposedly perpetrated by Cuban operatives—to inflame the public into supporting an overwhelming military operation against the island. In the face of such revelations, belief in submarine-projected holograms hardly ranks as credulity.

The Lords of Futurewar

The March 31, 1997 issue of Defense Week magazine published a fascinating article regarding the U.S. Air Force's entry into the field of "computer warfare" through the creation of an entire division—unnamed, but whose operating code was given as AF/XOIOW—to be headed by Lt. Col. Jimmy Miyamoto.

The new USAF division would be responsible for what the article describes as "offensive" computer warfare, meaning attacks upon military and civilian targets in order to achieve supremacy in the field. Coordinating its operations with all of the major government agencies, AF/XOIOW would employ its UAV's (unmanned aerial vehicles like Dark Star and Predator) to destroy enemy computing and communication systems, inject viruses into enemy weapon systems and computer links and other offensive tactics that would make Darth Vader smile.

But the most suggestive of all of these "futurewar" tactics includes the use of holograms for military purposes. The article goes on to describe a quasi-computer warfare or psychological warfare operations program initially conceived during the Gulf War. Holographic projections of this sort would include the projection of three dimensional, holographic images as decoys, including "the appearance of an angry God" over the battlefield.

The Defense Week story goes on to say that the Pentagon has openly included the use of such holograms as part of its non-lethal weapons program, but the program vanished from sight around 1994, becoming part of the much written-of "black projects". In late 1991, the JFK Center and School for Special Warfare appears to have looked into a PSYOPS holographic system able to "project persuasive messages and three-dimensional images of clouds, smoke, rain, buildings...even and including religious figures and images...the use of these holograms as persuasive messages shall have worldwide applications."

Military use of holograms appears to be widespread enough that the possibility was the very first thing that came to the mind of Major Gen. Wilfried de Brouwer during the Belgian UFO Wave of the early 1990s. Declaring himself skeptical about the triangular UFO first reported on November 29, 1989, de Brouwer stated his belief that the cause of the phenomenon could be ascribed to "laser beams or holograms."

Projection Booths in the Sky?

While cases such as the Lovera incident suggest that use of non-human imagery for unknown purposes appears to be undergoing tests in Argentina, outrageous though it may seem, there is the further question of whether the UFO phenomenon itself is holographic—that the bright lights and strange creatures being reported for the past fifty years are no more "real" than the light issuing from a cine projector.

The possibility is broached in Norman Briazak and Simon Mennick's The UFO Handbook (Citadel,1978), who suggest the interesting possibility that UFOs— or rather, their images— are being "beamed" to us from distant worlds for unknown reasons, perhaps serving no greater purpose than bewildering us, much like a human might deliberately seek to perplex a household pet by reflecting a light of a wall. The authors then posit an even more interesting possibility—that the flying objects are projected by a non-human device located somewhere outside the Earth but within our solar system, being "triggered" by certain activities on our own planet (wars, earthquakes, volcanic activity and other situations in which unidentified flying objects tend to be seen). While it is true that other advanced civilizations may be interested in being alerted when a younger one is about develop sophisticated technology, such a device could alert them (a good example being the black monolith in Arthur C. Clarke's 2001: A Space Odyssey) to the fact. However, why would the same device conceivably alert us to the same fact by projecting UFOs in our skies?

"The UFO-hologram theory is one of many explanations offered by ufologists to account for UFOs," write Briazak and Mennick, "However, most ufologists do not seriously consider this theory as a viable explanation."

Dr. Frank Salisbury, in his paper "Are UFOs from Outer Space?" (Proceedings of the First International UFO Congress, ed. Curtis Fuller. NY: Warner, 1980) added his voice to the debate on holographic saucers: "[...] maybe the UFOs are not tangible objects; they are three-dimensional projected holographs. This has been suggested often in recent years...I know of one case in the Uintah Basin where an Indian shot at a UFO with his deer rifle and heard the bullet ricochet off...but I thought, what if those who project the holograph up there are so clever that they are prepared to for people to shoot at them and have a recording of ricochet to play at that exact moment?"

A careful examination of UFO case histories reveals the existence of situations in which the above could apply, such as a midwestern case from the 1970s in which a rancher fired at a "Bigfoot"-like entity which disappeared, and a Pennsylvania entity from the same time frame in which a housewife fired a shotgun blast against a Bigfoot at close range, producing the same disappearance in flash of light. In her Glimpses of Other Realities (LMH Productions, 1993), Linda Moulton-Howe suggests that such cases, "combined with others about translucent beings, [have] provoked speculation that we humans are being manipulated by an intelligence that has sophisticate technology that can make us see anything it wants us to see. Some beings might even be holographic projections."

In the sequel to her 1993 work, Howe mentions the curious case of Jim Sparks, who allegedly witnessed non-human forces "morphing" into the shapes of law enforcement personnel and then military officers bedecked with ribbons.

A personal abduction experience posted to the internet by Janet Russell (http://members.aol.com/texfilez/beyond.html) describes further interaction with beings that appear to lack any type of physical reality. In 1962, she had an experience in which one of the so-called "Nordic" aliens resembled a holographic projection from a certain angle.

Stefan Duncan raises he possibility that holograms may have been used to create the August 1997 spectacle over Mexico City (known as el OVNI de Polanco, after of the upscale neighborhood over which the event allegedly occured) in the April 1998 issue of AUFON (American UFO News): "Were there military members or special effects people crouched down, aiming laser beams over Mexico City to produce holographic images?

Could such illusions be the result of highly advanced non-human holography, or very advanced human military holographic techniques employed on unsuspecting humans for experimental purposes? Howe subsequently cites the work of abductee Anna Hayes, who believes that "negative ETs" are planning to stage a holographic Second Coming of Christ to spread confusion among the faithful. Such an operation would be more likely to fit a "psy-ops" agenda than that of bona fide space explorers, should there be any, and the Cuban events of 1982, plus the Pentagon's own admission of experimenting with holography, reinforce the likelihood of an terrestrial answer to the mystery.

Probably the most distinguished researcher in the UFO field, Jacques Vallée looked into the stranger areas of the phenomenon and their intersections with clearly human, politico-military agendas as early as 1979 in his landmark Messengers of Deception and made specific mention of advances in psychological warfare in his book Dimensions (1987) in which he mentions the use of recordings of "primitive gods" in an effort to frighten tribespeople, and development of the Mitralux system by the U.S. military—a projector capable of displaying 85mm slides against cloud banks and physical structures.

In an interview with conspiracy writer Jonathan Vankin, Vallée mentioned a story involving the mass suicide of the saucer-cult known as Order of the Solar Temple: more than fifty cultists willingly laid down their lives in both Europe and North America. This cult, according to the interview, employed holographic projectors purchased in the United States to reinforce individual group members' belief in alien salvation. Vallée also mentions that the German Army was already using primitive slides and projectors to cast images against the sky to demoralize their adversaries during the First World War, proving there is really nothing new under the sun.

MATRIX OF THE MIND

Jose Delgado's "Physical Control of the Mind"

MATRIX OF THE MIND

MATRIX OF THE MIND

Natural Fate Versus Human Control:

The Process of Ecological Liberation and Domination

Manifestations of life depend on a continuous interplay of natural forces. Worms and elephants, mosquitoes and eagles, plankton and whales display a variety of activities on the land, in the air, and in the sea with a putpose-or lack of it-which escapes human understanding, obeying sets of laws which antedate the appearance of human intelligence.

In the animal kingdom, existence of the genetic code represents a biological determination of anatomical and functional characteristics in the newborn. The growth and development of organisms after birth proceed according to a natural fate imposed by the correlations between individual structure and environmental circumstances. The fact that about 300 million years ago all the world's creatures lived in the sea did not depend on their own volition but on biological evolution and ecological factors. The appearance of dinosaurs 80 million years ago in the Triassic period, their supremacy on earth, and their peak in power 30 million years later were determined not by the will of these animal which had disproportionately small brains and were probably rather stupid, but by a propitious warm and sticky climate which provided a soft slosh of water everywhere and land covered with a tangle of greenery, juicy palms, and huge fernlike trees extending almost to the North Pole. The catastrophic end of the age of gigantic reptiles was simply the result of their inability to adapt themselves to a change in weather and lack of food. At the beginning of the Cenozoic era 70 million years ago, the air was drier and cooler than before. High plains emerged from shallow seas and ponds, and hard wood forests towered in place of ferns and palms. This changing ecology was unsuitable for dinosaurs and because they lacked the intelligence to understand their situation, to improve their food supply, or to modify their diet, natural fate forced these giants into extinction, and in their place small, warm-blooded, furry mammals slowly grew in size and number.

The appearance of man approximately one million years ago meant only the flourishing of one more kind of animal which shared with the others most bio-

MATRIX OF THE MIND

logical laws and a complete dependence on natural forces. Men, like elephants and frogs, possessed lungs, bones, and brains; pumping of blood by the heart and other physiological phenomena were - and still are - very similar in all mammals, and proceeded according to preestablished mechanisms beyond awareness or voluntary control. Personal destiny was determined by a series of biological and environmental circumstances which could not be foreseen, understood, or modified, Natural fate meant that man, along with all animals, suffered the inclemencies of the weather, being decimated by cold temperatures, starvation, and all kinds of parasites and illnesses. He did not know how to make a fire ori a wheel, and he was not yet able to influence the functions of his own body or to modify his environment.

A decisive step in the evolution of man and in the establishment of his superiority over other living creatures was his gradual achievement of ecological liberation. Why should man accept unnecessary hardships? Why should he be wet because the rain was failing, or cold because the sun was hidden, or be at killed because predators were hungry? Why should he not cover his body with the soft skins of animals, construct tools and shelter, collect food and water? Slowly the first sparks of intelligence began to challenge natural fate, Herds Of cattle Were a more reliable source of food than hunting in the forest. Some fields were stripped of the vegetation which was growing according to capricious ecological destiny, and were placed tinder cultivation by man.

Attention was gradually directed toward the human body, and skills were learned for the treatment of injuries. Broken limbs no longer meant permanent disfunctiozi but could be repaired by transitory application of branches tied with vegetable fibers. Personal experience was not lost, but could be transmitted from generation to generation; the accumulating culture preserved through a gradually elaborated spoken and written language represented a continuous advance of civilization. Men learned to ivork together, to exchange skills and knowledge, and to join their efforts to improve their circumstances. Curiosity grew continuously, and endless questions were formulated about the observed reality. Ecological liberation could progress not by hiding inside caves but by facing danger, and man challenged the immense power of natural forces, using a lever to lift weights heavier than muscular power could manage, tricking the wind to push sailing ships through the ocean, and taming the rivers to turn the grinding stones of the mills. Thus began the process of man's ecological domination, the victory of human intelligence over the fate of a mindless nature -a victory without precedent in the history of other animal species. Biological adaptation enabled man to survive under extreme climatic conditions including arctic areas, dry deserts, high altitudes, and hot tropics, but it was the intellectual and material development of civilization that really brought about the present degree of ecological

MATRIX OF THE MIND

liberation and domination. The winning of a considerable degree of independence from natural elements permitted human beings to direct their intelligence
and energy toward endeavors more interesting than mere survival. The signs of
man's power slowly extended throughout the world, transforming the earth's surface with cultivated fields, with cities, and with roads; joining oceans; tunneling
through mountains; harnessing atomic power; and reaching for the stars. In spite
of the problems associated with the development of civilization, the fact is that
today the charting of our lives depends more on intelligent decisions than on ecological circumstances. The surrounding medium of modern societies is not nature, as in the past, but buildings, machines, and culture, which are man-made
products. Modem medicine has created a healthier environment by reducing infant mortality, diminishing the number and gravity of illnesses, and consider- ably
increasing the span of life. According to the biological law of only a few centuries
ago, pestilence desolated mankind from time to time, insects spread infections,
more than half of the newborn died before the age of three, old age began at
thirty or forty, and only a minority survived to the age of fifty. Scientific knowledge has modified our own biology, providing better diet, hygienic practices,
and pharmacological and surgical treatment.

Viewing evolution in terms of the opposition of human in- telligence to natural fate has a dramatic appeal which empha- sizes the relative importance of each
factor in the determination of events. In reality, however, we should accept the
fact that the existence of man, together with all of his attributes and crea- tions,
including his own ecological liberation and domination, is actually and inescap-
ably the result of natural fate. Man did not invent man. No conscious efforts Were
ever made to design- or modify-the anatomical structure of his brain. Because the
development of wings was a result of biological evolution, we cannot claim that
birds have liberated themselves from the pull of gravity by flying in the air in
defiance of natural laws. The fact that birds fly means that they have achieved one
step of ecological liberation, escape from gravity by using the lifting support of
the wind, Birds can live and play in the air above all other earthbound creatures.
Their wings were a gracious gift of evolution which did not require knowledge of
physics, mathematical calculations, or even the desire to own wings. Nature seems
to be highly imaginative but excessively slow; many millions of years passed from
the beginning of life on earth to the appearance of flying animals. The period
from the emergence of the human mind to the invention of the airplane was much
shorter. The tremendous acceleration in accomplishments was determined by
the development of the unique powers of imagination and reason; and it may be
expected that human inventions will have an increasing role in the control of activities on earth. Birds fly, and man thinks. Liberation from and domination of
many natural elements have changed ecology, and are also influencing the needs,
purpose, and general organization of human life, especially in the following as-

MATRIX OF THE MIND

pects.

Freedom of Choice

In contrast with the limitations felt by our ancestors and by members of still primitive societies, we enjoy nearly endless possibilities to pursue interests and activities of our own choice. Modern life is not bound by the physical restrictions of geography; our voices can be transmitted with the speed of light to anyone around the world; on television we can see events in any co unity as they actually occur; and we can travel to distant lands at supersonic speeds. We are not limited in food intake by our hunting skills. Instead, we may have available a variety of supermarkets ivhich display the culinary products of many countries. In the acquisition of knowledge we are no longer limited to verbal contact, but have access to many centers of learning equipped with increasingly effective teaching aids, where the different aspects of man's recorded history are collected and preserved.. We can select from a wide variety of entertainment, careers, ideas, and religions. Even parenthood can be planned, and the birth of children controlled, by the use of medical knowledge and contraceptive devices.

Today our activities are less determined by adaptation to nature than by the ingenuity and foresight of the human mind which recently has added another dimension to its spectrum of choices - the possibility of investigating its own physical and chemical substratum.

Limitation and regimentation of our activities are imposed mainly by education, legislation, social pressure, and finances - which are creations of civilizationrather than by environmental determination, as was formerly the case. Civilized man has surrounded himself with a multirude of instruments which magnify his senses, skills, strengths, and the speed with which he can travel, without realizing, perhaps, that in his drive to be free from natural elements, he was creating a new kind of servitude dominated by levers, engines, currency, and computers. The concerns of earlier times for crops and predators were supplanted by economic worries, industrial problems, and the threat of atomic overkill. Despite the tremendous increase in possible courses of action, the freedom an individual enjoys is becoming more tied to mechanization which is replacing the natural environment as a determinant of behavior. Liberation from ecology is paralloled by a mechanized dependence which absorbs considerable manpower for the invention, construction, and maintenance of machines. The possibility of independent behavior is certainly contingent on the availability of different paths of conduct. But the element most essential to its achievement is awareness of the many factors influencing our actions in order to assure us that our responses will not be automatic, but deliberate and personal. As René Dubos has said, "The need to choose is perhaps the most constant aspect of conscious human life; it constitutes

MATRIX OF THE MIND

both its greatest asset and its heaviest burden" (69).*

Awareness

The qualities which most distinctly separate man from other animals are the awareness of his own existence and the capacity and to resist and even change what appears to be his natural fate. The degree of individual awareness differs according to personal circumstances. Consciousness is a rather expensive luxury in terms of time and effort, and we use it sparingly while performing many daily tasks based on complex series of automatic responses. Walking, for example, requires a tedious process of motor learning in early life, but once the necessary cerebral formulas for controlling movements have been established, we pay no attention to the onset, strength, speed, timing, and sequences of muscular performance; we simply stand up and walk while our minds are occupied with other thoughts. All these processes are automatic and, to a considerable extent, are characteristic of each individual. We can, however, refocus our attention on any motor aspect of walking and re-educate and modify the motor formulas to improve the elegance and gracefulness of movement, or to mimic the gait of sailors, tramps, or cowboys, as actors do.

Stopping at a red light does not require a decision because we are highly trained and conditioned to perform this action. If we pause to analyze our behav-

124

ior, we may be aware of the motor activity involved in stepping on the brakes and of the reasons that we are stopping and obeying the traffic rules which only then may be questioned or even ignored. Choice is not involved in automatic responses, but if we appraise the reasons and circumstances surrounding our actions, new avenues of response are created. This applies to emotional reactions and social behavior as well as to motor activity.

Awareness is increased by knowledge of the mechanisms of the considered phenomenon. For instance, an expert is likely to notice any peculiar car engine noises, perceiving auditory signals which may not be detected by untrained drivers. Knowledge of the structure and mechanisms of the motor improves the probability of foreseeing and preventing possible breakdowns and also of correcting malfunctioning parts.

To a considerable degree, our behavior is composed of automatic responses to sensory inputs, but if we knew the genetic determinants, cultural elements, and intracerebral mechanisms involved in various kinds of behavioral performance, we could come closer to understanding the motivations underlying our actions. If we were cognizant of the factors influencing our behavior, we could accept or reject many of them and minimize their effects upon us. The result would be a decrease in automatism and an increase in the deliberate quality of our responses to the environment. Awareness introduces greater individual responsibility in behavioral activities.

Responsibility

Primitive man did not have the choice of going to the movies, reading a book, or watching television. He was fully occupied searching for food and fighting for survival. Today's many behavioral alternatives require that we make a conscious effort to understand and evaluate the different possibilities, perhaps to modify or repress emotional reactions to them, and finally, to select a course of action. In many cases, these processes are performed at the subconscious level, and responses flow effortlessly; at other times we are aware of an impending act an impending act and its possible alternatives, and arriving at a decision may be difficu and tiring. The conscious selection of one path among many places greater responsibility on the individual because his activities are not determined by automatic mechanisms or external factors beyond his control. Intelligent judgment is based on an individual's personal qualities and especially on his ability to evaluate possible solutions. Individual choice entails assuming accountability for the direction of personal destiny, and the greater one's awareness and freedom, the greater the responsibility. In a small social group such as a tribe, the consequences of the leader's choice are rather limited, while in highly organized contemporary societies, the decisions of governmental co elites will affect large numbers of

MATRIX OF THE MIND

people. The political actions of these powerful officials concerning foreign aid, cultural ex-change, and peace and war will affect life in most parts of the world. We should remember that decision-making always involves the activity of intracerebral mechanisms which, as yet, are little known.

Accumnulation of Power

Industrial and technological developments have created unparalleled resources with immense constructive and destructive potentials. Already we have conquered the natural obstacles of rivers, seas, and mountains, and they are no longer insurmountable barriers to the activities of man. At the same time, we have accumulated megatons of atomic energy capable of obliterating all forms of life in the world.

Instruments have been invented to increase a rniltionfold the perceptivity of our senses, the power of our muscles, and our ability to process information. In addition to increasing our material power, we have greatly improved our capacity to organize and use available resources. Plans for the development of cities, industries, research, education, and the economy in general are carefully formulated by experts, and these plans are essential for the organization and evolution of our society. These developments again introduce the question of responsibility in the choice of objectives to be reached. Because of the magnitude of our material and intellectual powers, the directive resolutions made by elite groups may be decisive for the development of scientific and economic fields of endeavor, for the evolution of civilization in general, and for the very existence of man.

Major nations are constantly faced with the choice of how to use power, and conscious efforts are made to reach intelligent decisions which are expressed as national goals such as overcoming poverty, landing a man on the moon, or meeting timetables for industrial, agricultural, and scientific development. Because our resources are not unlimited, a major effort in one field, such as armaments or outer space exploration, restricts the development of other less-favored areas. The application of human energy to the control of natural forces is continually increasing, and perhaps it is time to ask if the present orientation of our civilization is desirable and sound, or whether we should re-examine the universal goals of mankind and pay more attention to the primary objective, which should not be the development of machines, but of man himself.

Sensory Dependence of the Adult Mind

Even if reception of sensory information is accepted as totally essential for the onset and development of mental functions, it is more or less explicitly assumed that an adult has a wellestablished mental capacity which functions with relative independence of the environment. Individuality, initiative, and free will are expressed in the ability to accept or reject ideas and select behavioral responses. A man can isolate himself, meditate, and explore the depths of his own thoughts. To a great extent education, especially in Occidental cultures, is based on the belief that individual personality is a self-contained and relatively independent entity with its own destiny, well differentiated from the surroundings, and able to function by itself even when isolated from earth and traveling in an orbiting capsule.

A more detailed analysis of reality, however, shows that cerebral activity is essentially dependent on sensory inputs from the environment not only at birth but also throughout life. Normal mental functions cannot be preserved in the absence of a stream of information coming from the outside world. The mature brain, with all its wealth of past experience and acquired skills, is not capable of maintaining the thinking process or even normal awareness and reactivity in a vacuum of sensory deprivation: The individual mind is not self-sufficient.

Support for this statement derives from neurophysiological and psychological experimentation. In mammals, the central organization of motor activity is localized in special regions of the cerebral cortex where muscles and ideokinetic formulas are represented. The motor pathways descend through the spinal cord and emerge through the ventral roots to form plexus and motor nerves. As should be expected, experimental destruction in animals or pathological damage in man of the ventral roots produces complete motor paralysis because the cerebral impulses cannot reach the muscle target. Considering the input side, we know that all sensory information from the periphery, including proprioceptive impulses from the muscles, is carried by the dorsal roots of the spinal cord. As anticipated, destruction of all dorsal roots produces a loss of sensation, but in addition, there is also a paralysis of the musculature as pronounced as when the motoi- roots are interrupted. These experiments show that in the absence of sensory information, motor activity is totally disrupted. The brain and motor pathways are not sufficient in themselves, and for proper motor behavior, sensory inputs are absolutely necessary.

The studios of Sprague et al. (217) in the cat confirmed the importance of incoming information for normal functioning of the brain. These authors destroyed the lateral portion of the upper midbrain, including the main sensory pathways, and they observed that, in addition to the expected marked sensory deficit, the cats exhibited a lack of affect, aggression, and pleasurable responses, and did not solicit petting. The animals remained mute, expressionless, and showed minimal autonomic responses but in spite of this passivity, they showed hyperexploratory activity with incessant stereotyped wandering, sniffing, and searching as if hallucinating. "Without a patterned afferent input to the forebrain via the lemnisci, the remaining portions of the central nervous system . . . seem incapable of elaborating a large part of the animal's repertoire of adaptive behavior" (217).

Psychological data also confirm the essential importance of continuous reception of inputs, Experiments on sensory deprivation in animals and man have shown that maintenance of normal mental activity is difficult or impossible when sensory information is reduced and, moreover, that monotonous sensation is aversive. Animals and humans require novelty and continual and varied stimulation from their surroundings.

Perception of the environment has positive reinforcing properties, and when monkeys were confined in a cage, they would press levers and perform other instrumental responses for the reward of opening a little window and looking at the outside world. Curiosity derives from expectancy of novel sensory stimulation and motivates exploratory behavior in both animals and man, while boredom has negative reinforcing properties and is related to the absence of novel sensory inputs (16, 95). To be entertained means to be provided with new and changing sensations, mainly visual and auditory. Primitive man probably derived pleasure from looking at the changing beauty of nature, w hich retains its fascination to the present day. Civilization has provided the technical means for a far greater choice of inputs, and a major portion of our time, effort, mental activity, and economic resources are now devoted to entertainment through books, theaters, radio, television, museums, and other cultural media.

Symbolically we may speak about "psychic energy" as the level of intracerebral activity which could perhaps be identified in neurophysiological terms by electrical and chemical processes located at specific neuronal fields. This psychic energy may be considered a main determinant of the quantity of intellectual and behavioral manifestations. While this energy obviously depends on cerebral physiology (and indirectly on the health of the whole body), its actual source is extracerebral because mental activity is not a property of neurons, but is contingent on the received information which activates stored information and past experiences, creating emotions and ideas.

To be alone with our own mind is not enough. Even if all past experiences are included, the exclusion of new perceptions creates serious functional difficulties. This has been shown for instance in the studies of Hebb and his group (18, 103) in which college students were asked to lie comfortably on beds in soundproof, lighted cubicles, wearing translucent goggles to minimize optic sensation and gloves with cardboard cuffs to limit tactual perception. The purpose of this isolation experiment was not to cut out all sensory stimulation, but only to remove patterns and symbolic information. Most of the subjects expected to spend their idle time alone reviewing their studies, planning term papers, or organizing ideas for lectures. The surprising result-for the investigators as well as for the participantswas that the students "were unable to think clearly about anything for any length of time, and their thought process seemed to be affected in other ways." After several hours of isolation, in any of them began to see images, such as "a rock shaded by a tree, " "a procession of squirrels," or "prehistoric animals walking about in a jungle." Initially the subjects were surprised and amused but after a while their hallucinations became disturbing and vivid enough to interfere with sleep. The students had little control over these phenomena which, in some cases, included acoustic as well as optic perceptions such as people talking, a music box playing, or a choir singing in full stereophonic sound. Some subjects reported sensations of movement or touch, or feelings of "otherness," or that another body was lying beside them on the bed. Isolation also tended to increase the belief in supernatural phenomena and several of the students reported that for a few days after their isolation experiment, they were afraid that they were going to see ghosts. The conclusion was that "a changing sensory environment seems essential for human beings. Without it, the brain ceases to function in an adequate way and abnormalities of behavior develop" (103).

In patients with long-term hospital confinement in bed or in an iron lung or body cast, psychotic-like symptoms have appeared including anxiety, delusions, and hallucinations which did not respond to standard medical or psychiatric treatynent but were easily alleviated by social contact or by sensory stimulation from a radio or television set (141).

In our century the classic punishment of solitary confinement has been combined with sleep deprivation and used in psychological warfare. Exhaustion and decreased sensory inputs are known to cause mental disturbances and reduce defense mechanisms, and they have been effectively manipulated during "brainwashing" or "thought reform" procedures to indoctrinate prisoners (141, 244).

The literature on sensory deprivation is voluminous (197) and shows conclusively that the cerebral cortex requires a stream of stimulation for the preservation of behavioral and mental normality. We should realize, therefore, that our cerebral and mental functions rely on the umbilical cord of sensory inputs and become disrupted if isolated from the environmont. This fact has been recognized by philosophers and is reflected in the words of Ortega y Gasset (167) who wrote: "Man has no nature; what he has is a history," and "I am I and my circumstance." The recognition of environmental inputs as a part of personal identity is one of the important contributions of Ortega, and this idea is presented in Meditations on Quixote (i66), when one of the characters states that "circumstantial reality forms the other half of my person," and "rcabsorption of circumstances is the specific destiny of man." A similar thought is expressed in Tennyson's poem "Ulysses" when Ulysses says, "I am a part of all that I have met."

MATRIX OF THE MIND

Ortega's position is important to philosophical thinking, but we should probably go further and question the existence of that half of personal identity thought not to originate in the environment. If we could erase all individual history, all circumstances and experiences, would there be anything left of our personality? The brain would remain and neuronal nets would perhaps continue their spiking activity, but devoid of history of past experiences and knowledge-there could be no mental activity and the mind would, in fact, be an Aristotelian tabula rasa. Let us remember with Dobzhansky (64) that "genes determine not 'characters' or 'traits' but reactions or response." The frame of reference and the building blocks of our personality are the materials received from the outside. The role of cerebral mechanisms, which to a great extent are also determined by previous experience, is to receive, bias, combine, and store the received information, but not to create it. Originality is the discovery of novel associations between previously received information. We must realize that the anatomical structure of the brain has not evolved perceptibly in the past several millenniums of man's history; what has changed is the amount of information received by the brain and the training to deal with it. The major differences between a cave man and a modern scientist are not genetic but environmental and cultural.

For centuries philosophical tradition has accepted the existence of the "I," "soul," or "ego" as an entity, more or less metaphysical, relatively independent of the environment (and perhaps even of the genes), which is the "essence" that endows individual man with his unique personal identity and character. istics, and may later be threatened or disallowed by the social medium.

The concept of this mythical "I" is so strong that it has permeated the thinking of authors as original and revolutionary as Marcuse. In *One-dimensional Man* (151), he distinguishes between true and false needs, declaring:

False are those which are superimposed upon the individual by particular social interest in his repression.... Most of the prevailing needs to relax, to have fun, to behave and consume in accordance with the advertisements, to love and hate what others love and hate, belong to the category of false needs ... which are determined by external forces over which the individual has no control.... The only needs that have an unqualified claim for satisfaction are the vital one - nourishment, clothing, lodging.

According to Marcuse, inner freedom "designates the private space in which man may become and remain 'himself.'... Today the private space has been invaded and whittled down by technological reality."

The basic questions are obviously, who is this "himself," and what is the origin of its structural elements? Is there any way to provide the experience which will form a baby's mind except by means of the "external powers" of parents, teach-

130

MATRIX OF THE MIND

ers, and culture over which the baby has no control? Are we then going to classify a child's needs as false because they were inculcated? Where is the inner man?

Marcuse's pleas for "intellectual freedom" and his criticism of "material and intellectual needs that perpetuate obsolete forms of the struggle for existence" are certainly valid, but the state of unqualified liberty cannot be supposed to exist for the infant who is totally dependent physically and psychologically on his surroundings. Freedom must be taught and created.

The mutual dependence of the individual and the "psychic environment" or "noosphere" has been elaborated by Teilhard de Chardin (223), who wrote that the Universal and Personal "grow in the same direction and culminate simultaneously in each other ..." the "Hyper-Personal" consciousness at the "Omega point." While it is true that each of us personally receives, interprets, and feels the world around us, why should our individual half be opposed to the noospheric half? Teilhard de Chardin, like Ortega y Gasser and most other philosophers, accepts the existence of the quasi-mystical, inviolable self, an entity somehow identified with the individual mind, ego, or personality, which is related to the environment but has a relatively independent existence.

Recent neurophysiological and psychological studies discussed here reveal that this is not the case. The origin of memories, emotional reactivity, motor skills, words, ideas, and behavioral patterns which constitute our personal self can be traced to outside of the individual. Each person is a transitory composite of materials borrowed from the environment, and his mind is the intracerebral elaboration of extracerebral information. The "personal half" is a regrouping of elements of the environment. For the final result, which is manifested as individual reactivity and behavioral responses, the building blocks from culture are more decisive than the individual substratum within which the regrouping is performed.

It is impressive that this is actually the philosophy, as described by Lévi-Strauss (142), of the Bororo Indians, a very primitive tribe living by the Vermelho River in the Arfiazon jungles of Brazil. For the Bororo, a man is not an individual but a part of a sociological universe. Their villages exist "for all eternity," forming part of the physical universe along with other animate beings, celestial bodies, and meteorological phenomena. Human shape is transitory, midway between that of the fish and the arara. Human life is merely a department of culture. Death is both natural and anticultural, and whenever a native dies, damage is inflicted not only on his relatives but on society as a whole. Nature is blamed and Nature must pay the debt; therefore, a collective hunt is organized to kill some sizable animal ' if possible a jaguar, in order to bring home its skin, teeth, and nails which will constitute the dead man's mori, his everlasting personal value.

MATRIX OF THE MIND

The conclusion that human beings are part of culture does not deny the fact that "individuals" have "individual" reactions and that their brains are unique combinations of elements, but simply points to the source and quality of the factors of personal identity. The cerebral mechanisms which allow us to receive, intei7pret, feel, and react, as well as the extracerebral sources of stimuli, can and should be investigated experimentally. Then we shall gain a new awareness of the structure of the individual and its relations with the surrounding noosphere.

Working Hypothesis for the Experimental Study of the Mind

One of the most importnat consequences of recent scientific discoveries is the new attitude toward the course of human life. This attitude has modified our traditional acceptance of fatalistic determination by unknown factors related to heredity, body functions, and environment, and has intensified the search for knowledge and technology to direct our lives more intelligently. The genetic code is being unraveled, introducing the possibility that some time in the future, we may be able to influence heredity in order to avoid illnesses like Mongolism or in order to promote transmission of specific anatomical and functional characteristics. Neurophysiological investigation has established correlations between mental phenomena and physicochemical changes in the central nervous system, and specific electrical responses of different areas of the brain can be identified following sensory stimulation of the eye with patterns, shapes, or movements. Advances in other scientific areas have proved that mental functions and human behavior can be modified by surgery (frontal lobotomy), by electronics (brain stimulation), and by chemistry (drug administration), thus placing the mind within experimental reach.

The ability to influence mental activity by direct manipulation of cerebral structures is certainly novel in the history of man, and present objectives are not only to increase our understanding of the neurophysiological basis of mind but also to influence cerebral mechanisms by means of instrumental manipulation.

The working hypotheses may be sumriiarized as follows: (1) There are basic mechanisms in the brain responsible for all mental activities, including perceptions, emotions, abstract thought, social relations, and the most refined artistic creations. (2) These mechanisms may be detected, analyzed, influenced, and sometimes substituted for by means of physical and chemical technology. This approach does not claim that love or thoughts are exclusively neurophysiological phenomena, but accepts the obvious fact that the central nervous system is absolutely necessary for any behavioral rnanifestation. It plans to study the mechanisms involved. (3) Predictable behavioral and mental responses may be induced by direct manipulation of the brain. (4) We can substitute intelligent and purposeful determination of neutonal functions for blind, automatic responses.

132

MATRIX OF THE MIND

In any evaluation of experimental results, we should remember that there is always a congruence between the methodological approach and findings obtained, in the sense that if we study the brain with an oscilloscope, we can expect information about spike potentials and other electrical data but not about the chemical composition of the neurons. Psychological reactions and behavioral performance often escape neurophysiological methodology, and a coordinated interdisciplinary approach is needed. Music does not exist in a single note but is the product of a spatiotemporal sequence of many sounds. Mental activity does not emanate front the activity of single neurons but from the interaction of many neuronal fields. Rage, for example, is characterized by changes in electrochemical, autonomic, sensory, and motor functions which are overtly expressed in social relations. Some electrical manifestations of rage have been recorded as discharges at the single neuronal level, but the phenomenon involves multilevel responses, and for its proper investigation the whole organism should be observed in a social setting.

The development of new methodology to explore and communicate with the depth of the brain while the experimental subject engages in spontaneous or evoked activities now enables the scientist to analyze and control basic neurological mechanistns of the mind and represents a unique means of understanding the material and functional bases of individual structure. The future should see collaboration between those investigators who formerly studied neuronal physiology while disregarding behavior and other scientists who have been interested in behavior while ignoring the brain.

Summary

Autonomic and somatic functions, individual and social behavior, emotional and mental reactions may be evoked, maintained, modified, or inhibited, both in animals and in man, by electrical stimulation of specific cerebral structures. Physical control of many brain functions is a demonstrated fact, but the possibilities and limits of this control are still little known.

Experimental Control of Brain Functions in Behaving Subjects

In our present technological environment, we are used to the idea that machines can be controlled from a distance by means of radio signals.

In our present technological environment, we are used to the idea that machines can be controlled from a distance by means of radio signals. The doors of a garage can be opened or closed by pushing a button in our car; the channels and volume of a television set can be adjusted by pressing the corresponding knobs of a small telecollimand instrument without moving from a comfortable armchair; and even orbiting calmules can now be directed from tracking stations on

MATRIX OF THE MIND

earth. These accomplishments should familiarize us with the idea that we may also control the biological functions of living organisms from a distance. Cats, monkeys, or human beings can be induced to flex a limb, to reject food, or to feel emotional excitement under the influence of electrical impulses reaching the depths of their brains through radio waves purposefully sent by an investigator.

This reality has introduced a variety of scientific and philosophical questions, and to understand the significance, potentials, and limitations of brain control, it is convenient to review briefly the basis for normal behavioral activity and the methodology for its possible artificial modification, and then to consider some representative examples of electrical control of behavior in both animals and man.

Physicochemical Bases of Behavioral Activity

In the vegetable as well as in the animal kingdom, the dynamics of biological processes are related to ionic movements and electrical changes across the membranes which separate cells from the surrounding medium. For example, during the process of photosynthesis, the leaf of a tree captures energy from the sun and a negative potential is created on its receptive surface. In a similar manner, activation of a squid axon, a frog muscle, or the human brain is accompanied by a negative wave which invades cellular membranes and then disappears. This transmembrane change of potential induces a flow of electrical currents into the cellular cytoplasm and surrounding conducting fluids. Cellular activity may therefore be investigated by recording the electrical potentials appearing across the membranes or by detecting differences in potential which appear in the extraceiltilar fluid, even if the recording electrodes are placed at a considerable distance from the electromotive source. This is the basic principle of recording electrical activity of the heart (electrocardiogram = EKG) through electrodes placed on the extremities, or of studying electrical potentials of the brain (electroencephalogram = EEG) by means of leads attached to the scalp. If electrodes are placed closer to the source of negativity, for example in the depth of the brain, recordings will be more accurate and may reveal the location of generators of electrical activity. Conversely, by using an external potential, an electrical field may be established through the extracellular fluid, and some of this current flows through the cellular membranes, modifying their charge and permeability and producing the self-propagating process called "stimulation."

In order to stimulate, it is necessary to reduce quickly the positive charge which normally exists on the surface of a resting cell until it reaches a critical point of local depolarization. Then the ionic permeability of the membrane is modified, triggering a pre-established sequence of electrical and chemical phenomena. Excitation takes place in the vicinity of the iterative electrode (cathode) because the application of negative charges will neutralize the normally existing positivity at the external part of the cellular membrane. When stimulation is over, the positive polarity is re-established on the membrane surface with the aid of energy provided by specific chemical reactions, and the cell is ready for a new stimulation. The relatively simple processes of depolarization and repolarization of cell membranes are the essential elements of neuronal excitation, and they are responsible for the extraordinary complexity of all behavioral performance.

Our knowledge gap between understanding electrical events at the cellular level and deciphering the chain of phenomena taking place during the response of a whole organism is certainly formidable. How can we explain activities such as walking, problem solving, or ideation in terms of polarization and repolarization of membranes? Behavior certainly cannot occur without concomitant spike potentials and ionic exchanges, but the same statement holds true for oxygen and sugar consumption, and we must differentiate the mechanisms supporting basic nonspecific cellular activities, such as metabolic requirements, from the mechanisms more specifically related to behavioral responses. Electrical activity of the neurons seems to have the dual role of indicating nonspecific activity and transmitting coded information. This ability to transmit coded information is the most important and least understood property of the nerve cell, and it represents the functional unit for nervous communication. In architecture, given a number of brick units an infinite number of different houses can be constructed. We need to know both the properties of the individual bricks and the pattern of their organization in order to ascertain the properties and qualities of the final building. The characteristics of behavioral responses are determined by the combination of many depolarization phenomena, organized in space and repeated sequentially in time. Their arrangement is often so cornplex that it defies experimental analysis, and we must begin by examining very simple phenomena. The squid axon was for years a popular object of investigation in neuropliysiology, Great caution should be observed, however, when applying experimental results with that preparation to the understanding of motor responses or mental activity. We should remember that knowledge of the letters of the alphabet will not explain the meaning of a phrase or reveal the beauty of a poem.

In addition to investigating the spontaneous changes in membrane potentials, we can artificially depolarize membranes by electrical stimulation of cerebral neuronal pools in order to investigate their functional organization and behavioral consequences for the whole organism. Both of these experimental approaches should be used simultaneously in order to correlate cellular functions with behavioral results. Our present knowledge of the physicachemical bases of biological activity, which has an extensive bibliography (23, 182, 203), permits statement of the following principles: (1) All behavioral manifestations including their mental aspects require the existence of waves of negativity accompanied by electrical and chemical changes at the cellular level. (2) Membrane depolarization, artificially induced by electrical or chemical means, may be followed by observable behavioral manifestations. (3) While the complexity of these responses is extraordinary and many of their aspects are unknown, explanations of motor behavior and psychic activity do not require "vital spirits" or any other metaphysical principle because they are related to physical and chemical laws which can be investigated experimentally.

The classical experiments of Galvani, showing that the legs of a decapitated frog contract in response to electrical stimulation, are repeated many times every year in high school and college laboratories. These simple experiments demonstrate that a process of life, muscle contraction, can be elicited at the will of the investigator as many times as electricity is applied to the tissue. In the absence of stimulation, the legs do not contract. If the cells of the muscle are dead, excitability and contractability are lost and the preparation does not respond. The contraction of the frog's legs is similar regardless of whether the muscle is stimulated directly through its motor nerve or through the brain, and this muscle action is also comparable to its activation during voluntary movements of the intact frog. The applied electricity does not create the limb movement but acts only as a depolarizing agent, starting a chain of events which depends on the properties of the stimulated organ.

The reliability and apparent simplicity of the muscle contraction may be misleading because in reality the contraction depends on tremendously complex processes Nvhich include: depolarization of the testing membrane, changes in its permetbility, precipitous exchange of potassium, sodium, and other ions, creation of electrical fields, reorientation of proteic molectiles within the muscle fiber with a shortening in the length of its chain, decomposition and synthesis of adenosin triphosphate, exchange of phosphoric acids, degradation of hexosapliospliate into lactic acid, and many other enzymatic and biochemical reactions which follow each other according to a genetically determined plan within the muscle fiber and independent from the agent which initiates them. The *mechanisms for contraction and relaxation of the muscle fiber are pre-established in the biological structure of the cells. Electricity, like the nervous system itself, acts as a trigger for these processes.* This principle is fundamental for an understanding of the electrical control of biological functions. Organisms are composed of a large number of biological sequences, some of them inherited and others learned through experience. When a chain reaction has started, it proceeds according to an intrinsic plan which can be modified by feedback or by the arrival of new stimulations. In some cases the trigger may be nonspecific and, for example, muscular contraction can be initiated by mechanical, thermal, osmotic, chemical, electrical, or neuronal stimulation. In investigations of the brain as well as the muscle, electrical

MATRIX OF THE MIND

activation is preferable because it is not harmful for the cells and permits repeated studies of the same biological processes. By applying electricity we can activate pre-established functional mechanisms of a structure and discover its possible role in spontaneous behavior, By means of ESB (electrical stimulation of the brain) it is possible to control a variety of functions - a movement, a glandular secretion, or a specific mental manifestation, depending on the chosen target. Necessary methodology and examples of selected results are discussed in the following chapters.

Methodology for Direct Communication with the Brain

The depth of the central nervous system can be reached very easily through the natural windows of sensory receptors. Stimuli such as patterns of light travel fast front the eye's retina through optic pathways to the visual cortex located in the occipital lobe. Would it be possible to explore the local activity of cortical neurons during the process of symbolic perception? Could we evoke similar sensations by direct stimulation of specific neurons? Can we reach the mind of an individual without using the normal ports of sensory entry? Can we direct the functions of the brain artificially? These and similar problems have attracted the interest of many investigators, but the brain is well protected by layers of membranes, spinal fluid, bone, and teguments, a formidable shield which for a long time has kept the secrets of mental functions away from scientific curiosity.

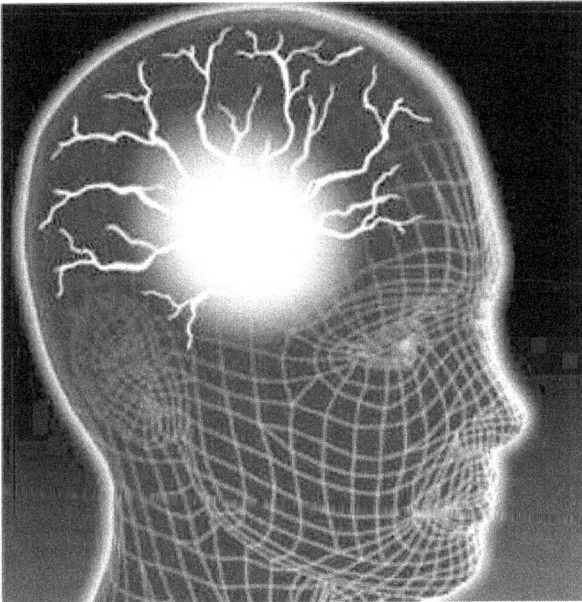

Implantation of Electrodes in Animals

Starting in the last century, many investigators have explored the brain, first in animals and recently in human patients as part of diagnosis and therapy. In these studies it was necessary to open both skin and skiill, and because the procedure was painful it was mandatory to uoo anesthesia. It blocked pain perception, but it also inhibited some of the most important functions of the nervous system. Emotions, consciousness, and free behavior were certainly absent under heavy sedation, and for many years scientists directed their attention to sleeping subjects and overlooked the complexity of awake brains. Textbooks of cerebral physiology were concerned with pathways, connections, reflexes, posture, and movement; mental functions and behavior were considered to belong to a different discipline.

MATRIX OF THE MIND

The methodological breakthrough which made it possible to study the brain of behaving animals came in the 1930s when W.R. Hess (106) devised a procedure to implant very fine wires within the brain of anesthetized cats. After the effects of anesthesia had disappeared, the relatively free and normal animal could be electrically stimulated by connecting long leads to the terminals of the implanted electrodes. This procedure was refined in the early 1950s (47, 49) by reducing the size of the electrodes while increasing the number of intracerebral contacts and using aseptic precautions during implantation. Surgical accuracy in reaching chosen cerebral targets was also improved by means of micromanipulators and a precise system of anatomical coordinates which made it possible to reach similar structures in different subjects. Using biologically inert materials such as gold, platinum, or stainless steel wires insulated with teflon allows the electrodes to be left inside of the brain indefinitely. A diagram of the cerebral implantation of one assembly of seven contacts is shown in Figure I and the X ray of the head of a monkey after implantation is seen in Figure 2. Through a small opening in the skull, the shaft is introduced down to a predetermined depth and is secured with dental cement at the point where it passes through the skull. Then the upper portion of the shaft is bent over the bone surface and secured again a short distance away, and the terminal socket is exteriorized on the head. Each contact of the socket corresponds to a determined point in the depth of the brain which is accessible merely by plugging in a connector, a procedure as simple as connecting any electrical appliance to a wall outlet. This technique has been used for ESB in thousands of animals in many laboratories around the world, and there is ample experience of its efficiency, accuracy, and safety, resolving the initial skepticism that introduction of wires into the brain would be technically difficult, dangerous for the subject, and grossly disruptive of normal functions. It is true that implantation of electrodes destroys neurons along the path of penetration, breaking capillary vessels and later producing a local reaction involving the formation of a thin fibrotic capsule along the implantation tract. It has been proven, however, that local hemorrhage is neglible and that because of the well-known functional redundancy of neural tissue with abundance of duplication in its circuits, the destruction of a relatively small group of neurons does not produce any detectable deficit. The thin reactive encapsulation is electrically conductive and is not an obstacle to stimulation or recording. Beyond this 0.1-0.2 millimeter capsule, the brain appears histologically normal. judged by the absence of abnormal electrical activity, the reliability of effects evoked by ESB, and the consistency of thresholds of excitability through months of experimentation, the electrodes seem to be well tolerated. Some of our monkeys have had electrodes in their heads for more than four years. The anchorage is very solid, and after some initial pulling and scratching of the terminal sockets, the monkeys seem to ignore their presence.

As shown in Figure 3, as many as 100 contacts have been implanted in the

MATRIX OF THE MIND

brain of some chimpanzees without any noticeable neurophysiological or behavioral disturbance, and in several monkeys, contacts have been placed in areas as critical and delicate as the respiratory centers of the medulla without any surgical problems. Electrodes have been used in laboratory animals such as rats, cats, and monkeys, and also in less frequently studied species including crickets, roosters, dolphins, and brave bulls.

Electrodes in the Human Brain

Our present knowledge of the central nervous system is based principally on investigations in animals. Experience has shown that many questions about implantation in humans, such as biological tolerance of electrodes by the neural tissue, can be successfully answered in cats or in lower species. Some of the electrochemical events of neural conduction can be analyzed just as adequately in squids as in mammals, and for certain studies of memory, the octopus has proven an excellent subject. The rat has been - and still is - the animal preferred by experimental psychologists because it is a small and inexpensive mainmal which can be used in large quantities to provide behavioral results suitable for statistical evaluation. The limited behavioral repertory of lower animals, however, cannot be compared with the complex activities of monkeys and apes. These species, being closer relatives of man, are more appropriate subjects for the neurophysiological study of intelligent behavior, and when we want to investigate the highest psychological functions of the brain which involve verbal communication, there is no possible substitute for man himself.

The human brain, like any other part of the body, may suffer traumatic accidents, rumors, or illnesses, and it has often been necessary to explore the affected areas in order to identify structtires, assess abnormality of the tissues, test excitability, and learn the location of important functions which should not be disrupted during surgical procedures. Conscious participation of the patient was required in some of these explorations, for example, to ascertain whether the aura of epileptic attacks could be triggered by electrical stimulation of a specific cortical point@ thus providing information about the possible source of epileptic discharges which could be removed by surgery. For this kind of investigation the brain was exposed under local anesthesia, presenting an exceptional opportunity to study behavioral and psychological responses evoked by ESB in fully awake subjects. The most extensive work in this area has been carried out by Penfield and his associates in Montreal (174), and a considerable number of similar studies have been performed by other neurosurgeons as well (2, 8, 97, 124, 163, 215).

Exploration of the exposed brain has, however, some obvious limitations. It has to be brief to avoid prolongation of surgery; electrodes are usually held in place by hand, causing variability in the applied mechanical pressure; the exposed brain is subject to possible thermal, mechanical, and chemical trauma; the cortical areas are identified only by visual inspection; and the physical and psychological stress of the patient undergoing operation introduces factors difficult to control. Most of these handicaps can be avoided with the use of implanted electrodes, and given the experience of aiiinial experimentation it was natural that sorile investigators should contemplate the application of this methodology to patients for diagnostic and therapelitic purposes (19, 59, 98). Neurosurgeons had already proved that the central nervous system is not as delicate as most people believe, and during therapeutic surgery parts of the cerebral tisstie have been cut, frozen, cauterized, or ablated with negligible adverse effects on the patients. Exploratory introduction of needles into the cerebral ventricles is a well-known and relatively safe clinical procedure, and since electrodes are smaller in diameter than these needles, their introduction into the brain should be even less traumatic. Experience has confirmed the safety and usefulness of long-term implantation of electrodes in man, and the procedurehas been used in specialized medical centers around the world to help thousands of patients suffering from epilepsy, involuntary movements, intractable pain, anxiety neurosis, and other cerebral disturbances. In general several assemblies of fine electrodes with a total of twenty to forty contacts are placed on the surface and/or in the depth of the brain, with the terminal connectors exteriorized through the scalp and protected by a small head bandage (see Figure 4). In some cases the electrodes have remained for nearly two years with excellent tolerance.

Leaving wires inside of a thinking brain may appear unpleasant or dangerous, but actually the many patients who have undergone this experience have not been concerned about the fact of being wired, nor have they felt any discomfort due to the presence of conductors in their heads. Some women have shown their feminine adaptability to circumstances by wearing attractive hats or wigs to conceal their electrical headgear, and many people have been able to enjoy a normal life as outpatients, returning to the clinic periodically for examination and stimulation. In a few cases in which contacts were located in pleasurable areas, patients have had the opportunity to stimulate their own brains by pressing the button of a portable instrument, and this procedure is reported to have therapeutic benefits.

Chronically implanted electrodes enable careful diagnostic explorations to be performed without time limit, and repeated electrical excitations or well-conttolled coagulations can be graded according to the reactions of the patient. As a bonus, important information about psychophysiological correlations, providing direct knowledge about the cerebral basis of human behavior, is being acquired. In our studies (60, 109, 150), an interview situation was selected as the method most likely to offer a continuous supply of verbal and behavioral data.

MATRIX OF THE MIND

While the electrical activity of eight pairs of cerebral points was being recorded, we taped about one hour of conversation between therapist and patient. Notes of the observable behavior were also taken, During the interview, electrical stimulations of the brain were applied for 5 seconds with intervals of three or more minutes, and each significant point was explored several times.

Two girls who were suffering from epileptic seizures and behavioral disturbances requiring implantation of electrodes in the brain for diagnostic and therapeutic purposes. Under the cap, each patient wean a "stimoceiver," used to stimulate the brain by radio and to send electrical signals of brain activity by telemetry while the patients are completely free within the hospital ward (60).

Two-way Radio Comunication with the Brain

Electronic technology has reached a high level of sophistication, and two-way radio communication with automobiles, airplanes, and outer space vehicles is commonplace today. The notable lag in development of similar instrumentation for communciation with the depth of the brain reflects the already mentioned unbalanced evolution of our technological civilization, which seems more interested in accumulating power than in understanding and influencing the basic mechanisms of the human mind.

This gap is now being filled, and it is already possible to equip animals or human beings with minute instruments called "stimoceivers" for radio transmission and reception of electrical messages to and from the brain in completely unrestrained subjects. Microminiaturization of the instrument's electronic components permits control of all parameters of excitation for radio stimulation of three different points within the brain and also telemetric recording of three channels of intracerebral electrical activity. In animals, the stimoceiver may be anchored to the skull, and different members of a colony can be studied without disturbing their spontaneous relations within a group. Behavior such as aggression can be evoked or inhibited. In patients, the stimoceiver may be strapped to the head bandage, permitting electrical stimulation and monitoring of intracerebral activity without disturbing spontaneous activities.

Stimoceivers offers geat promise in the investigation, diagnosis, and therapy of cerebral disturbances in man. Preliminary information about use in patients with temporal lobe seizures (see Figure 4) has demonstrated the following advantages over other methods of intracerebral exploration (60): (1) The patient is instrumented simply by plugging the stimoceiver to the head sockets. (2) There is no disturbance of the spontaneous individual or social behavior of the patient. (3) The subject is under continuous medical supervision, and stimulations and recordings may be made day and night. (4) Studies are carried out during spontaneous social interactions in the hospital environment without introducing fac-

141

tors of anxiety or stress. (5) The brain in severely disturbed patients may be explored without confinement to a recording room. (6) As connecting wires are not necessary there is no risk of dislodgment of electrodes during abnormal behavior. (7) Therapeutic programed stimulation of the brain can be prolonged for any necessary amount of time.

It is reasonable to speculate that in the near future the stimoceiver may provide the essential link from man to computer to man, with a reciprocal feedback between neurons and instruments which represents a new orientation for the medical control of neurophysiological functions. For example, it is conceivable that the localized abnormal electrical activity which announces the imminence of an epileptic attack could be picked tip by implanted electrodes, telemetered to a distant instrument room, tape-recorded, and analyzed by a computer capable of recognizing abnormal electrical patterns. identification of the specific electrical disturbance could trigger the emission of radio signals to activate the patient's stimoceiver and apply an electrical stimulation to a determined inhibitory area of the brain, thus blocking the onset of the convulsive episode.

This speculation is supported by the following experiments completed in June, 1969, in collaboration with Drs. Johnston, Wallace, and Bradley. Chimpanzee Paddy (Figure 3), while free in her cage, was equipped with a stimoceiver to telemeter the brain activity of her right and left amygdaloid nuclei to an adjacent room, where these waves were received, tape-recorded, and automatically analyzed by an on-line analog computer. This instrument was instructed to recognize a specific pattern of waves, a burst of spindles, which was normally present in both amygdaloid nuclei for about one second several times per minutes The computer was also instructed to activate a stimulator, and each time the spindles appeared, radio signals were sent back to Paddy's brain to stimulate a point in her reticular formation known to have negative reinforcing properties. In this way electrical stimulation of one cerebral structure was contingent on the production of a specific EEG pattern by another area of the brain, and the whole process of identification of information and command of action was decided by the on-ine computer.

Results showed that about two hours after the brain-to-computer-to brain feedback was established, spindling activity of the amygdaloid nucleus was reduced to 50 per cent; and six days later, with daily two-hour periods of feedback, spindles were drastically reduced to only 1 per cent of normal occurrence, and the Chimpanzee was quieter, less attentive, and less motivated during behavioral testing, although able to perform olfactory and visual tasks without errors.

The computer was then disconnected, and two weeks later the EEG and Paddy's behavior returned to normal. The experiment was repeated several times with similar results, supporting the conclusions that direct communication can be established between brain and computer, circunivening normal sensory organs, and also that automatic learning is possible by feeding signals directly into specific neuronal structures without conscious participation.

One of the limiting factors in these studies was the existence of wires leading from the brain to the stimoceiver outside of the scalp. The wires represented a possible portal of entry for infection and could be a hindrance to hair grooming in spite of their small size. It would obviously be far more desirable to employ minute instruments which could be implanted completely beneath the skin. For this purpose we have developed in our laboratory a small three-channel stimulator which can be placed subcutaneously and which has terminal leads to be implanted within the liraiii (Figure 6). The instrument is solid state, has no batteries, and can work indefinitely. Necessary electrical energy, remote control of parameters of stimulation, and choice of channels are provided by transdermal coupling, using a small coil which is activated by frequency-modulated radio signals. In February, 1969, an experiment was begun in monkey Nona and in chimpanzee Suzi who were equipped with subcutaneous stimulators to activate their brains from time to time for the rest of their lives. Terminal contacts were located in motor pathways in order to evoke flexion of the contralateral leg, an effect simple enough to be observed and quantified without difficulty. Study of Nona and Suzi and preliminary investigations in other animals have demonstrated that subcutaneous instrutiientation is efficient, reliable, and well tolerated. Behavioral responses were consistent, and local motor excitabilily was not modified by repeated experimentation. Thus the technical problems of stimulating any dc sired area of the brain for as long as necessary in the absence of conductors passing through the skin have been solved, therapeutic and scientific possibilities have been multiplied, and the comfort of subjects has been considerably increased.

The next technical step will be to combine transdermal stimulation of the brain with

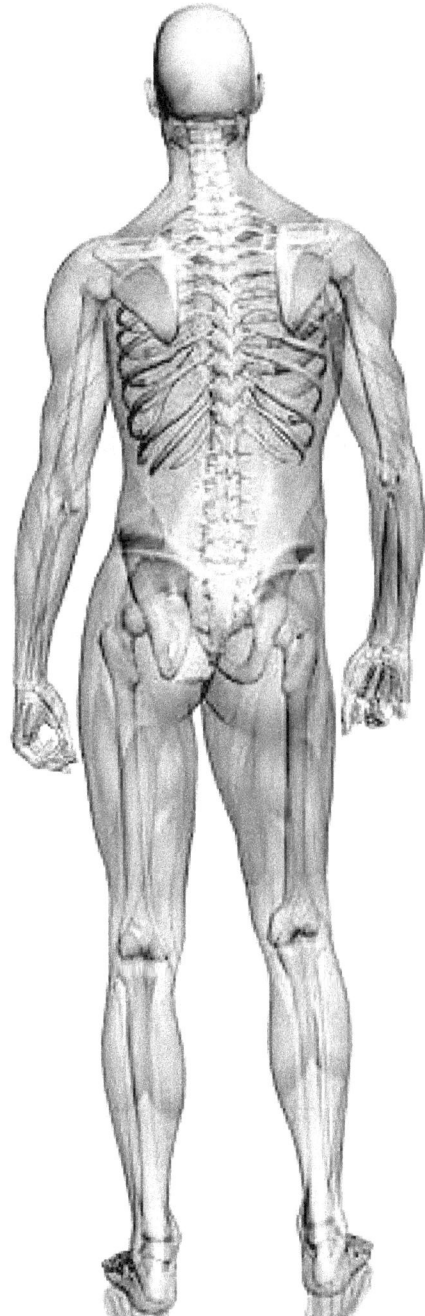

MATRIX OF THE MIND

transdermal telemetry of EEG. In this case the stimoceiver will not be outside the skin as it was in Paddy (Figure 3), nor will it be limited to only transdermal stimulation (Figure 6) as in Nona and Suzi: the whole instrument will be totally subcutaneous. The technology for nonsensory communication between brains and computers through the intact skin is already at our fingertips, and its consequences are difficult to predict. In the past the progress of civilization has tremendously magnified the power of our senses, muscles, and skills. Now we are adding a new dimension: the direct interface between brains and machines. Although true, this statement is perhaps too spectacular and it requires cautious clarification. Our present knowledge regarding the coding of information, mechanisms of perception, and neuronal bases of behavior is so elemental that it is highly improbable that electrical correlates of thoughts or emotions could be picked up, transmitted, and electrically applied to the suitable structure of a different subject in order to be recognized and to trigger related thoughts or emotions. It is, however, already possible to induce a large variety of responses, from motor effects to emotional reactions and intellectual manifestations, by direct electrical stimulation of the brain. Also, several investigators have learned to identify patterns of electrical activity (which a computer could also recognize) localized in specific areas of the brain and related to determined phenomena such as perception of smells or visual perception of edges and movements. We are advancing rapidly in the pattern recognition of electrical correlates of behavior and in the methodology for two-way radio communication between brain and computers.

Fears have been expressed that this new technologies with it the threat of possible unwanted and unethical remote control of the cerebral activities of man by other men, but as will be discussed later, this danger is quite improbable and is outweighed by the expected clinical and scientific benefits. Electronic knowledge and microminiaturization have progressed so much that the limits appear biological rather than technological. Our greatest need is for more experimental information about the neuronal mechanisms related to behavioral and mental processes, and research in unrestricted subjects promises to reveal new understanding of normal minds and more efficient therapy of disturbed brains.

Electrical Stimulation
of the Brain (ESB)

The diameter of the pupil can be electrically controlled as if it were the diaphragm of a photographic camffa. Above, the normal eyes, and below, constriction of the right pupil evoked by stimulation of the hypothalamus Some effects of ESB such as this are indefatigable and can be maintained for days as long stimulation is applied (61).

MATRIX OF THE MIND

The master control for the whole body resides in the brain, and the new methodology of implanted electrodes has provided direct access to the centers which regulate most of the body's activities. The brain also constitutes the material substratum of mental functions, and by exploring its working neurons we have the possibility of investigating experimentally some of the classical problems of mind-brain correlations. In addition to new answers, implantation of electrodes has introduced new problems: Is it feasible to induce a robotlike performance in animals and men by pushing the buttons of a cerebral radio stimulator? Could drives, desires, and thoughts be placed under the artificial command of electronics? Can personality be influenced by ESB? Can the mind be physically controlled?

In scientific literature there is already a substantial amount of information demonstrating the remarkable effects induced by ESB. The heart, for instance, can be stopped for a few beats, slowed down, or accelerated by suitable stimulation of determined cortical and subcortical structures, illustrating the physiological reality that it is the brain which controls the heart, and not vice versa. Respiratory rate and amplitude have been driven by ESB; gastric secretion and motility have also been modified by brain stimulation; the diameter of the pupil can be adjusted at will (Figure 7) from maximum constriction to maximum dilatation, as if it were a photographic camera, simply by changing the intensity knob of an electric stimulator connected with the hypothalamic region of the brain (61). Most visceral functions have been influenced by ESB, as have sensory perceptions, motor activities, and mental functions. Rather than examine each type of finding in detail, we have selected a few typical examples to illustrate the main aspects of electrical control of the brain and its behavioral consequences.

Motor Responses

Behavior is the result of motor activities which range from a simple muscular twitch tc, the creation of a work of art. If we consider the skill involved in nest building, the strategies of fighting animals, or the precision of piano playing, it is obvious that these activities are not solely the result of physical and chemical processes of muscular contraction but depend on conscious direction-on the refined complexity of their cerebral command.

Very little is known about the automatic aspects of voluntary acts, how purpose is related to performance, or how contractions are organized in time and space. Present methodology, however, has placed some of these questions within experimental reach. The fact that ESB can induce simple movements was discovered in the nineteenth century, and today we know that the cerebral organization of motility is located mainly in the cortex of the parietal lobe. Stimulation of this area induces movements on the opposite side of the body, while its destruction

MATRIX OF THE MIND

results in paralysis. These findings have been expressed in attractive diagrams showing the motor areas of the brain as an "homunculus" lying upside down in the parietal cortex, with a big face and a big thumb, like a caricature of a little man in charge of motility. This image was partly responsible for consideration of the cortex as the supreme and intelligent organizer of behavior.

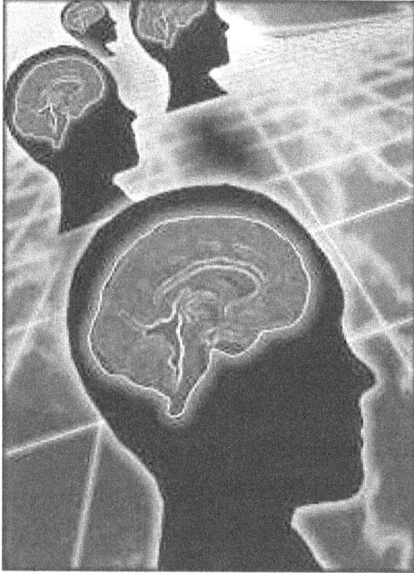

However, further research demonstrated that motor responses obtained from this cortex are rather crude and that other areas in the depth of the brain have a decisive role in the organization of skilled motility. Modern concepts suggest that the cortex should not be considered the highest hierarchical structure of the motor system or even the starting point of motor impulses, but rather a way station, one more link in the loops of sensorymotor correlations. The multiplicity and complexity of motor representation is logical when we consider the tremendous variety of behavioral manifestations which constitute the only means of communication between the individual and his surroundings. This relation requires a motor performance with precise temporal and spatial coordination among many functional units and the processing of a great deal of information for the adjustment and guidance of movements and for instantaneotis adaptation to changes in circumstances. Because of the complexity of these mechanisms, it has been assumed that the artificial ESB could never induce refined and purposeful motor performance. The surprising fact is that, depending on its location, electrical stimulation of the brain is able to evoke not only simple responses but also complex and well-organized behavior which may be indistinguishable from spontaneous activity.

Motor Activation in Animals

A classical experiment for medical students is to anesthetize a rabbit or other small mammal and to expose its brain in order to stimulate the motor cortex. In this way simple responses, such as contraction or extension of the limbs, may be demonstrated. These responses usually involve a small group of muscles, are stereotyped, and lack adaptability, but in spite of these limitations students are generally impressed by seeing the movements of an animal placed under the command of a human being. The demonstration is far more elegant if the experimental animal is completely awake and equipped with electrodes implanted in the brain. Then the responses appear more physiological, and we can investigate the mutual influence of spontaneous and evoked motility.

146

MATRIX OF THE MIND

Electrical stimulation of the right-side motor cortex produced flexion of the left hind limb proportional in amplitude to the electrical intensity used. Observe the animal's harmonious postural adaptation to the evoked movement and lack of emotional disturbance. During these experiments cats were alert and friendly m usual, purring and seeking to be petted.

Electrical Stimulation of the right-side motor cortex of a cat may produce flexion of the left hind leg with an amplitude of movement proportional to the applied intensity. For example, in one experiment when the animal was standing on all fours, the intensity of 1.2 milliamperes evoked flexion of the leg barely off the ground. At 1.5 milliamperes, the hind leg rose about 4 centimeters, and when 1.8 milliamperes were applied, leg flexion was complete (Figure 8). The evoked movement began slowly, developed smoothly, reached its peak in about two seconds, and lasted until the end of the stimulation. This motor performance could be repeated as many times as desired, and it was accompanied by a postural adjustment of the whole body which included lowering of the head, raising of the pelvis, and a slight weight shift to the left in order to maintain equilibrium on only three legs, The electrical stimulation did not produce any emotional disturbance, and the cat was as alert and friendly as usual, rubbing its head against the experimenter, seeking to be petted, and purring.

If, however, we tried to prevent the evoked effect by holding the left hind leg with our hands, the cat stopped purring, struggled to get free, and shook its leg. Apparently the evoked motility was not unpleasant, but attempts to prevent it were disturbing for the animal, suggesting that stimulation produced not a blind motor movement but also a desire to move, and the cat cooperated spontaneously with the electrical command, adjusting its posture before performing the leg flexion. It was evident that the animal was not in a hurry and took its time in preparing for the induced movement. Preliminary adjustments were not seen if the cat's posture was already adequate for the leg flexion. In cases of conflict between the spontaneous movements of the animal and those elicited by the experimenter, the final result depended on the relative strength of the opposing signals. For example, if the cat was walking, threshold stimulations of i.2 milliamperes for slight leg flexion were ineffective. If the cat was stimulated while jumping off a table to reach food, stronger intensities of up to 1.5 milliamperes, which usually evoked a clear motor response, were also ineffective; physiological activity seemed to override the artificial excitation and the cat landed with perfectly coordinated movements. If the intensity was increased to 2 milliamperes, stimulation effects were prepotent over voluntary activities; leg flexion started during the jump, coordination was disrupted, and the cat landed badly. A similar experiment is described on page 186.

In monkeys, electrical stimulation of motor areas has evoked contralateral movements similar to those described for the cat. The stimulated animal showed no signs of fear or hostility (Figure 9), nor did he interrupt his spontaneous behavior, such as walking, climbing, or eating. Evoked and spontaneous movements influenced each other, and the final response was a combination of both.

Simultaneous stimulation of two cerebral points with opposite effects could establish a dynamic balance without any visible effect. For example, if excitation of one point produced turning of the head to the right and another one produced turning to the left, the monkey did not move his head at all when both points were stimulated. This equilibrium could be maintained at different intensity levels of simultaneous stimulation.

Brain stimulation of different areas has elicited most of the simple movements observed in spontaneous behavior, including frowning, opening and closing the eyes, opening, closing, and deviation of the mouth, movements of the tongue, chewing, contraction of the face, movements of the cars, turns, twists, flexions, and extensions of the head and body, and movements of the arms, legs, and fingers. We must conclude that most if not all of the possible simple movements can be evoked by electrical stimulation of the brain.

Movements, loss of equilibrium (as shown in Figure 10), and epileptiform convulsions have also been produced, depending on the cerebral area and parameters of stimulation investigated.

Turning now to more complex responses, we must realize that normal activities in animals and man involve a succession of different acts well coordinated in space and in time. Walking, for example, is a displacement of the body with alternate flexion and extension of the extremities requiring refined control of strength, amplitude, and speed for the contraction of different groups of muscles with precise timing and mutual correlation aimed toward a common goal. In addition, postural adaptation and corrective movements of the head and body are necessary. To induce walking in an animal by programed electrical stimulation of individual muscles would be a formidable task requiring the wiring of perhaps too muscles, the use of a complex cornputer, sophisticated timing mechanisms, large numbers of stimulators with instantaneously adjustable intensities, many sensors, and the help of a team of scientists and technicians, in addition to a cooperative animal and a measure of good luck. The surprising fact is that electrical pulses applied directly to the brain activate cerebral structures which possess the necessary functional complexity to induce walking with apparently normal characteristics.

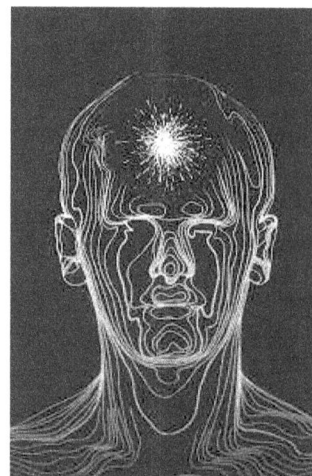

MATRIX OF THE MIND

In one of our experiments, monkey Korn was sitting in the colony cage picking some food when radio stimulation of his thalamus, located in the center of the brain, began. The animal slowly got up and started walking around the cage on all fours at a speed of about 1 meter per second, without bumping against the walls or against other animals, in a normal manner without any signs of anxiety, fear, or discomfort. At the end of 5 to 10 seconds of stimulation, the monkey calmly sat down and resumed picking food. As soon as stimulation was reapplied, Kuru re-sumed walking around the cage. In some studies this effect was repeated as often as sixty times in one hour.

The speed and pattern of a motor response vary according to the cerebral structure stimulated. The effect most often observed in cats and monkeys, obtained by stimulation of limbic structures and extrapyramidal pathways, is walking in circles. Usually the response begins with slow head turning, followed by body turning, getting up, and walking around the cage. In other studies, during stimulation of the fimbria of the fornix, a monkey ran around the cage at a speed of 2.4 meters per second, showing excellent coordination and orientation, avoiding obstacles or other animals in its path. In this experiment, as shown in Figure 11, one monkey in the colony learned to press a lever in the cage which triggered radio stimulation of the test animal. Repetition of these excitations produced conditioning in the stimulated monkey.

Another type of complex motor response induced by ESB has been described as sequential behavior (54) in which different patterns of behavior follow each other in a precise order, as indicated in the following typical example. Monkey Ludy had one contact implanted in the red nucleus, and when it was stimulated for 5 seconds, the following effects appeared (see Figure 12): (1) immediate interruption of spontaneous activity; 2) change in facial expression; (3) turning of the head to the right; (4) standing on two feet; (5) circling to the right; (6) walking on two feet with perfect balance, using both arms to maintain equilibrium during bipedestation; (7) climbing a pole; (8) descending to the floor; (9) uttering a growl; (10) threatening and often attacking and biting a subordinate monkey; (11) changing aggressive attitude and approaching the rest of the group in a friendly manner; (12) resuming peaceful spontaneous behavior. This complex sequence of events took place during ten to fourteen seconds always in the same order but with considerable flexibility in the details of performance. Ludy avoided obstacles in her path, walked with excellent coordination, and used normal strategies in her fights. The sequential response was so reliable that it persisted after 20,000 stimulations repeated once every minute. Demonstrating the specificity of evoked effects, Figure 13 shows Ludy's very different response evoked by radio stimulation of another red nucleus point located three millimeters away.

The monkey at left has learned to press the lever inside the cage which The monkey at left has learned to press the lever inside the cage which triggers radio stimulation of another monkey in the fimbria of the fornix, inducing fast running with excellent coordination. After repetition of these excitations, conditioning is established in the stimulated animal who shows restlessness and stands in a cage corner ready to start the running response as soon as another monkey approaches the lever.

Stimulation of the red nucleus in monkey Ludy produced a response which included turning of the head, walking on two feet, turning around, and other sequential effects. The experiment was repeated more than 20,000 times with reliable performance (54).

Radio stimulation of Ludy in another red nucleus point 3 millimeters away produces only the simple response of yawning. If the monkey was sleeping, brain stimulation was less effective.

Many questions were aroused by these experiments. Why was Ludy walking on two feet? Why the chain of behavioral events? Why was she aggressive a few seconds after the end of stimulation? More studies are needed in order to understand these problems, but the fact that similar sequences have been evoked in other monkeys indicates that we are dealing with rather specific mechanisms of intracerebral organization.

When reviewing tire motor responses that can be induced by electrical stimulation several important limitations should be considered: (i) *Lack of predictability*: When a point of the brain is stimulated for the first time, we cannot predict the effects which may be evoked. When the upper part of the motor cortex is stimulated, it is highly probable that the contralateral hindlimb will contract, but we cannot foresee the quality of this movement or the participation of other body muscles, or know whether this response will affect the whole leg or only the foot. Once the evoked effect is known, repeated stimulations gives predictable results provided that the experimental situation is constant. (2) *Lack of purpose*: In some cases the evoked response is directed by the animal in a purposeful way, but the movements and sequential responses are usually out of context, and there is no reason or purpose for yawning, flexing a hand, or walking around, apart from ESB. It is important to differentiate these aimless motor responses from other types of behavior described later in which the aim is of primary importance an t e motor performance secondary. (3) *No robot performance*: Brain stimulation activates cerebral mechanisms which are organized for motor performance, but it cannot replace them. With the present state of the art, it is very unlikely that we could electrically direct an animal to carry out predetermined activities such as opening a gate or performing an instrumental response. We can induce pleasure or punishment and therefore the motivation to press a

MATRIX OF THE MIND

lever, but we cannot control the sequence of movements necessary for this act in the absence of the animal's own desire to do so. As will be discussed later, we can evoke emotional states which may motivate an animal to attack another or to escape, but we cannot electrically synthesize the complex motor performance of these acts.

Motor Effects in Man

The most common effect obtained by electrical stimulation of the human brain is a simple motor response such as the contraction of an extremity. This effect is often accompanied by lack of voluntary control of the muscles involved, and occasionally it is limited to a local paralysis without any other observable symptoms. In general, the evoked contractions are simple in performance, artificial in character, lacking purpose, and without the elegance of spontaneous motility. For example, in one of our patients, stimulation of the left parietal cortex through implanted electrodes evoked a flexion of the right hand starting with contraction of the first two fingers and continuing with flexion of the other fingers. The closed fist was then maintained for the rest of the 5-second stimulation. This effect was not unpleasant or disturbing, and it developed without interrupting ongoing, behavior or spontaneous conversation. The patient was aware that his hand had moved involuntarily but he was not afraid and only under questioning did he comment that his arm felt "weak and dizzy." When the patient was warned of the oncoming stimulation and was asked to try to keep his fingers extended, he could not prevent the evoked movement and commented, "I guess, Doctor, that your electricity is stronger than my will." If this stimulation was applied while the subject was voluntarily using his hand, for instance to turn the pages of a magazine, this action was not blocked but the induced hand flexion distorted voluntary performance and resulted in crumpling and tearing of pages. In our experience and in reports by other investigators, electrical stimulation of the motor cortex has not induced precise or skillful movements, and in all cases the evoked responses have been clumsy and abnormal.

Excitation of the supplementary motor area, located near the main motor cortex, may induce three types of effects (174): (1)

There can be postural changes, in which the movement starts slowly and attains a determined end point with more or less general involvement of the body.

(2) The movements can have a phasic character such as pawing with the hand, stepping with the foot, or flexing and extending the fingers or wrist. (3) The response can consist of uncoordinated movements. Of special interest is the possibility of activating paralyzed limbs by means of ESB. For example, one patient was suffering from sudden paralysis of the left arm and leg probably caused by an embolus, and after four years he had begun to experience burning pain in the left side of his body which was exacerbated by touching his left thorax or arm. After other treatments failed, two surgical interventions were performed to ablate parts of the sensorimotor cortex, and it was observed that electrical stimulation in the supplementary motor area produced vocalization, raising of the paralyzed arm, and other motor responses. These effects were similar to those evoked in other patients without paralysis. Thus it is clear that the supplementary cortex has pathways independent from the classical motor pathways and that evoked movements may be independent from the integrity of the main motor representation in the cortex.

ESB apparently produces similar results whether applied to the motor area of a child or an adult, of a manual laborer or of an accomplished artist. Skills and refined movements not stem to be represented in the cortex, or at least they have not been aroused by its electrical stimulation. The motor cortex is probably like a large keyboard located on the efferent side, dealing with the output of activity, able to play the strings of muscular contraction and to produce movements, but requiring the direction of other cerebral structures which as yet are little known.

In contrast to these effects, ESB may evoke more elaborate responses. For example, in one of our patients, electrical stimulation of the rostral part of the internal capsule produced head turning and slow displacement of the body to either side with a well-oriented and apparently normal sequence, as if the patient were looking for something. This stimulation was repeated six times on two different days with comparable results. The interesting fact was that the patient considered the evoked activity spontaneous and always offered a reasonable explanation for it. When asked "What are you doing?" the answers were, "I am looking for my slippers," "I heard a noise," "I am restless," and "I was looking under the bed." In this case it was difficult to ascertain whether the stimulation had evoked a movement which the patient tried to justify, or if an hallucination had been elicited which subsequently induced the patient to move and to explore the surroundings.

There are very few clinical reports of complex movements evoked by ESB which are comparable to the sequential responses observed in monkeys, and this may indicate that cerebral organization is less stereotyped in man than in animals. Temporal lobe stimulation in man has induced automatisms, including

MATRIX OF THE MIND

fumbling with surgical drapes or with the patient's own hands, and well-organized movements aimed at getting off the operating table. Usually these evoked automatisms have not been remembered. Vocalizations and more or less intelligible speech may also be included among complex motor responses, although) they represent the activation of motor and ideational mechanisms. Vocalizations have been obtained by stimulation of the motor area in the precentral gyros and also of the supplementary motor area in both hemispheres. The response usually consists of a sustained or interrupted cry with a vowel sound which occasionally has a consonant component (174).

Hell and Heaven Within the Brain:

The Systems for Punishment and Reward

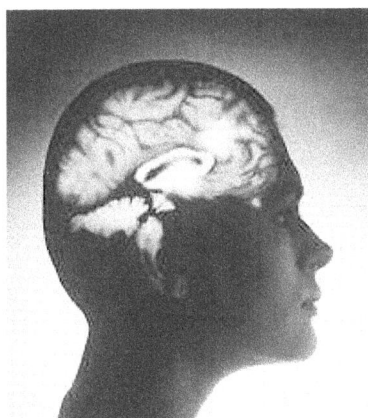

When man evolved above other powerful animals, the size and complexity of his brain increased, giving him superior intelligence along with more anguish, deeper sorrow, and greater sensitivity than any other living creature. Man also learned to enjoy beauty, to dream and to create, to love and to hate. In the education of children as well as in the training of animals, Punishment and reward constitute the most powerful motivations for learning. In our hedonistic orientation of life to minimize pain and seek pleasure, we often attribute these qualities to the environment without realizing that sensations depend on a chain of events which culminates in the activation of determined intracerebral mechanisms. Physical damage, the loss of a beloved child, or apocalyptic disaster cannot make us suffer if some of our cerebral structures have been blocked by anesthesia. Pleasure is not in the skin being caressed or in a full stomach, but somewhere inside the cranial vault.

At the same time pain and pleasure have important psychic and cultural components related to individual history. Men inhibited by sortie extraordinary tribal or religious training to endure discomfort have been tortured to death without showing signs of suffering. It is also known that in the absence of physical injury, mental elaboration of information may produce the worst kind of suffering. Social rejection, guilt feelings, and other personal tragedies may produce greater autonomic, somatic, and psychological manifestations than actual physical pain.

There is strong reluctance to accept that such personal and refined interpretations of reality as being afraid and being in love are contingent on the membrane depolarization of determined clusters of neurons, but this is one aspect of emotional phenomena which should not be ignored. After frontal lobotomy, cancer patients have reported that the pain persisted undiminished, but that their subjective suffering was radically reduced, and they did not complain or request as much medication as before surgery. Lobotomized patients reacted to noxious stimuli as much, if not more, than before their operations, jumping at pinpricks and responding quickly to objective tests of excessive heat, but they showed decreased concern. It seems that in the frontal lobes there is a potentiating mechanism for the evaluation of personal suffering, and after lobotomy the initial sensation of pain is unmodified, while the reactive component to that feeling is greatly diminished. This mechanism is rather specific of the frontal lobes; bilateral destruction of the temporal lobes fails to modify personal suffering.

Important questions to resolve are: Do some cerebral structures have the specific role of analyzing determined types of sensations? Is the coding of information at the receptor level essential for the activation of these structures Not too long ago, many scientists would have dismissed as naive the already demonstrated fact that punishment and reward can be induced at will by manipulating the controls of an electrical instrument connected to the brain.

Perception of Suffering

In textbooks and scientific papers, terms such as "pain receptors," "pain fibers," and "pain pathways" are frequently used, but it should be clarified that peripheral nerves do not carry sensations. Neuronal pathways transmit only patterns of electrical activity with a message that must be deciphered by the central nervous system, and in the absence of brain there is no pain, even if some reflex motor reactions may still be present. A decapitated frog cannot feel but will jump away with fairly good motor coordination when pinched in the hind legs. During competitive sports or on the battlefield, emotion and stress may temporarily block the feeling of pain in man, and often injuries are not immediately noticed. The cerebral interpretation of sensory signals is so decisive that the same stimulus may be considered pleasant or unpleasant depending on circumstances. A strong electrical shock on the feet scares a dog and inhibits its secretion of saliva. If, however, the same "painful" excitation is followed for several days by administration of food, the animal accepts the shock, wagging its tail happily and salivating in anticipation of the food reward. Some of these dogs have been trained to press a lever to trigger the electric shock which preceded food. During sexual relations in man, bites, scratches, and other potentially painful sensations are often interpreted as enjoyable, and some sexual deviates seek physical punishment as a source of pleasure.

The paradox is that while skin and viscera have plentiful nerve endings for sensory reception, the brain does not possess this type of innervation. In patients under local anesthesia, the cerebral tissue may be cut, burned, pulled apart, or

MATRIX OF THE MIND

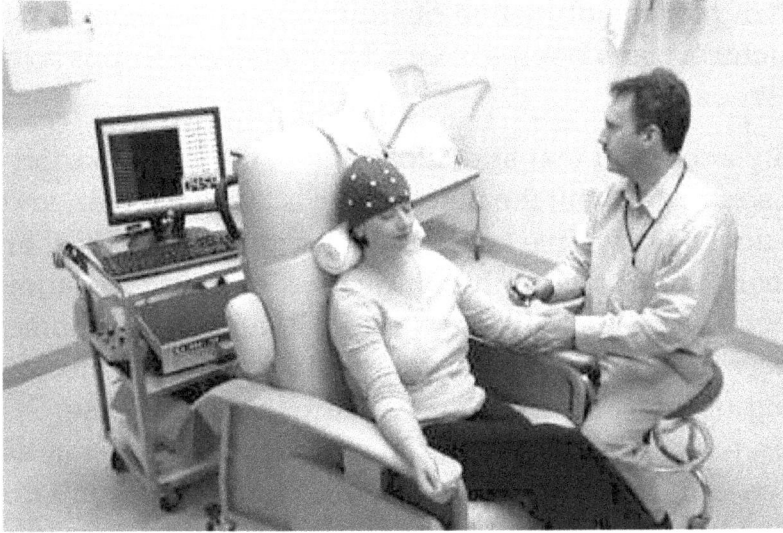

frozen without causing any discomfort. This organ so insensitive to its own destruction is, however, the exquisite sensor of information received from the periphery. In higher animal species there is sensory differentiation involving specialized peripheral receptors which code external information into electrical impulses and internal analyzers which decode the circulating inputs in order to give rise to the perception of sensations.

Most sensory messages travel through peripheral nerves, dorsal roots, spinal cord, and medulla to the thalamic nuclei in the brain, but from there we lose their trail and do not know where the information is interpreted as painful or pleasurable, or how affective components are attributed to a sensation (212, 220).

Although anatomical investigations indicate that thalamic fibers project to the parietal "sensory" cortex, stimulation of this area does not produce pain in animals or man. No discomfort has been reported following electrical excitation of the surface or depth of the motor areas, frontal lobes, occipital lobes, cingulate gyros, and many other structures, while pain, rage, and fear have been evoked by excitation of the central gray tegmentum, and a few other regions.

Animals share with man the expressive aspect of emotional manifestations. When a dog wags its tail, we suppose it is happy, and when a cat hisses and spits we assume that it is enraged, but these interpretations are anthropomorphic and in reality we do not know the feelings of any animal. Several authors have tried to correlate objective manifestations with sensations; for example, stimulation of the cornea of the eye provokes struggling, pupillary dilatation, and rise of blood pressure (87), but these responses are not necessarily related to awareness of feelings, as is clearly demonstrated by the defensive ability of the decapitated frog. Experimental investigation of the mechanisms of pain and pleasure is handicapped in animals by their lack of verbal communication, but fortunately we can investigate whether an animal likes or dislikes the perceived sensations by analyzing its instrumental responses. Rats, monkeys, and other species can learn to press a lever in order to receive a reward such as a food pellet or to avoid something unpleasant such as an electric shock to the skin. By the voluntary act of instrumental manipulation, an animal expresses whether or not the food, shock, or brain stimulation is desirable, allowing for the objective qualification of the sensation. In this way, many cerebral strictures have been explored to identify their positive or negative reinforcing properties.

At present it is generally accepted that specific areas of the brain participate in the integration of pain sensations, but the mechanism is far from clear, and in our animal experiments we do not know if we are stimulating pathways or higher centers of integration. The concept of a straight conduction of pain messages from the periphery up to the central nervous system was too elemental. Incoming messages are probably processed at many levels with feedbacks which modify the sensitivity and the filtering of information at many stages including the peripheral receptor level. Brain excitation, therefore, may affect transmission as well is the elaboration of inputs and feedback modulation. Electrical stimuli do not carry any specific message because they are a monotonous repetition of similar pulses, and the fact that they constitute a suitable trigger for central perception of pain means that the reception of a patterned code is not required, but only the nonspecific activation of neuronal pools which are accessible to investigation. In addition to the importance of these studies for finding better therapies for the alleviation of pain, there is another aspect which has great social interest: the possible relations between pain perception and violence.

Violence Within the Brain

The chronicle of human civilization is the story of a cooperative venture consistently marred by self-destruction, and every advance has been accompanied by increased efficiency of violent behavior. Early man needed considerable physical strength -,end skill to defend himself or attack other men or beasts with stones, arrows, or swords, but the invention of explosives and subsequent development of firearms have made unskilled individuals more powerful than mythical warriors of the past. The technology for destruction has now placed at the disposal of man a vast i arsenal of ingenious weapons which facilitate all forms of violence including crimes against property, assassinations, riots, and wars, threatening not only individual life and national I stability but the very existence of civilization.

Ours is a tragically unbalanced industrial society which devotes most of its resources to the acquisition of destructive power and invests insignificant effort in the search which could provide the true weapons of self-defense: knowledge of the mechanisms responsible for violent behavior. They are necessarily related with intracerebral processes of neuronal activity, even if the triggering causality may reside in environmental circumstances. Violence is a product of cultural environment and is an extreme form of aggression, distinct from modes of self-expression required for survival and development under normal conditions. Man

MATRIX OF THE MIND

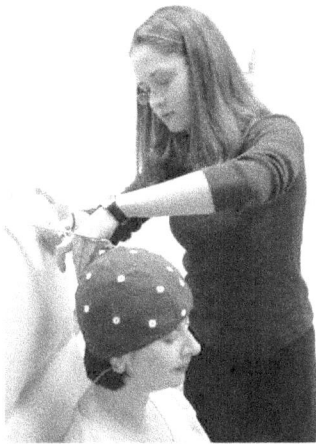

may react to unpleasant or painful stimuli with violence-he may retaliate even more vigorously than he is attacked-but only if he has been taught by his culture to react in this manner. A major role of education is to "build internal controls in human beings so that they can withstand external pressures and maintain internal equilibrium" (157). We should remember that it is normal for an animal to urinate when the bladder is full and to mount any available female during the mating season, but that these behaviors may be controlled in man through training. The distinctly human quality of cerebralization of behavior is possible through education.

Human aggression may be considered a behavioral response characterized by the exercise of force with the intent to inflict damage on persons or objects. The phenomenon may be analyzed in three components: inputs, determined by environmental circumstances perceived through sensory receptors and acting upon the individual; throughputs, which are the personal processing of these circumstances through the intracerebral mechanisms established by genetic endowment and previous experiences; and outputs, represented by the expressions of individual and social behavior which constitute the observable manifestations of aggression. Increasing awareness of the need to investigate these subjects has already resulted in the creation of specialized institutes, but surprisingly enough the most essential element in the whole process of violence is usually neglected. Attention is directed to economic, ideological, social, and political factors and to their consequences, which are expressed as individual and mass behavior, while the essential link in the central nervous system is often forgotten. It is, however, an incontrovertible fact that the environment is only the provider of sensory inputs which must be interpreted by the brain, and that any kind of behavior is the result of intracerebral activity.

It would be naive to investigate the reasons for a riot by recording the intracerebral electrical activity of the participants, but it would be equally wrong to ignore the fact that each participant has a brain and that determined neuronal groups are reacting to sensory inputs and are subsequently producing the behavioral expression of violence. Both neurophysiological and environmental factors must be evaluated, and today methodology is available for their combined study. Humanity behaves in general no more intelligently than animals would under the same circumstances, and this alarming reality is due largely to that spiritual pride which prevents men from regarding themselves and their behavior as parts of nature and as subject to its universal laws" (148). Experimental investigation of the cerebral structures responsible for aggressive behavior is an essential counterpart of social studies, and this should be recognized by sociologists as well as biologists.

In animals, the first demonstration that offensive activity could be evoked by ESB was provided by Hess (I 05), and it has subsequently been confirmed by numerous investigators. Cats under electrical stimulation of the periventricular gray matter acted "as if threatened by a dog," responding with unsheathed claws and well-aimed blows. "The animal spits, snorts or growls. At the same time the hair on its back stands on end, and its tail becomes bushy. Its pupils widen sometimes to their maximum, and its ears lie back or move back and forth to frighten the non-existing enemy" (106). In these experiments it is important to know how the cat really feels. Is it aware of its own responses? Is the hostility purposefully oriented to do harm? Or is the entire phenomenon a pseudoaffective reaction, a false or sham rage containing the motor components of offensive display without actual emotional participation? These issues have been debated over the years, but today it is clear that both sham and true rage can be elicited by ESB depending on the location of stimulation. Excitation of the anterior hypothalamus may induce a threatening display with hissing and growling which should be interpreted as false rage because, as shown in Figure 14, the display was not directed against other animals. When other cats reacted by hissing and attacking the stimulated animal, it did not retaliate or escape and simply lowered its head and flattened its ears, and these brain stimulations could not be conditioned to sensory cues.

In contrast, true rage has been demonstrated in other experiments. As shown in Figure 15, stimulation of the lateral hypothalamus produced an aggressive display clearly directed toward attack against investigators with whom relations had previously been friendly (above); learning of instrumental responses, such a rotating a paddle wheel, in order to stop the brain stimulation (below). In this way the cat expresses its dislike of being stimulated in a particular area (53).

The stimulated animal started prowling around looking for fights with other subordinate animals, but avoided the most powerful cat in the group. It was evident that brain stimulation had created a state of increased aggressiveness, but it was also clear that the cat directed its hostility intelligently, choosing the enemy and the moment of attack, changing tactics, and adapting its movements to the motor reaction of its opponents Brain stimulation determined the affective state of hostility, but behavioral performance depended on the individual characteristics of the stimulated animal, including learned skills and previous experiences. Stimulations were usually tested for 5 to 10 seconds, but since it was important to know the fatigability of the effect, a longer experiment was performed, reducing the applied intensity to a level which did not evoke overt rage. The experimental subject was an affectionate cat which usually sought petting and ported while it was held in the experimenter's arms. Then it was introduced into the colony with five other cats and was radi4p stimulated continuously for two hours. During this period the animal sat motionless in a corner of the cage, uttering barely audible growls from time to time. If any other cat approached, the stimulated animal started hissing and threatening, and if the experimenter tried to pet it, the growls increased in intensity and the animal often spat and hissed. This hostile attitude disappeared as soon as the stimulation was over, and the cat became as friendly as before. These experiments demonstrated that brain excitation could modify reactions toward normal sensory stimuli and could modulate the quality of the responses in a way similar to modulation during spontaneous emotional states.

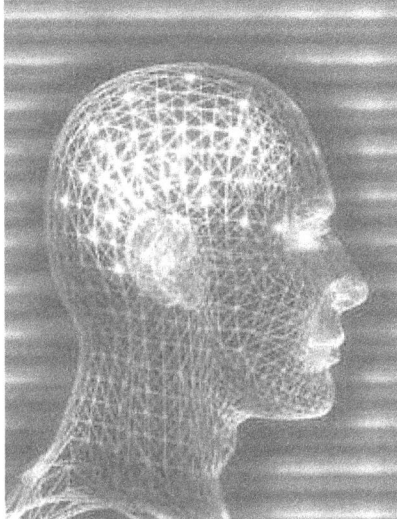

They usually express their submissiveness by grimacing, crouching, and offering sexual play. In several colonies we have observed that radio stimulation of specific points in the thalamus or central gray in the boss monkey increased his aggressiveness and induced well-directed attacks against other members of the group, whom he chased around and occasionally bit. It was evident that his hostility was oriented purposefully and according to his previous experience because he usually attacked the other male who represented a challenge to his authority, and he always spared the little female who was his favorite partner.

A high-ranking monkey expresses rage by attacking submissive members of the colony, but what would he the consequences of stimulating the brain of lower-ranking animals? Could they be induced to challenge the authority of other monkeys, including perhaps even the boss, or would their social inhibitions block the electrically induced hostility? These questions were investigated in one colony by changing its composition to increase progressively the social rank of one member, a female named Lina, who in the first grouping of four animals ranked lowest, progressing to third rank in the second group and to second rank in the third group. Social dominance was evaluated during extended control periods using the criteria of number of spontaneous agonistic and sexual interactions, priority in food getting, and territoriality. On two successive mornings in each colony Lina was radio stimulated for 5 seconds once a minute for one hour in the nucleus posterolateralis of the thalamus. In all three colonies, these stimulations induced Lina to run across the cage, climb to the ceiling, lick, vocalize, and according to her social status, to attack other animals. In group I, where l,ina was submissive, she tried to attack another monkey only once, and she was threatened or attacked 24 times. In group 2 she became more aggressive (24 occurrences) and was attacked only 3 times, while in group 3 Lina attacked other monkeys 79 times and was not threatened at all. No changes in the number of agonistic acts were observed in any group before or after the stimulation hour, showing that alterations in Lina's aggressive behavior were determined by ESB.

In summary, intraspecies aggression has been evoked in cats and monkeys by electrical stimulation of several cerebral structures, and its expression is dependent on the social setting. Unlike purely motor effects including complex sequences which have no social significance, an artificially evoked aggressive act may be directed against a specific group member or may be entirely suppressed, according to the stimulated subject's social rank.

Many questions remain to be answered. Which cerebral areas are responsible for spontaneous aggressive behavior? By what mechanisms are environmental inputs interpreted as undesirable? How does cultural training influence the reactivity of specific cerebral areas? Can neurophysiological mechanisms of violence be re-educated, or are individual responses set for life after early imprinting? It is interesting that application of ESB modified the interpretation of the environment, changing the peaceful relations of a group of animals into sudden overt hostility. The same sensory inputs provided by the presence of other animals, which were neutral during control periods, were under ESB the cue for a ferocious and well-directed attack. Apparently brain stimulation introduced an emotional bias which altered interpretation of the surroundings.

While neurophysiological activity may be influenced or perhaps even set by genetic factors and past experience, the brain is the direct interpreter of environmental inputs and the determinant of behavioral responses. To understand the causes and plan remedies for intraspecific aggression in animals and man require knowledge of both sociology and neurophysiology. Electricity cannot determine the target for hostility or direct the sequences of aggressive behavior, which are both related to the past history of the stimulated subject and to his immediate adaptation to changing circumstances. Artificially triggered and spontaneously provoked aggression have many elements in common, suggesting that in both cases similar areas of the brain have been activated.

While individual and collective acts of violence may seem rather distant from the electrical discharges of neurons, we should remember that personality is not in the environment but in the nervous tissue. Possible solutions to undesirable aggression obviously will not be found in the use of ESB. This is only a methodology for investigation of the problem and acquisition of necessary information about the brain mechanisms involved. It is well known that medical treatment of cardiac patients is based on anatomical and physiological studies of the heart, and that without this information it would not have been possible to dis-

MATRIX OF THE MIND

cover new drugs or to give effective medical advice. Similarly, without knowledge of the brain it will be difficult to correlate social causality with individual reactivity.

Anxiety, Fear, and Violence Evoked by ESB in Man

Anxiety has been considered the alpha and omega of psychiatry. It is one of the central themes of existential philosophy, and it shades the normal - and abnormal - life of most human beings. Several emotional states may be classified under the heading of anxiety, including fear, fright, panic, and terror, which are variations of the same basic experience. One of the most complex mental disturbances, unreasonable or excessive anxiety, including phobias and compulsive obsessions, often does not respond to standard therapies, and in some instances it has been improved by electrocoagulation of discrete areas of the frontal pole. Grey Walter (234) has claimed an 85 per cent total social recovery in a group of sixty patients with anxiety and obsessions treated with carefully dosified coagulations made through electrodes implanted in the frontal lobes.

Without entering into semantic discussions, we may consider anxiety an emotional state of conscious or subconscious tension related to real or imaginary threats to psychological or physical individual integrity. A mild degree of anxiety may mobilize, while excessive degrees may paralyze somatic and mental activity. Beyond a certain limit, anxiety has unpleasant characteristics. In normal circumstances, it is produced, as is any other emotion, by sensory inputs from the environment and by recollections, both of which require mental elaboration of messages which may be influenced by humoral and neuronal factors. In addition, there is abundant evidence that anxiety and fear may be induced as either a primary or a secondary category of response by direct electrical stimulation of the brain. The perception or expectancy of pain can be frightening, and in some cases when ESB produced localized or generalized discomfort, patients have expressed concern about continuation of the exploratory procedures. In addition to the natural fear of possible further discomfort, there may have been a component of primary anxiety which would be difficult to evaluate.

Destruction of discrete parts of the thalamus produces relief from anxiety neurosis and obsessive-compulsive neurosis which is probably related to the interruption of tonic pathways to the frontal lobes. Stimulation of the thalamic nucleus, however, very seldom produces anxiety, and the reports of patients are limited to feelings of weakness, being different, dizziness, floating, and something like alcoholic intoxication (214).

Clearer demonstrations of direct induction of fear without any other accompanying sensations have been reported by several investigators. Lesions in the medial thalamus give effective pain relief with a minimal amount of sensory loss,

161

and for this reason this area has often been explored electrically in cancer patients. In some cases it has produced acute anxiety attacks, which one patient vividly described as: "It's rather like the feeling of having just been missed by a car and leaped back to the curb and went B-r-r-r." Something in his guts felt very unpleasant, very unusual, and he certainly did not want to feel like that again (73). The surprising fact is that the unpleasant sensation of fear was felt in one side of the body, contralateral to the brain stimulation, Sweet (221) has reported the case of a very intelligent patient, the dean of a graduate school, who after a unilateral sympathectomy to treat his upper limb hyperhydrosis, found that his previous and customary sensation of shivering while listening to a stirring passage of music occurred in only one side and he could not be thrilled in the sympathectomized half of his body. These cases were interesting because emotions are usually experienced in a rather diffuse and bilateral fashion unless innervation has been specifically interrupted.

The role of the thalamus in the integration of fear is also suggested by the study of a female patient whose spontaneous crippling attacks of anxiety of overwhelming intensity had led to several suicide attempts and a chronic state of depression and agitation quite refractory to drugs and psychotherapy. Stimulation of the dorsolateral nucleus of the thalamus evoked precisely the same type of attack at a level of symptomatology directly proportional to the applied intensity. It was possible to find the electrical threshold for a mild anxiety or to increase it to higher levels simply by turning the dial of the stimulator. "One could sit with one's hand on the knob and control the level of her anxiety" (73).

In one of our female patients, stimulation of a similar area in the thalamus induced a typical fearful expression and she turned to either side, visually exploring the room behind her. When asked what she was doing, she replied that she felt a threat and thought that something horrible was going to happen. This fearful sensation was perceived as real, and she had a premonition of imminent disaster of unknown cause. The effect was reliable on different days and was not altered by the use of lights and a movie camera to document the finding. Her motor activity and choice of words varied according to the environmental setting, but her facial expression and acute sensation of nonspecific, unexplainable, but real fear were similar following different stimulations. The response started with a delay of less than one second, lasted for as long as the stimulation, and did not leave observable aftereffects. The patient remembered her fear but was not upset by the memory.

Some patients have displayed anxiety and restlessness when the pallidum was stimulated at frequencies above 8 cycles per second, and they also perceived a constriction or warmth in the chest (123). A few reported a "vital anxiety in the left chest," and screamed anxiously if the stimulation was repeated. Intense emotional reactions have been evoked by stimulation of the amygdaloid nucleus, but responses varied in the same patient even with the same parameters of stimulation. The effect was sometimes rage, sometimes fear. One patient explained, "I don't know what came over me. I felt like air animal" (100).

The sensation of fear without any concomitant pain has also been observed as a result of ESB of the temporal lobe (230). This effect may be classified as "illusion of fear" (174) because there was obviously no real reason to be afraid apart from the artificial electrical activation of some cerebral structures. In every case, however, fear is a cerebral interpretation of reality which depends on a variety of cultural and experiential factors with logical or illogical reasons. The fact that it can be aroused by stimulation of a few areas of the brain allows the exploration of the neuronal mechanisms of anxiety, and as a working hypothesis we may suppose that the emotional qualities of fear depend on the activation of determined structures located probably in the thalamus, amygdala, and a few other as yet unidentified nuclei. This activation usually depends on the symbolic evaluation of coded sensory inputs, but the threshold for this activation may be modified-and also reached-by direct application of ESB. Knowledge of intracerebral mechanisms of anxiety and fear will permit the establishment of a more rational pharmacological and psychiatric treatment of many suffering patients, and may also help its to understand and ameliorate the increasing level of anxiety in our civilization.

It is also known that in some tragic cases, abnormal neurological processes may be the causal factor for unreasonable and uncontrollable violence. Those afflicted may often hurt or even kill either strangers or close family members usually treated with affection. A typical example was J. P., a charming and attractive 20-year-old girl with a history of encephalitis at the age of eighteen months and many crises of temporal lobe seizures and grand mal attacks for the last ten years (6o). Her main social problem was the frequent and unpredictable occurrence of rage which on more than a dozen occasions resulted in an assault on another person such as inserting a knife into a stranger's myocardium, or a pair of scissors into the pleural cavity of a nurse. The patient was committed to a ward for the criminally insane, and electrodes Were implanted in her amygdala and hippocampus for exploration of possible neurological abnormalities. As she was rather impulsive, confinement in the EEG recording room was impractical, and she bocame one of the first clinical cases instrumented with a stimoceiver, which made it possible to study intracerebral activity without restraint (see Figure 4). Depth recordings taken while the patient moved freely around the ward demonstrated marked electrical abnormalities in both amygdala and hippocampus. Spontaneous periods of aimless walking coincided with an increase in the number of high-voltage sharp waves. At other times, the patient's speech was spontaneously inhibited for several minutes during which she could not answer any questions although she retained partial comprehension and awareness. These periods coincided with bursts of spike activity localized to the optic radiation (Figure 17). Transitory emotional excitement was related with an increase in the number and duration of 16-cycles-per-second bursts; but the patient read papers, conversed with other people, and walked around without causing any noticeable alterations in the telemetered intracerebral electrical activity.

During depth explorations, it was demonstrated that crises of assaultive behavior similar to the patient's spontaneous bursts of anger could be elicited by radio stimulation of contact 3 in the right amygdala. A 1.2 milliampere excitation of this point was applied while she was playing the guitar and singing with enthusiasm and skill. At the seventh second of stimulation, she threw away the guitar and in a fit of rage launched an attack against the wall and then paced around the floor for several, minutes, after which she gradually quieted down and resumed her usual cheerful behavior. This effect was repeated on two different days. The fact that only the contact located in the amygdala induced rage suggested that the neuronal field around contact 3 was involved in the patient's behavior problem, and this finding was of great clinical significance in the orientation of subsequent treatment by local coagulation.

The demonstration that amygdaloid stimulation may induce violent behavior has also been provided by other investigators. King (128) has described the case of a woman with feelings of depression and alienation, with an extremely flat tone of voice and a facial expression which was blank and unchanging during interviews, who upon stimulation of the amygdala with 5 milliamperes had greatly altered vocal inflections and an angry expression. During this time she said, "I feel like I want to get up from this chair! Please don't let me do it! Don't do this to me, I don't want to be mean!" When the interviewer asked if she would like to hit him, the patient answered, "Yeah, I want to hit something. I want to act something and just tear it up. Take it so I won't! " She then handed her scarf to the interviewer who gave her a stack of paper, and without any other verbal exchange, she tore it into shreds saying, "I don't like to feel like this." When the level of stimulation was reduced to 4 milliamperes, her

MATRIX OF THE MIND

attitude changed to a broad smile, and she explained, "I know it's silly, what I'm doing. I wanted to get up from this chair and run. I wanted to hit something, tear up something-anything. Not you, just anything. I just wanted to get up and tear. I had no control of myself." An increase in intensity up to 5 milliamperes again resulted in similar aggressive manifestations, and she raised her arm as if to strike.

It is notable that although the patients seemed to be out of control in these two instances of electrically induced aggression, they did not attack the interviewer, indicating that they were aware of their social situation. This finding is reminiscent of the behavior of stimulated monkeys who directed their aggressiveness according to previous experience and social rank and did not dare to challenge the authority of well-established bosses, Apparently ESB can induce a state of increased violent reactivity which is expressed in accordance with individual structure and environmental circumstances. We may conclude therefore that artificially evoked emotional change is only one more factor in the constellation of behavioral determinants.

Pleasurable Excitation of the Animal Brain

It is surprising that in science as well as in literature more attention has been paid to suffering than to happiness. The central theme of most novels is tragedy, while happy books are hard to find; excellent monographs have been published about pain, but similar studies of pleasure are nonexistent. Typically, in the monumental Handbook of the American Physiological Society (75), a full chapter is devoted to pain, and pleasure is not even listed in the general subject index. Evidently the pursuit of happiness has not aroused as much -scientific interest as the fear of pain.

In Psychological literature the study of reward is well represented, but even there it has been considered a second-rate sensation and perhaps an artifact of a diminution of pain. It has been postulated that a truly "pleasant" sensation could not exist because organisms have a continuous tendency to minimize incoming stimuli. Pleasure was thus considered a subjective name for the diminution of drive, the withdrawal of a strong stimulation, or the reduction of pain. This "pain reduction" theory (154) has been fruitful as a basis for psychological investigations, but it is gloomy to think that we live in a 'world of punishment in which the only reality is suffering and that or brain can perceive different degrees of pain but no real pleasure. Interest in the earlier ideas of hedonism has been renewed by recent experimental studies. According to this theory, pain and pleasure are relatively independent sensations and can be evoked by different types of stimuli which are recognized by separate cerebral mechanisms. Behavior is considered to be motivated by stimuli which the organism, tries to minimize (pain) or by stimuli which the organism tries to maximize (pleasure). The brain is thought to have

165

different systems for the reception of these two kinds of inputs, and the psychological of pleasure or reward can be determined not only by tile state termination of pain but also by the onset of primary pleasure. The discovery of two anatomically distinct mechanisms in the brain, one for punishment, as mentioned earlier, and one for reward, provides a physiological basis for the dualistic motivation postulated in hedonism (62, 165).

The surprising fact is that animals of different species, including rats, cars, and monkeys, have voluntarily chosen to press a lever which provides electrical stimulation of specific cerebral areas. The demonstrations are highly convincing because animals which initially pressed a lever to obtain the reward of sugar pellets later pressed at similar or higher rates when electrical stimulation was substituted for food. These experiments showed conclusively that the animals enjoyed the electrical impulses which were delivered only at their own demand. Watching a rat or monkey stimulate its own brain is a fascinating spectacle. Usually each lever pressing triggers a brief 0.5-to-1.0 second brain stimulation which can be more rewarding than food. In a choice situation, hungry rats ran faster to reach tile self-stimulation lever than to obtain pellets, and they persistently pressed this lever, ignoring food within easy reach. Rats have removed obstacles, run mazes, and even crossed electrified floors to reach the lever that provided cerebral stimulation.

Not all areas of the brain involved in pleasurable effects appear equally responsive. The highest lever-pressing rates (of up to a remarkable 5,000 times per hour) were recorded by animals self-stimulating in the posterior hypothalamus; excitation of rhinencephalic structures (of only about 200 times per hour) was considered moderately rewarding; and in sensory or motor areas, animals self-stimulated at merely a chance level (of 10 to 25 times per hour), and these areas were classified as neutral. As should be expected, when stimulation was shifted from rewarding areas to nuclei in the punishment system in the same animals, they pressed the lever once and never went back, showing that in the brain of the same animal there were two different groups of structures, one rewarding and the other aversive.

A systematic analysis of the neuroanatomical distribution of pleasurable areas in the rat (164) shows that 6o per cent of the brain is neutral, 35 per cent is rewarding, and only 5 per cent may elicit punishing effects. The idea that far more brain is involved in pleasure than in suffering is rather optimistic and gives hope that this predominance of the potential for pleasurable sensations can be developed into a more effective behavioral reality.

Because of the lack of verbal communication with animals, any ideas about what kind of pleasure, if any, may be experienced during ESB is a matter of speculation. There are some indications, however, that the perceived sensations could be related to anatomical differentiation of primary rewards of food and sex, because hungry animals self-stimulated at a higher rate in the middle hypothalamus, while administration of sexual hormones to castrated rats increased their lever pressing of more lateral hypothalamic points.

The controversial issue of how these findings in animals may relate to human behavior and the possible existence of areas involved in pleasure in the human brain has been resolved by the information obtained in patients with implanted electrodes.

Human Pleasure Evoked by ESB

On the basis of many studies during cerebral surgery, Penfield (174) has said of anger, joy, pleasure, and sexual excitement in the human brain that "so far as our experience goes, neither localized epileptic discharge nor electrical stimulation is capable of awakening any such emotion. One is tempted to believe that there are no specific cortical mechanisms associated with these emotions." This statement still holds true for the cerebral cortex, but studies in human subjects with implanted electrodes have demonstrated that electrical stimulation of the depth of the brain can induce pleasurable manifestations, as evidenced by the spontaneous verbal reports of patients, their facial expression and general behavior, and their desire to repeat the experience. In a group of twenty-three patients suffering from schizophrenia (98), electrical stimulation of the septal region, located deep in the frontal lobes, produced an enhancement of alertness sometimes accompanied by an increase in verbal output, euphoria, or pleasure. In a more systematic study in another group of patients, further evidence was presented the rewarding effects of septal stimulation (20, 99). One man suffering from narcolepsia was provided with a small stimulator and a built-in counter which recorded the number of times that he voluntarily stimulated each of several selected points in his brain during a period of seventeen weeks. The highest score was recorded front one point in the septal region, and the patient declared that pushing this particular button made him feel "good" as if he were building up to a sexual orgasm, although he was not able to reach the end point and often felt impatient and anxious. His narcolepsia was greatly relieved by pressing this ' septal button." Another patient with psychomotor epilepsy also enjoyed septal self-stimulation, which again had the highest rate of buttton pressing and often induced sexual thoughts, Activation of the septal region by direct injection of acetylcholine produced local electrical changes in two epileptic patients and a shift in iiiood from disphoria to contentment and euphoria, usually with concomitant sexual motivation and some "orgastic sensations."

Further information was provided by another group of sixty-five patients

MATRIX OF THE MIND

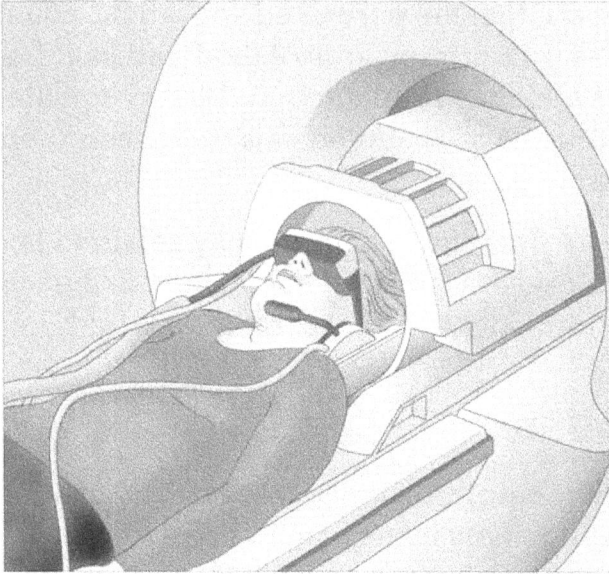

suffering from schizophrenia or Parkinson's disease, in whom a total of 643 contacts were implanted, mainly in the anterior part of the brain (201). Results of ESB were grouped as follows: 360 points were "Positive I," and with stimulation "the patients became relaxed, at ease, had a feeling of well-being, and/or were a little sleepy." Another 31 points were "Positive II," and "the patients were definitely changed . . . in a good mood, felt good. They were relaxed, at ease, and enjoyed themselves, frequently smiling. There was a slight euphoria, but the behavior was adequate." They sometimes wanted more stimulations. Excitation of another eight points evoked behavior classified as "Positive III," when "the euphoria was definitely beyond normal limits. The patients laughed out loud, enjoyed themselves, and positively liked the stimulation, and wanted more." ESB of another 38 points gave ambivalent results, and the patients expressed occasional pleasure or displeasure following excitation of the same area. From three other points, responses were termed "orgasm" because the patients initially expressed enjoyment and then suddenly were completely satisfied and did not want any more stimulation for a variable period of time. Finally, from about two hundred other points, ESB produced unpleasant reactions including anxiety, sadness, depression, fear, and emotional outbursts. One of the moving pictures taken in this study was very demonstrative, showing a patient with a sad expression and slightly depressed mood who smiled when a brief stimulation was applied to the rostral part of the brain, returning quickly to his usual depressed state, to smile again as soon as stimulation was reapplied. Then a ten-second stimulation completely changed his behavior and facial expression into a lasting pleasant and happy mood. Some mental patients have been provided with portable stimulators which they have used in self-treatment of depressive states with apparent clinical success.

These results indicate the need for careful functional exploration during brain surgery in order to avoid excessive euphoria or depression when positive or negative reinforcing areas are damaged. Emotional instability, in which the subject bursts suddenly into tears or laughter without any apparent reason, has been observed following some neurosurgical interventions. These major behavior problems might have been avoided by sparing the region involved in emotional regulation.

MATRIX OF THE MIND

In our own experience, pleasurable sensations were observed in three patients with psychomotor epilepsy (50, 58, 109). The first case was V.P., a 36-year-old female with a long history of epileptic attacks which could not be controlled by medication.

Electrodes were implanted in her right temporal lobe and upon stimulation of a contact located in the superior part about thirty millimeters below the surface, the patient reported a pleasant tingling sensation in the left. side of her body "from my face down to the bottom of my legs." She started giggling and making funny comments, stating that she enjoyed the sensation "very much." Repetition of these stimulations made the patient more communicative and flirtatious, and she ended by openly expressing her desire to marry the therapist. Stimulation of other cerebral points failed to modify her mood and indicated the specificity of the evoked effect. During control interviews before and after ESB, her behavior was quite proper, without familiarity or excessive friendliness.

The second patient was J.M., an attractive, cooperative, and intelligent 30-year-old female who had suffered for eleven years from psychomotor and grand mal attacks which resisted medical therapy. Electrodes were implanted in her right temporal lobe, and stimulation of one of the points in the amygdala induced a pleasant sensation of relaxation and considerably increased her verbal output, which took on a more intimate character. This patient openly expressed her fondness for the therapist (who was new to her), kissed his hands, and talked about her immense gratitude for what was being done for her. A similar increase in verbal and emotional expression was repeated when the same point was stimulated on a different day, but it did not appear when other areas of the brain were explored. During control situations the patient was rather reserved and poised.

The third case was A.F., an 1 1-year-old boy with severe psychomotor epilepsy. Six days after electrode implantation in both temporal lobes, his fourth tape-recorded interview was carried out while electrical activity of the brain was continuously recorded and 5-second stimulations were applied in a prearranged sequence at intervals of about four minutes. The interviewer maintained an air of friendly interest throughout, usually without initiating conversation. After six other excitations, point LP located on the surface of the left temporal lobe was stimulated for the first time, and there was an open and precipitous declaration of pleasure. The patient had been silent for the previous five-minute interval, but immediately after this stimulation lie exclaimed, "Hey! You can keep me here longer when you give me these; I like those." He went on to insist that the ongoing brain tests made him feel good. Similar statements with an emphatic expression of "feeling good" followed eight of a total sixteen stimulations of this point during the ninety-minute interview. Several of these manifestations were accompanied by a statement of fondness for the male interviewer, and the last one was accompanied

MATRIX OF THE MIND

by a voluptuous stretch. None of these manifestations appeared during the control prestimulation period of twenty-six minutes or during the twenty-two minutes when other points were excited. Statistical analysis of the difference between the frequency of pleasurable expressions before and after onset of stimulations proved that results were highly significant (P

The open expressions of pleasure in this interview and the general passivity of behavior could be linked, more or less intuitively, to feminine strivings. It was therefore remarkable that in the next interview, performed in a similar manner, the patient's expressions of confusion about his own sexual identity again appeared following stimulation of point LP. He suddenly began to discuss his desire to get married, but when asked, "To whom?" he did not immediately reply. Following stimulation of another point and a one-minute, twenty-second silence, the patient said, "I was thinking-there's-I was saying this to you. How to spell 'yes'-y-e-s. I mean y-o-s. No! 'You' ain't y-e-o. It's this. Y-o-u." The topic was then completely dropped. The monitor who was listening from the next room interpreted this as a thinly veiled wish to marry the interviewer, and it was decided to stimulate the same site again after the prearranged schedule had been completed, During the following forty minutes, seven other points were stimulated, and the patient spoke about several topics of a completely different and unrelated content. Then LP was stimulated again, and the patient started making references to the facial hair of the interviewer and continued by mentioning pubic hair and his having been the object of genital sex play in the past. He then expressed doubt about his sexual identity, saying, "I was thinkin' if I was a boy or a girl-which one I'd like to be." Following another excitation he remarked with evident pleasure: "You're doin' it now," and then he said, "I'd like to be a girl."

In the interpretation of these results it is necessary to consider the psychological context in which electrical stimulation occurs, because the personality configuration of the subject, including both current psychodynamic and psychogenetic aspects, may be an essential determinant of the results of stimulation. Expression of feminine strivings in our patient probably was not the exclusive effect of ESB but the expression of already present personality factors which were activated by the stimulation. The balance between drive and defense may be modified by ESB, as suggested by the fact that after one stimulation the patient said without apparent anxiety, "I'd like to be a girl," but when this idea was presented to him by the therapist in a later interview without stimulation, the patient became markedly anxious and defensive. Minute-to-minute changes in personality function, influenced by the environment and by patient-interviewer relations, may modify the nature of specific responses, and these variables, which are difficult to assess, must be kept in mind.

MATRIX OF THE MIND

Friendliness and Increased Conversation
Under Electrical Control

Human relations evolve between the two opposite poles of love and hate which are determined by a highly complex and little understood combination of elements including basic drives, cultural imprinting, and refined emotional and intellectual characteristics. This subject has so many semantic and conceptual problems that few investigators have dared to approach it experimentally, and in spite of its essential importance, most textbooks of psychology evade its discussion. To define friendliness is difficult although its identification in typical cases is easy, and in our daily life we are continuously evaluating and classifying personal contacts as friendly or hostile. A smiling face, attentive eyes, a receptive hand, related body posture, intellectual interest, ideological agreement, kind words, sympathetic comments, and expressions of personal acceptance are among the common indicators of cordial interpersonal relations. The expression of friendship is a part of social behavior which obviously requires contact between two or more individuals. A mutually pleasurable relation creates a history and provides each individual with a variety of optic, acoustic, tactile, and other stimuli which are received and interpreted with a "friendly bias." The main characteristic of love and friendship is precisely that stimuli coming from a favored person are interpreted as more agreeable than similar stimuli originating from other sources, and this evaluation is necessarily related to neuronal activity.

Little is known about the cerebral mechanisms of friendliness, but as is the case for any behavioral manifestation, no emotional state is possible without a functioning brain, and it may be postulated that some cerebral structures are dispensable and others indispensable both for the interpretation of sensory inputs as amicable and for the expression of friendship. Strong support for this idea derives from the fact, repeatedly proved in neurosurgery, that destruction of some parts of the brain, such as the motor and sensory cortices, produces motor deficits without modifying affective behavior, while ablation of the frontal lobes may induce considerable alteration of emotional personality. Further support has been provided by electrical stimulation of the frontal lobes, which may induce friendly manifestations.

In patient A. F., mentioned earlier in connection with pleasurable manifestations, the third inter-view was characterized by changes in the character and degree of verbal output following stimulation of one point in the temporal cortex. Fourteen stimulations were applied, seven of them through point RP located in the inferolateral part of the right frontal lobe cortex, and the other seven through contacts located on the cortex of the right temporal lobe and depth of the left and right temporal lobes. The interview started with about five minutes of lively conversation, and during the next ten minutes the patient gradually quieted down

171

until he spoke only about five seconds during every subsequent two-minute period. Throughout the interview the therapist encouraged spontaneous expression by reacting compassionately, by joking with, urging, and reassuring the patient, and by responding to any information offered. The attitude never produced more than a simple reply and often not even that.

In contrast to this basic situation, there were six instances of sharp increase in verbal communication and its friendly content. Each of these instances followed within forty seconds after stimulation of point RP. The only exception was the last excitation of this point when the voltage had been changed. The increases in verbal activity were rapid bat brief and without any consistency in subject material, which was typical for the patient. Qualification and quantification of the patient's conversation was made by analyzing the recorded typescript which was divided into two-minute periods and judged independently by two investigators who had no knowledge of the timing or location of stimulations. Comparison of the two-minute periods before and after these stimulations revealed a verbal increase from seventeen to eighty-eight words -and a greater number of friendly remarks, from six to fifty-three. These results were highly significant and their specificity was clear because no changes in verbalization were produced by stimulation of any of the other cerebral points. It was also evident that the evoked changes were not related to the interviewer's rather constant verbal activity. It was therefore concluded that the impressive increase in verbal expression and friendly remarks was the result of electrical stimulation of a specific point on the cortex of the temporal lobe.

Hallucinations, Recollections, and Illusions in Man

Hallucinations may be defined as false perceptions in the absence of peripheral sensory stimulation, and they probably depend on two processes: (1) the recollection of stored information and (2) its false interpretation as an extrinsic experience entering through sensory inputs. Very little is known about the cerebral mechanisms responsible for these phenomena, but apparently the frontotemporal region of the brain is somehow involved because its electrical stimulation may evoke hallucinations.

In some patients electrical stimulation of the exposed temporal lobe has produced the perception of music. Occasionally it was a determined tune which could be recognized and hummed by the subject, and in some cases it was as if a radio or record were being played in the operating room. The sound did not seem to be a recollection but resembled an actual experience in which instruments of an orchestra or words of a song were heard (174). These artificially induced hallucinations were not static but unfolded slowly while the electrode was held in place. A song was heard from beginning to end and not all at once; in a dream, familiar places were seen and well-known people spoke and acted.

Like spontaneous memories, the recollections induced by ESB could bring back the emotions felt at the time of the original experience, suggesting that neuronal mechanisms keep an integrated record of the past, including all the sensory inputs (visual, auditory, proprioceptive, etc.) and also the emotional significance of events. Electrical stimulation activated only one memory without reawakening any of the other records which must be stored in close proximity. This fact suggests the existence of cerebral mechanisms of reciprocal inhibition which allow the orderly recall of specific patterns of memory without a flood of unmanageable amounts of stored information. In no case has brain stimulation produced two psychical experiences at the same time, and the responses have been on an all-or-nothing basis.

In one of our patients, complex sensory hallucinations were evoked on different days when the depth of the tip of the left temporal lobe was electrically stimulated. The patient said, "You know, I just felt funny, just now. . . . Right then all of a sudden somethin' else came to me - these people -the way this person talked. This married couple-as though the fellow came into my mind-as though like he was saying somethin' like oh my mind drifted for a minute-to somethin' foolish... It seemed like he was coming out with some word - sayin' some word silly."

The fact that stimulation of the temporal lobe can induce complex hallucinations may be considered well established, and this type of research represents a significant interaction between neurophysiology and psychoanalysis (133). The mechanism of the evoked hallucinations, however, is far from clear, and it is difficult to know whether the experiences are new creations based on the recombination of items from memory storage and thus equivalent to psychotic hallucinations, or if the experiences are simply an exact playback of the past. In either case, the applied electricity is not "creating" a new phenomenon but is triggering the orderly appearance at the conscious level of materials from the past, mixed in some cases with present perceptions. The order in the stream of perceived information is perhaps one of the most interesting qualities of this behavior because it indicates something about the mechanisms for storage of information in the brain. Memory does not seem to be preserved as single items but as inter-related collections of events, like the pearls on a string, and by pulling any pearl we have access to the whole series in perfect order. If memory were organized in this way, it would be similar to the strings of amino acids forming molecules of proteins and carrying genetic messages. Electrical stimulation may increase general neuronal excitability; and the memory traces which at this moment have a lower threshold may consequently be reactivated, reaching the perceptual level and forming the content of the hallucinatory experience while exerting a reciprocal inhibit ory influence upon other traces. The excitability of individual traces

MATRIX OF THE MIND

may be modified by environmental factors and especially by the ideological content of the patient's thoughts prior to stimulation. Thus electrical excitation of the same point may produce a series of thematically related hallucinatory experiences with different specific details, as was the case in the patients that we have investigated.

All sensory inputs suffer distortion during the normal process of personal interpretation, which is determined to a great extent by past experience and depends heavily on cultural factors. A baby looking at the moon may extend his arms in an attempt to catch it without realizing the remoteness of celestial bodies. By comparing past and present experiences, we learn to evaluate distance, size, intensity, and other qualities of inputs. The mechanisms for these evaluations do not seem to be genetically determined and are related to neuronal activity which may be influenced by direct stimulation of the brain. We must remember that our only way to be in touch with external reality is by transducing physical and chemical events of the surroundings into electrical and chemical sequences at the sensory receptor level. The brain is not in touch with the environmental reality but with its symbolic code transmitted by neuronal pathways. Within this frame of personal distortion, our lives evolve within a range of "normality." Beyond this range, the distortion of perceptions qualifies as illusion. Illusions occur in a wide variety of regressed mental states, during moments of keen anticipation, and as a primary manifestation in some epileptic discharges. An hallucination is a false perception in the absence of sensory inputs, while an illusion requires an external sensory source which is misinterpreted by the individual. This distinction is convenient, and it will be observed in our discussion, although in practice the terms often overlap.

The following phenomena have been observed in patients: (1) illusions (visual, auditory, labyrinthine, memory or déjà vu, sensation of remoteness or unreality, (2:) emotions (loneliness, fear, sadness), (3) psychical hallucinations (vivid memory or a dream as complex as life experience itself, and (4) forced thinking (stereotyped thoughts crowding into the mind). The first three groups of phenomena have been induced by different intracerebral stimulations. The most commonly reported effect has been the illusion of familiarity or déjà vu, which is characterized by surprise, interruption of conversation, and immediate spontaneous reporting that something unusual had just happened. For example, after a stimulation in the inferolateral part of the frontal lobe, one patient began to reply to the interviewer's question but suddenly stopped and said, "I was thinkin' - it felt like someone else was asking me that before." Occasionally a previously initiated statement would be completed, but there was always an overt desire to express the perceived experience. The effect was clearly felt as intrusive although not disturbing. After several of these experiences, the patient recognized the special quality of the phenomena and said, for example, "Hey - I had another strike. I have a feeling that someone once told me that before." The reliability of the response was remarkable, as was the consistency of its reporting, which was spontaneous and in most cases unsolicited. Each instance consisted usually of a reference to a remark made by the patient or the observer just before or during the moment of stimulation. The ideational content of the déjà vu was therefore dissimilar following each stimulation, but it always referred to the theme of the ongoing conversation.

The common feature was the sensation, expressed by the patient, that the words, ideas, or situation were similar to a previous experience. There was no new perception, only the interpretation of a novel input as one already known and familiar. There was no anxiety or fear in the perception of these illusions, and the apparent effect was one of interested surprise with a rather pleasant, amusing quality which made the patient more alert and communicative. He was eager to report that something similar had happened before, and the word "before" was used in reporting most of these incidents. No lasting traces could be detected, and after the sensation of familiarity had been expressed, the patient's behavior continued in the same vein as before stimulation.

Knowledge of the cerebral mechanisms of psychic activities is so elemental that it would not be wise to speculate about the neuronal causality of illusions of familiarity. However, the fact that they may be elicited with reliability indicates the probable existence of interpretive functions in a determined area of the brain and opens the way for further experiments studies of how sensory inputs are processed by the individual. Penfield supposes that the cortex of the temporal lobe has a ganglionic mechanism which is utilized in the personal assessment of experiential reality regarding distance, sound, sight, intensity, strangeness, or familiarity of sensory inputs. This mechanism would be relatively independent from the mechanism utilized in the recording of contemporary experience and could be affected by epileptic abnormality or by direct brain stimulation. If we accept this hypothesis, we may assume that artificial influencing of electrical and chemical neuronal physiology could play a decisive role in the interpretation of reality with some independence from past experience and personal structure.

Inhibitory Effects in Animals and Man

The existence of inhibitory functions in the central nervous system was described in the last century by Sechenov (198), Pavlov (171), and other founders of Russian psychology. Inhibition is a well-known phenomenon, and it has been the main theme of several recent symposiums (14, 63, 77). In spite of its importance, information about inhibitory mechanisms has not yet been integrated into the general body of scientific knowledge, and no chapter is devoted to this subject in

MATRIX OF THE MIND

most neurophysiological, psychological, and pharmacological textbooks. This lack of interest is surprising because as Morgan (158) wrote eighty years ago, "When physiologists have solved the problem of inhibition they will be in a position to consider that of volition," and modern investigators maintain that inhibition and choice, rather than expression and learning, are the central problems of psychology (63). A shift in interest among scientists seems necessary to give inhibition its deserved importance, and the layman should also be aware of the decisive role of inhibition in the performance of most of our daily activities.

The sound of a theater crowd at intermission is a continuous roar without intelligible meaning. During the performance, however, noises and, individual conversations must be inhibited so that the voices of the actors can be heard. The brain is like a monumental theater with many millions of neurons capable of sending messages simultaneously and in many directions. Most of these neurons are firing nearly continuously, and their sensitivity is like that of an enormous synaptic powder barrel which would explode in epileptic convulsions in the absence of inhibitory elements (122). During the organized performance of behavioral responses, most neurons and pathways must remain silent to allow meaningful orders to circulate toward specific goals. Inhibition is as important as excitation for the normal physiology of the brain, and some structures have specialized inhibitory functions. It should therefore be expected that, in addition to inducing the many types of activities described in previous sections, ESB can also block performance of such activities by exciting pools of neurons whose role is to inhibit these specific responses.

To behave is to choose one pattern among many. To think we must proceed in some orderly fashion repressing unrelated ideas; to talk we must select a sequence of appropriate words; and to listen we need to extract certain information from background noise. As stated by Ashby, we must "dispose once and for all of the idea...that the more communication there is within the brain the better" (6). As we know by personal experience, one of the problems of modern civilization is the confusion produced by a barrage of sensory inputs. We aye optically and acoustically assaulted by scientific literature, news media, propaganda, and advertisements. The defense is to inhibit the processing of sensory stimuli. Conscious and unconscious behavioral inhibition should not be considered passive

MATRIX OF THE MIND

processes but active restraints, like holding the reins of a powerful horse, which prevent the disorderly display of existing energies and potentialities.

Within the central nervous system, the reticular formation seems to be especially differentiated to modulate or inhibit the reception of sensory impulses, and some other cerebral structures including the thalamus, septum, and caudate nucleus also possess important inhibitory properties which can be activated by ESB. Three types of inhibitory processes may be induced by electrical stimulation: (1) sleep, which usually starts slowly and can easily be interrupted by sensory stimuli; (2) general inhibition, which affects the whole body, starts as soon as ESB is applied, and persists in spite of sensory stimulation; and (3) specific inhibition, which appears immediately, affects only a determined pattern of behavior such as aggression or food intake, and may or may not be modified by sensory impulses.

One example of sleep induced in a monkey by application of ESB is shown in Figure 18. After 30 seconds of stimulation in the septal area, the animal's eyes started closing, his head lowered, his body relaxed, and he seemed to fall into a natural state of sleep. In response to noise or to being touched, the animal would slowly open his eyes and look around with a dull expression for a few seconds before falling asleep again. Similar results have been obtained in free-ranging monkeys stimulated by radio. In this situation there was a gradual diminution of spontaneous activity, and then the animals began to doze, closing their eyes and assuming a typical sleeping posture with heads down and bodies curved over the knees. Theoretically it should be possible to treat chronic insomnia by brain stimulation, or to establish an artificial biological clock of rest and activity by means of programed stimulation of inhibitory and excitatory areas of the brain, but these challenging possibilities still require further investigations.

Motor arrest is an impressive effect consisting of sudden immobilization of the experimental animal in the middle of ongoing activities, which continue as soon as stimulation is over. It is as if a motion picture projector had been stopped, freezing the subjects in the position in which they were caught. A cat lapping milk has been immobilized with its tongue out, and a cat climbing stairs has been stopped between two steps.

Other types of inhibitory effects are more specific and restricted to only one determined behavioral category. Typical examples are the inhibition of food intake, aggressiveness, territoriality, and maternal behavior. As these specific inhibitions influence general activities, they could pass unnoticed do not if the experimental situation was not properly arranged. Obviously inhibition of appetite cannot be demonstrated in the absence of food, nor can changes in maternal behavior be investigated when no babies are present. One example of how a hungry monkey loses appetite under the influence of brain excitation is presented in Figure 19. At the sight of a banana, the animal usually shows great interest, leaning forward to take the fruit, which he eats voraciously and with evident pleasure. However, his appetite is immediately inhibited as soon as the caudate nucleus is electrically stimulated. Then the monkey looks with some interest at the banana without Teaching for it, and may even turn his face away, clearly expressing refusal. During stimulation the animal is well aware of his surroundings, Reacting normally to noises, moving objects, and threats, but he is just not interested in food. If a monkey is stimulated when his mouth is full of banana, he immediately stops chewing, takes the banana out of his mouth, and throws it away.

Close to the hunger inhibitory area there is a region which is involved in inhibition of aggressive behavior. When this part of the caudate nucleus is stimulated (Figure 2o), the normally ferocious macacus rhesus becomes tranquil, and instead of grabbing, scratching, and biting any approaching object, he sits peacefully and the investigator can safely touch his mouth and pet him. During this time the animal is aware of the environment but has simply lost his usual irritability, showing that violence can be inhibited without making the animal sleepy or depressed. Identification of the cerebral areas responsible for ferocity would make it possible to block their function and diminish undesirable aggressiveness without disturbing general behavioral reactivity.

Similar results have been obtained in chimpanzees, and one example is presented in Figure 19. Chimpanzee Carlos was an affectionate animal who enjoyed playing with the investigators and had learned a variety of tricks including throwing and catching a ball. Enticed by an expected food reward, he sat voluntarily in the restraining chair where recordings and experiments were conducted. Like most chimpanzees, Carlos was rather temperamental and was easily provoked into a tantrum by being punished, frustrated, or merely teased. He liked to be touched by people he knew but not by strangers. Figure 21 (left) shows his defensive, anxious reaction when approached by an unfamiliar investigator. His fear and aggressive manifestations were, however, completely inhibited during electrical stimulation of the caudate nucleus, as shown in Figure 21 (right). The animal displayed no emotion, appeared peaceful, and could be teased without any resulting disturbance.

Other experiments in monkeys have also confirmed the pacifying possibilities of ESB. In the autocratic social structure of a monkey colony the boss enjoys a variety of privileges such as choosing female partners, feeding first, displacing other animals, and occupying most of the cage while the other monkeys avoid his proximity and crowd together in a far comer (s ee Figure 22). This hierarchical position is maintained by subtle communication of gestures and postures: a boss may look directly at a submissive member of the group who will glance only furtively at his superior, and the boss may paw the floor and threaten by opening his mouth or uttering a warning cry if any low-ranking animal does not keep a suitable distance. This social dominance has been abolished by stimulation applied for 5 seconds once a minute for one hour to the caudate nucleus in the boss monkey. During this period the animal's facial expression appeared more peaceful both to the investigator and to the other animals, who started to circulate freely around the cage without observing their usual respect. They actually ignored the boss, crowding around him without fear. During the stimulation hour, the boss's territoriality completely disappeared, his walking time diminished, and he performed no threatening or aggressive acts against other monkeys in the colony. It was evident that this change in behavior had been determined by brain stimulation because about ten minutes after ESB was discontinued, the boss had reasserted his authority and the other animals feared him as before. His territoriality was as well established as during control periods, and he enjoyed his customary privileges.

Figure 22 (NOT SHOWN)

Monkey colonies from autocratic societies in which the territorially of the boss is clearly shown. He occupies more than half of the cage (above). Radio stimulation of an inhibitory area of the brain (below) modifies the boss's facial expressions, and the other monkeys crowd fearlessly around the former boss in his own corner.

The old dream of an individual overpowering the strength of a dictator by remote control has been fulfilled, at least in our monkey colonies, by a combination of neurosurgery and electronics, demonstrating the possibility of intraspecies instrumental manipulation of hierarchical organization. As shown in Figure 23, a monkey named Ali, who was the powerful and ill-tempered chief of a colony, often expressed his hostility symbolically by biting his hand or by threatening other members of the group. Radio stimulation in Ali's caudate nucleus blocked his usual aggressiveness so effectively that the animal could be caught inside the cage without danger or difficulty. During stimulation he might walk a few steps, but he never attempted to attack another animal. Then a lever was attached to the cage wall, and if it was pressed, it automatically triggered a five seconds' radio stimulation of Ali. Front time to time some of the submissive monkeys touched the lever, which was located close to the feeding tray, triggering the stimulation of Ali. A female monkey named Elsa soon discovered that Ali's aggressiveness could be inhibited by pressing the lever, and when Ali threatened her, it was repeatedly observed that Elsa responded by lever pressing. Her attitude of looking straight at the boss was highly significant because a submissive monkey would not dare to do so, for fear of immediate retaliation. The total number of Ali's aggressive acts diminished on the days when the lever was available, and although

MATRIX OF THE MIND

Elsa did not become the dominant animal, she was responsible for blocking many attacks against herself and for maintaining a peaceful coexistence within the whole colony.

Appeasement of instinctive aggressiveness has also been demonstrated in an animal species which for generations has been bred to increase its ferocious behavior: the brave bull. Some races of bulls have been genetically selected for their aggressive behavior just as others have been bred for farm work or meat supply. Brave bulls are stronger and more agile than their tamer relatives, and these differences in appearance and behavior must be supported at the neurophysiological level by different mechanisms of responses. The sight of a person, which is neutral for a tame bull, will trigger a deadly attack in a brave one. If we could detect functional differences in the brains of these two breeds we could discover some clues about the neurological basis of aggression. This was the reason for implanting electrodes in the brains of several bulls. After surgery, different cerebral points were explored by radio stimulation while the animal was free in a small farm ring. Motor effects similar to those observed in cats and monkeys were evoked, including head turning, lifting of one leg, and circling. Vocalizations were often elicited, and in one experiment to test the reliability of results, a point was stimulated too times and too consecutive "moo's" were evoked.

It was also repeatedly demonstrated that cerebral stimulation produced inhibition of aggressive behavior, and a bull in full charge could be abruptly stopped, as shown in Figure 24. The result seemed to be a combination of motor effect, forcing the bull to stop and to turn to one side, plus behavioral inhibition of the aggressive drive. Upon repeated stimulation, these animals were rendered less dangerous than usual, and for a period of several minutes would tolerate the presence of investigators in the ring without launching any attack.

Maternal behavior is one of the instincts most widely shared by mammals, and a baby rhesus monkey enjoys the first months of his life resting in the arms of the mother, who spends most of her time hugging, nursing, grooming, and taking care of him. If the pair are forcibly separated, the mother becomes very disturbed and expresses her anxiety by prowling about restlessly, threatening observers, and calling to her baby with a special cooing sound. It is promptly reciprocated by the little one, who is also extremely anxious to return to the protective maternal embrace. This strong bond can be inhibited by ESB, as demonstrated in one of our colonies, consisting of Rose and Olga with their respective babies, Roo and Ole, plus a male monkey. Maternal affection was expressed as usual without being handicapped by the presence of electrodes implanted in both females (Figure 25). Several simple motor effects evoked by ESB (such as head turning or flexion of the arm) did not disrupt mother-infant relations, but when a 10-second radio stimulation was applied to the mesencephalon of Rose, an aggressive attitude was evoked with rapid circling around the cage and self-biting of the hand, leg, or flank. For the next eight to ten minutes, maternal instinct was disrupted, and Rose completely lost interest in her baby, ignoring his tender calls and rejecting his attempts to approach her. Little Roo looked rather disoriented and sought refuge and warmth with the other mother, Olga, who accepted both babies without hesitation. About ten minutes after ESB, Rose regained her natural maternal behavior and accepted Roo in her arms. This experiment was repeated several times on different days with similar disruptive results for the mother-infant relation. It should be concluded, therefore, that maternal behavior is somehow dependent on the proper functioning of rnesencephalic structures and that short ESB applied in this area is able to block the maternal instinct for a period of several minutes.

Information about inhibitory effects induced by electrical stimulation of the human brain is more limited than our knowledge about inhibition in animals. The subject has great importance, however, because one of the primary aims of human therapy is to inhibit undesirable sensations or excessive neuronal activities. Some patients experience a type of "intractable pain" which cannot be alleviated by the usual analgesic drugs, and their unbearable suffering could be blocked by direct intervention in brain structures where sensations reach the perceptual level of consciousness. Illnesses such as Parkinson's disease and chorea are characterized by continuous involuntary movements maintained by neuronal discharges originating in specific cerebral structures which could be inhibited by suitable therapy. Assaultive behavior constitutes one of the most disturbing symptoms of a group of mental illnesses and is probably related to the abnormal reactivity of limbic and reticular areas of the brain. Epilepsy is caused by explosive bursts of electrical discharges which might be inhibited at their original source. Anxiety poses very difficult therapeutic problems, and its basic mechanism might be traced to the increased reactivity of specific areas of the brain. All these disturbances could be cured, or at least diminished, if we had a better knowledge of their anatomical and functional bases and could inhibit the activity of neurons responsible for the phenomena.

In the near future, important advances may be expected in this field, and already we have some initial clinical information demonstrating that ESB can induce inhibitory effects in man. For example, ESB applied to the supplementary motor cortex has slowed down or completely arrested voluntary motor activity without producing pain or any concomitant loss of consciousness (174). In other cases, stimulation of the frontotemporal region has caused an "arrest response characterized by sudden cessation of voluntary movements which may be followed by confusion, inappropriate or garbled speech, and overt changes of mood (128, 186). More interesting from the therapeutic point of view is the fact that ab-

MATRIX OF THE MIND

normal hyperkinetic movements have been inhibited for the duration of the applied ESB, allowing patients to perform skilled acts which were otherwise impossible. In these cases, a small portable instrument could perhaps be used by the patient to stimulate his own brain in order to inhibit abnormal motility temporarily and restore useful skills (160).

Somnolence with inexpressive faces, tendency to lower the eyelids, and spontaneous complaint of sleepiness, but without impairment of consciousness, has been produced in some patients by stimulation of the fornix and thalamus (7, 199). In some cases, sleep with pleasant dreams has been induced, and occasionally sleep or awakening could be obtained from the same cerebral point by using a slow or high frequency of stimulation (96, 229). Diminished awareness, lack of normal insight, and impairment of ability to think have been observed by several investigators during excitation of different points of the limbic system (74, 120). Often the patients performed automatisms such . as undressing or fumbling, without remembering the incidents afterward. Some of our patients said they felt as if their minds were blank or as if they had been drinking a lot of beer. These results indicate that Consciousness may be related to specific mechanisms located in determined areas of the brain. They contrast with the full awareness preserved when other areas of the brain were stimulated.

Arrest of speech has been most common of all inhibitory effects observed during electrical stimulation of the human brain (8), and this fact is probably due to the extensive representation of the speech areas in the temporal lobe, and also to the facility of exploring verbal expression just by conversing with the patients. The most typical effect is cessation of counting. For example, one of our female patients was asked to count numbers, starting from one. When she had counted to fourteen, ESB was applied, and speech was immediately interrupted, without changes in respiration or in facial expression, and without producing fear or anxiety. When stimulation ceased seconds later, the patient immediately resumed counting. She said that she did not know why she had stopped; although she had heard the interviewer encouraging her to continue, she had been unable to speak, If the same stimulation was applied while the patient was silent, no effect could be detected by the observer or by the patient herself. In other cases, patients have been able to read and comprehend or to write messages that they were temporarily unable to verbalize (200).

It is known that ESB activation of pleasurable areas of the brain can inhibit pain perception in animals (42, 146), and similar results have also been reported in man, with an immediate relief of pain following septal stimulation (98). Because of the multiplicity of pathways in the nervous system which can transmit disagreeable sensations, it is often not possible to block all of them, and to alleviate unbearable suffering it may be easier to inhibit the cerebral structures involved in the psychological evaluation of pain, blocking the components of anxiety and diminishing the subjective sensation of unpleasantness.

There are also a few reports indicating that abnormal violence may be reduced by ESB: Heath has a movie showing a patient who self-stimulated his own brain in order to suppress an aggressive mood as it developed, and we have described a case in whom crises of antisocial conduct during which the patient attacked members of his own family were considerably diminished by repeated stimulations of the amygdaloid nucleus (60).

We are only at the beginning of our experimental understanding of the inhibitory mechanisms of behavior in animals and man, but their existence has already been well substantiated. It is clear that manifestations as important as aggressive responses depend not only on environmental circumstances but also on their interpretation by the central nervous system where they can be enhanced or totally inhibited by manipulating the reactivity of specific intracerebral structures.

Violence, including its extreme manifestation of war, is determined by a variety of economic and ideological factors; but we must realize that the elite who make the decisions, and even the individual who obeys orders and holds a rifle, require for their behavioral performance the existence of a series of intracerebral electrical signals which could be inhibited by other conflicting signals generating in areas such as the caudate nucleus. Inhibitory areas of the central nervous system can be activated by electrical stimulation as well as by the physiological impact of sensory inputs which carry messages, ideas, and patterned behavior. Reception of information from the environment causes electrical and chemical changes in the brain substance, and the stimuli shape the functional characteristics of individual interpretation and integration, determining the degree and quality of his reactions. Human relations are not going to be governed by electrodes, but they could be better understood if we considered not only environmental factors but also the intracerebral mechanisms responsible for their reception and elaboration.

Evaluation of Electrical Control of the Brain

Because the brain controls the whole body and all mental activities, ESB could possibly become a master control of human behavior by means of man-made plans and instruments. In previous sections we have described methodology for brain stimulation and many effects evoked by ESB. This section will discuss the meaning of these results, the mechanisms involved, the expected limitations, and the problems facing investigators. How physiological or artificial is the electrical activation of neurons? How predictable? Who is responsible for acts performed under ESB-the stimulated subject or the scientist? Which benefits or

MATRIX OF THE MIND

risks may be expected in the future? Can we modulate perception and expression by electrical means? Can we expect that brain investigation will provide a new conception of the human mind? These and other questions confront the investigator while he is sending radio messages to induce a muscle to contract, a heart to beat faster, or a sensation to be felt. Evaluation of these experiments requires the formulation of appropriate theoretical concepts and the design of working hypotheses.

Brain Stimulation Triggers Physiological Mechanisms

Electrical stimulation of the brain is in reality a rather crude technique based on the delivery of a monotonous train of pulses without modulation, without code, without specific meaning and without feedback to the pool of neurons which by chance is located within the artificial electrical field created by stimulation. Temporal and spatial characteristics and the complexity of multisynaptic relays, delays, and convergent and divergent correlations are also absent. The intensity of several volts usually employed in ESB is hundreds of times higher than spontaneous neuronal potentials, which are measured in millivolts.

It is reasonable, therefore, that doubts have been expressed about the normality of responses obtained by brain stimulation. It is difficult to compare normal behavior with electrically evoked effects, considering the complications of operative trauma, artificiality of experimental conditions, and lack of specificity of ESB (4). "Electrical stimulus, unlike physiological excitation, unselectively affects all elements of a similar threshold that lie within the radius of action of the electrodes" (107), and in the majority of cases cortical stimulation "has failed to elicit anything but fragments of skilled Movements" (224). Cobb (33) considers the greatest oversimplification the belief "among those not educated in physiology, that the electrical stimulation of a nerve or brain center closely resembles normal neuronal stimulation. Electrical stimulation, however, produces little that resembles the normal."

It is certainly true that many responses evoked by ESB are simple contractions of a small group of muscles without coordination, skill, or apparent purpose, and that many effects have abnormal characteristics far removed from the harmonious elegance of voluntary activities. It is also true, however, that with the development of technology to stimulate the brain in free subjects, many of the responses obtained in both animals and man are indistinguishable from spontaneous behavior. Sequential behavior, sexual activity, alimentary responses, walking, yawning, fighting, and many other effects documented in previous sections demonstrate conclusively that ESB can evoke purposeful, well-coordinated, skillful activities of great refinement and complexity. Patients have accepted evoked psychological changes, such as an increase in friendliness, as natural manifestations

MATRIX OF THE MIND

of their own personality and not as artificial results of the tests. The question to answer is not whether but how the application of a crude train of messageless electricity may result in the performance of a highly refined and complicated response.

To explain this apparent contradiction we Must consider the normal mechanisms of physiological performance. In a simple act such as the flexion of a limb, the nerve impulse initiates a very complex process which includes well-organized, sequential, metabolic activities and structural changes in the myoproteins resulting in the shortening of muscle fibers. These processes do not depend on neural impulses and have been established by genetic determination as intrinsic properties of muscular tissue unfolding in a similar way under nervous command or direct electrical excitation. Electricity does not create muscle contraction; it simply activates a pre-established pattern of response. At the neurological level, flexion of a limb requires the propagation of many well-organized impulses from the brain to the different groups of muscles, the processing of proprioceptive information from many regions, the adjustments of servomechanisms, visceral adaptations, and many other electrical, thermal, chemical, mechanical, and physiological -established phenomena and correlations. The applied electricity is only the depolarizing trigger of a group of neurons; it starts processes which once activated are relatively independent of the initial cause. Evoked behavior is like a chain reaction in which the final result depends more on the structure and organization of the components than on the trigger. To understand the role of electrical stimulation, we may ask whether the finger of the person pushing a button to launch a man into orbit is responsible for the performance of the complicated machinery or for the sequence of events. Obviously the finger, like a simple electrical stimulus, is only the trigger of a programmed series of interdependent events and cannot be accepted as the real cause of capsules orbiting around the earth.

A tentative explanation of some of the mechanisms involved in motor activities has been proposed in the theory of fragmental representation of behavior (53) which postulates that behavior is organized as fragments which have anatomical and functional reality within the brain, where they can be the subject of experimental analysis. The different fragments may be combined in different sequences like the notes of a melody, resulting in a succession of motor acts which constitute specific behavioral categories such as licking, climbing, or walking. The theory may perhaps be clarified with one example. If I wish to take a cookie from the table, this wish may be considered a force called "the starter" because it will determine the initiation of a series of motor acts. The starter includes drives, motivations, emotional perceptions, memories, and other processes. To take the cookie it is necessary to organize a motor plan, a mechanical strategy, and to decide among several motor choices, because the cookie may be taken with the left or right hand, directly with the mouth, or even by using the feet if one has simian skills. Choice, strategies, motor planning, and adjustments depend on a set of cerebral structures, "the organizer," which is different from the set employed by the starter, because the desire for cookies may exist in hungry people or in completely paralyzed patients, and the hands can move and reach the table for many different reasons even if there are no cookies. Finally, the actual contraction of muscles for the performance of the selected movement to reach the cookie-for example, rising the right hand-depends on a cerebral set, "the performer," different from the previous two, because motor representation of hands, mouth, and feet is situated in different areas of the brain, and the choice of muscle group to be activated is under the supervision of a given organizer. Naturally, there is a close correlation among these three basic mechanisms, and also between them and other cerebral functions. The concept of a brain center as a visible anatomical locus is unacceptable in modern physiology, but the participation of a constellation of neuronal groups (a functional set) in a specific act is more in agreement with our present knowledge. The functional set may be formed by the neurons of nuclei far from one another, for instance, in the cerebellum, motor cortex, pallidum, thalamus, and red nucleus, forming a circuit in close mutual dependence, and responsible for a determined act such as picking up a cookie with the right hand.

If we accept the existence of anatomical representation of the three functional sets - starter, organizer, and performer is logical that they can be activated by different types of triggers, and that the evoked results will be related to the previous experiences linked to the set. The same set, evoking a similar behavioral response, may be activated by physiological stimuli, such as sensory perceptions and ideations, or by artificial stimuli, such as electrical impulses. When we stimulate the brain through implanted electrodes we can, depending on the location of contacts, activate the starter, the organizer, or-the performer of different behavioral reactions, so that natural and artificial stimuli may interplay with one another, as has been experimentally demonstrated.

Electrical Activation of the "Will"

The theoretical considerations of the previous section may facilitate the understanding of so-called willful, free, or spontaneous behavior which to a great extent depends on pre-established mechanisms, some of them inborn and others

MATRIX OF THE MIND

acquired through learning. When a child takes his first steps or when an adult learns a new skill like tennis or typing, the initial movements are clumsy and require considerable attention and effort in every detail. Coordination progressively improves, unnecessary muscular tension diminishes, and the movements proceed with speed, economy, and elegance without being thought about. Acquisition of a skill means the automation of patterns of response with the establishment of spatial and temporal sequences. The voluntary aspects of willful activity are the purpose for it and the initiation of performance, while most of the details of complex movements and adaptation to changing circumstances are performed automatically. We may consider that the role of the will is mainly to trigger previously established mechanisms. Obviously the will is not responsible for the chemistry of muscular contraction, the electrical processes of neural transmission, or the intimate organization of responses. These phenomena depend on spindle discharges, cerebellar activation, synaptic junctions, reciprocal inhibitions, and many other mechanisms which are not only beyond consciousness but may be beyond our present knowledge and comprehension. The uniqueness of voluntary behavior lies in its initial dependence on the integration of a vast number of personal past experiences and present receptions.

Volition itself must be related to neuronal activities, and it may be asked whether either appropriate sensory perceptions or artificial electrical stimulation could induce neuronal pools involved in decision-making to discharge in a like manner. I shall not enter into the controversial issues of causality and determination of free behavior, but on the basis of experimental findings it is reasonable to assume that voluntary and electrical triggering can activate existing cerebral mechanisms in a similar way. If spontaneous and electrically evoked behavior involve participation of the same set of cerebral areas, then both types of behavior should be able to interact by modifying each others' inhibitory and excitatory influences. This possibility has been proved experimentally.

As described by Hess (107) and as observed also in our experiments, excitation of some points in the subthalamus of the cat induces a clockwise rotation of the head, and the effect of low intensity and low frequency (8 cycles per second) stimulation can be counteracted by the animal. The head starts rotating slowly and then is brought back to normal position by a quick voluntary jerk, the process repeating several times until stimulation ceases. If the intensity of stimulation is increased, the corrective movements disappear and rotation of the head progresses slowly but continuously, followed by rotation of the body on its longitudinal axis until the cat lies on its back. Then with a sudden jerk the animal abruptly completes the turn and springs to its feet. The explanation of these results may be as follows: During the initial part of the evoked head rotation, its abnormal position should produce normal proprioceptive and vestibular stimuli, starting a reflex reaction to slow down and counteract the electrically evoked effect. As soon as the cat is on its back, however, artificial and natural stimuli work together, the first to continue the turning, and the second to bring the animal to its usual horizontal position; the summation of these two actions would explain the sudden jerk. Interaction between evoked and spontaneous activity has also been observed during conditioning experiments with cats in which the animals often tried to suppress motor movements induced by ESB (89).

A clear example of algebraic summation between voluntary and evoked motility was observed in one of our cats with electrodes implanted in the left hidden motor cortex (48), Electrical stimulation induced an extension and raising of the right forepaw with proper postural adaptation. Offering of fish to the animal resulted in a similar extension and raising of the limb in order to seize the food. Simultaneous presentation of the fish and stimulation of the cortex produced a motor response of greater amplitude than usual; the cat miscalculated the necessary movement and overshot his target. He was unable to catch the food until he made a series of corrective adjustments, and then the fish was successfully captured and eaten. In addition to demonstrating the interrelation between evoked and spontaneous responses, this experiment also proved that the animal was aware of an artificial disturbance, and after a brief period of trial and error was able to correct its performance accordingly.

In the play of forces between spontaneous and evoked responses, which one is more powerful? Will one of them be prepotent over the other? Experimental results demonstrate that when there is a conflict in the response, the stronger stimulus dominates. For example, stimulation of the left sulcus presylvius with 0.6 milliamperes in a cat named Nero caused a small flexion of the right foreleg. When Nero was jumping from a table to the floor, the same excitation did not produce any visible effect, and the animal landed with perfect coordination, showing good voluntary control of all his limbs. Electrical flexion of the foreleg had therefore been completely inhibited by tire peremptory need to use the musculature in the jump, If stimulation intensity was increased up to 1.8 milliamperes, flexion of the limb appeared even when Nero was air-borne in the middle of a jump, and landing was disrupted by the inability to use the right foreleg. In general, electrical stimulation of the brain was dominant over voluntary behavior, provided that its intensity was sufficiently increased.

It is known that reflexes are predictable responses, rigidly patterned and blindly performed. Similarly, electrical excitation of a peripheral motor nerve induces a stereotyped movement with little adaptation to external circumstances. In contrast, willful activity generally has a purpose, and its performance is adapted for the attainment of a determined aim, with a continuous processing of proprioceptive and exteroceptive sensory information, with the use of feedback mechanisms, with capacity for instantaneous readjustment of the central command to adapt to changes in the environment, and with prediction of the future which requires spatiotemporal calculation of speed, direction, and strategies of moving targets. Depending on the location of cerebral stimulation, the responses obtained by ESB may either be similar to a blind reflex or have all the above-mentioned characteristics of voluntary activity.

Stimulation of some points in the motor cortex and motor pathways in the cat, monkey, and other animals may produce simple movements, such as the flexion of a limb, which are completely stereotyped and lack adaptation. These effects may be interpreted as the activation of efferent structures where the pattern of response has already been decided. At this level, the neural functions are of conduction rather than of integration and organization, and only minor variations are possible in the circulating impulses, regardless of whether their origin was spontaneous or artificial. To the contrary, there is plenty of evidence that many of the effects evoked by ESB are oriented toward the accomplishment of a specific aim with adaptation of the motor performance to unexpected changes in environmental circumstances. The following examples substantiate this statement.

In the cat, electrical stimulation of the inferior part of the sulcus presylvius consistently induced licking movements with well-organized opening and closing of the mouth and phasic protrusion of the tongue. Under anesthesia, the licking was automatic and purposeless; but in the awake, free-moving animal the response was directed toward some useful purpose, and the cat searched for a target to lick-food, the hands of the experimenter, the floor, or its own fur. In this case, motor performance and posture of the whole body adapted to the experimental setting, and in order to lick the investigator's hand, for example, the cat advanced a few steps and approached the hand even if it moved slowly away. Another example of adaptation to the environment is the "avoidance of obstacles" (48). Stimulation of the middle part of the presylvian sulcus in the cat induced a contralateral turning of the head in the horizontal plane. The effect was reliable, but when the movement was interrupted by placing an obstacle such as a book in its path, the animal modified its performance and raised its head to avoid the interposed obstacle before continuing the evoked head turning.

The adaptability of artificially induced cerebral responses to changes in the environment has been clearly demonstrated by rhesus monkeys' aggressive behavior which was selectively directed by the animals against their natural enemies within the group with a motor pattern of chasing and fighting which continuously changed according to the unpredictable strategies of those under attack. In this case, ESB evidently did not evoke a predetermined motor effect but an emotional state of increased aggressiveness which was served by pre-established motor skills and directed according to the previous history of social relations (53).

Similar experiments have been performed in roosters (111). If the bird was alone, motor restlessness was the only observable effect of ESB, while the same stimulation of a rooster in a group produced a state of increased aggressiveness and attacks on other birds. Sharp fighting ensued with perfectly coordinated, typical patterns of attack and defense in the group.

We may conclude that ESB can activate and influence some of the cerebral mechanisms involved in willful behavior. In this way we are able to investigate the neuronal functions rerated to the so-called will, and in the near future this experimental approach should permit clarification of such highly controversial subjects as "freedom," "individuality," and "spontaneity" in factual terms rather than in elusive semantic discussions. The possibility of influencing willful activities by electrical means has obvious ethical implications, which will be discussed later.

Characteristics and Limitations of Brain Control

The possibility of man's controlling the thoughts of other men has ranked as high in human fantasy as the control over transmutation of metals, the possession of wings, or the power to take a trip to the moon. Our generation has witnessed the accomplishment of so many nearly impossible tasks that today we are ready to accept almost anything. In the world of science, however, speculation and fantasy cannot replace truth.

There is already abundant evidence that ESB can control a wide range of functions, including motor activities and mental manifestations, in animals and in man. We know that by electrical stimulation of specific cerebral structures we can make a person friendlier or influence his train of thought. In spite of its spectacular potential, ESB has practical and theoretical limitations which should be delineated.

Predictability

When we get into a car and press the starter, the motor will almost certainly begin to run in a few seconds. The brain, however, does not have the simplicity of a machine. When electrodes are introduced into a cerebral structure and stimulation is applied for the first time, we really cannot predict the quality, localization, or intensity of the evoked effects. We do not even know that a response will appear. This is especially true for complex structures, like the amygdaloid region, which have great functional multiplicity; but it is also the case in relatively simple areas like the motor cortex. The anatomical and functional variability of the brain are factors which hinder prediction of ESB results (53). The importance of these limiting factors is compounded by alterations in regional activity related to changes in local, general, and environmental circumstances. We know that certain functions are represented in specific cerebral structures, but the precise location of a desired target requires careful exploration, and implantation of only a few contacts may be rather disappointing. After repeated explorations of a selected area in several subjects, predictability of the observed responses in that area for that species can be assessed with a higher degree of confidence. Present information about functional mapping in most cerebral areas is still rather incomplete.

Functional Monotony

Electrical stimulation is a nonspecific stimulus which always activates a group of neurons in a similar way because there is no coded neural message or feedback carried to the stimulating source. The responses, therefore, are repeated in a monotonous way, and any variability is related to changes in the stimulated subject. This functional monotony rules out the possibility that an investigator could direct a subject toward a target or induce him, like a robot, to perform any complex task under remote-controlled orders.

Science fiction has already imagined men with intracerebral electrodes engaged in all kinds of mischief under the perverse guidance of radio waves sent by some evil scientist. The inherent limitations of ESB make realization of this fantasy very remote. The flexion of a limb can be radio controlled and an emotional state could also be set remotely, but the sequences of responses and adaptation to the environment depend on established intracerebral mechanisms whose complexity cannot be duplicated by ESB. Even if we could stimulate different points of the brain through twenty or thirty channels, it would be necessary to have sensory feedback and computerized calculations for the programing of simple spatiotemporal sequences. Induced performance of more complex acts would be far beyond available methodology. It should be clarified that I am talking about directing each phase of a response, and riot about complex behavior such as lever pressing or fighting, which may be triggered by ESB but develops according to individual experiential circumstances which are beyond electrical control.

Skillful Performance

Many of the activities elicited by ESB certainly can be categorized as skillful. Pressing a lever, climbing a cage wall, and looking for a fight require good motor coordination and suitable processing of information. Walking on two feet, which has been repeatedly elicited in monkeys dorm- stimulation of the red nucleus (Figure 12), is another example of refined coordination and equilibrium seldom observed in spontaneous behavior.

These facts demonstrate that ESB may result in different types of skillful performance, but it must be understood that these responses represent the manifestation of skills already familiar to the subject. Motor learning requires the reception of sensory inputs not only from the environment but also from the performing muscles, and a relatively lengthy process of motor training is required to perfect reactions related to each type of performance and to store the appropriate ideokinetic formulas in the brain for future reference and use. Much of the brain participates in learning, and a monotonous train of pulses applied to a limited pool of neurons cannot be expected to mimic its complexity. The acquisition of a new skill is theoretically and practically beyond the possibilities of electrical stimulation, but ESB can create the desire to perform certain acts which may be skillful.

Individual Stability

Personal identity and reactivity depend on a large number of factors accumulated through many years of experience interacting with genetic trends within the complexity of neuronal networks. Language and culture are among the essential elements of individual structure. All these elements cannot be substituted for by the delivery of electricity to the brain. Memories can be recalled, emotions awakened, and conversations speeded up by ESB, but the patients always express themselves according to their background and experience. It is possible to disturb consciousness, to confuse sensory interpretations, or to elicit hallucinations during excitation of the brain. It is also possible to induce fear, pleasure, and chances in aggressive behavior, but these responses do not represent the creation of a new personality - only a change in emotionality or reactivity with the appearance of manifestations closely related to the previous history of the subject.

ESB cannot substitute one personality for another because electricity cannot replicate or influence all the innumerable factors which integrate individual identity. Contrary to the stories of science fiction writers, we cannot modify political ideology, past history, or national loyalties by electrical tickling of some secret areas of the brain. A complete change in personality is beyond the theoretical and practical potential of ESB, although limited modification of a determined aspect of personal reactions is possible. In spite of important limitations, we are certainly facing basic ethical problems about when, why, and how some of these changes are acceptable, and especially about who will have the responsibility of influencing the cerebral activities of other human beings.

Technical Complexity

Electrical stimulation of the central nervous system requires careful planning, complex methodology, and the skillful collaboration of specialists with knowledge and experience in anatomy, neurophysiology, and psychology. Several pre-

192

requisites, including construction of the delicate multilead electrodes and refined facilities for stereotaxic neurosurgery, are necessary. The selection of neuronal targets and appropriate parameters of stimulation require further sophistication and knowledge of functional brain mapping as well as electronic technology. In addition, medical and psychiatric experience is necessary in order to take care of the patient, to interpret the results obtained, and to plan the delivery of stimulations. These elaborate requirements limit the clinical application of intracerebral electrodes which like other modern medical interventions depends on team work, equipment, and facilities available in only a few medical centers. At the same time, the procedure's complexity acts as a safeguard against the possible improper use of ESB by untrained or unethical persons.

Functions Beyond the Control of ESB

We are in the initial steps of a new technology, and while it is difficult to predict the limits of unknown territory, we may suppose that cerebral manifestations which depend on the elaboration of complex information will elude electrical control. For example, reading a book or listening to a conversation involves reception of many messages which cannot be mimicked by ESB. A pattern of behavior which is not in the brain cannot be organized or invented under electrical control. ESB cannot be used as a teaching tool because skills such as playing the piano, speaking a language, or solving a problem require complex sensory inputs. Sequential behavior or even elemental motor responses cannot be synthesized by cerebral stimulation, although they are easily evoked if they have already been established in the excited area as ideokinetic formulas. Since electrical stimulation does not carry specific thoughts it is not feasible as a technique to implant ideas or direct behavioral performance in a specific context. Because of its lack of symbolic meaning, electricity could not induce effects comparable to some posthypnotic performances.

Medical Applications

The discovery of new therapies has been - and still is - a more pressing need in cerebral disorders than in other fields of medicine because of their greater consequences for the mental and somatic well-being of patients. Unfortunately, advances in this area have been relatively slow, partly because of the intrinsic complexity of the problems involved, and partly because of a traditional fear and reluctance to disturb or deal directly with the material substratum of mental activities. At the beginning of the century, the public was generally hostile to surgery and considered it almost obscene for a surgeon to look into the most intimate depths of the body (185). With cultural and scientific advances this prejudice has slowly receded, and the study of the human body is now recognized as essential for the advance of medicine. Sexual taboos have diminished, and even the scientific investigation of the phases and details of human intercourse has at last been undertaken. All of the organs of the body, including the heart, genitals, and brain, have been accepted as suitable subjects for research.

Implantation of electrodes inside the human brain is like installing a magic window to reveal the bursts of cellular discharges during functional activation of specific structures. The meaning of these bursts is often difficult to decipher, but some correlations between electrical patterns and behavioral effects have already been firmly established. The electrical line of communication has also been used to send simple messages to the depth of the brain in order to arouse dormant functions or to appease excessive neuronal firing. A new method was thus found to impose therapeutic order upon disorderly activity.

In spite of the tremendous potential offered by the direct access to the brain, medical applications were received with suspicion and strong criticism and have progressed rather slowly. The growing acceptance of even experimental surgical interventions in most organs including the human heart is in sharp contrast with the generally cold reception to the implantation of wires in the human brain, even though this procedure has been used in animals for forty years and has proved to be safe. The reasons are to a great extent related to the persistence of old taboos, in scientists as well as in laymen, and to the more logical fear of opening some Pandora's box.

As experience overcomes opposition, cerebral explorations are being extended to different hospitals around the world, as shown by several recent symposia (159, 182, 216).

Diagnosis

The spontaneous electrical activity of the brain (electroencephalogram or EEG) can be recorded by means of surface electrodes attached by conductive paste to the outside of the scalp. This is a standard procedure used for diagnostic purposes in several cerebral illnesses, such as epilepsy, which is characterized by episodes of increased amplitude and synchronization of neuronal activity which can be recorded and identified. Strong electrical disturbances may, however, he present in structures located in the depth of the brain which cannot be detected by scalp EEG (57), and in this case the use of intracerebral electrodes may provide essential diagnostic information. For example, psychomotor epilepsy has been alleviated by surgical removal of the tip of the temporal lobe where seizure activity originated, and in these cases it is imperative to identify the source of the fits and especially to decide whether they are unilateral or present on both sides of the brain. In spite of some controversial problems about the location, multiplicity, and migration of epileptic foci, there is general agreement that depth recordings through implanted electrodes can give valuable data unobtainable by any other means.

The expected correlations between scalp EEG and mental disturbances have failed to materialize in experimental studies, although some mentally ill patients have exhibited electrical abnormalities. Depth recordings have also failed to provide decisive information about these patients, and for example, the suggestion that septa] spikes might be typical of schizophrenia (98) has not been confirmed (57). The absence of significant data must be attributed to the lack of refinement of present methodology Disturbed functions must have a background of altered neuronal physiology which should be detectable if more knowledge of the mechanisms involved and more sophisticated techniques were available. One step in this direction is the analysis of electrical activity by means of auto-correlation and cross-correlation (23) in order to recognize periodicity of patterns among the noise of other signals. Computer analysis of power and spectral analysis of frequencies are also new tools which will increase the future scientific and diagnostic usefulness of electrical recordings. Depth recordings may also be used for localization of tumors inside the unopened skull to detect abnormally slow potential shifts from the tissue surrounding the neoplasm and the lack of spontaneous waves within the mass of tumoral cells.

In addition to knowledge derived from the study of spontaneous brain waves, other valuable information may be obtained by recording the alterations evoked in intracerebral electrical activity following application of sensory stimulation or ESB. Presentation of flashes of light with a stroboscope, or of auditory clicks, activates the corresponding cerebral analyzers and may unveil areas of excessive reactivity. Epileptic patients are especially sensitive to repeated flashes and may respond with an activation of dormant electrical abnormalities or even with a convulsive seizure. Administration of single or repeated electrical shocks may also help in the localization of malfunctioning neuronal fields. Systemic administration of drugs which increase or decrease brain excitability (such as metrazol or phenobarbital) can be used in conjunction with evoked potentials in order to test the specific pharmacological sensitivity of a patient, thus orienting his medical or postsurgical therapy.

Electrical stimulation of the brain during surgical interventions, or during therapeutical destruction of limited cerebral areas, is necessary in order to test local excitability and determine the functional localization of areas which must be spared. This is particularly important during the surgical treatment of Parkinson's disease, which requires freezing of cerebral tissue around the pallidum or thalamus, close to motor pathways in the internal capsule. Identification of these pathways is imperative in order to avoid their accidental destruction and the subsequent permanent motor paralysis of the patient.

MATRIX OF THE MIND

Therapy

The cerebral tissue around the electrode contact may be destroyed by electrocoagulation, passing a suitable amount of direct current. The main advantages of using implanted electrodes for this purpose, instead of open brain surgery, are that careful functional explorations are possible before and after the brain lesion is placed and, more importantly, that coagulation can be controlled and repeated if necessary over a period of days or weeks, according to the therapeutic results obtained. The procedure has been used for therapy of involuntary movements, intractable pain, focal epilepsy, and several mental disturbances including anxiety, fear, compulsive obsessions, and aggressive behavior. Some investigators report a remarkable therapeutic success in obsessive patients; others are more skeptical about the usefulness of depth electrodes and electrocoagulations in treating mental illness.

Electrical stimulation of specific structures has been used as a therapeutic procedure, and beneficial effects have been obtained in schizophrenic patients by repeated excitation of the septum and other areas which produce pleasurable sensations (99, 201, 233). In other cases of intractable pain, considerable improvement has also been reported, and some patients have been allowed to stimulate their own brains repeatedly by means of portable stimulators. In one patient, spontaneous bursts of aggressive behavior were diminished by brief periods of repeated stimulation of the amygdaloid nucleus (60).

One of the promising medical applications of ESB is the programing of long-term stimulations. Animal studies have shown that repeated excitations of determined cerebral structures produced lasting effects and that intermittent stimulations could be continued indefinitely. Some results in man have also been confirmatory. It should be emphasized that brain lesions represent an irreversible destruction while brain stimulations are far More physiological and conservative and do not rule out placing of lesions if necessary. One example may clarify the potential of this procedure. Nashold (160) has described the case of one patient, suffering from very severe intention tremor associated with multiple sclerosis, in whom stimulation of the dentate nucleus of the cerebellum produced an inhibition of the tremor with marked ipsilateral improvement of voluntary motility. The speculation was that a cerebral pacemaker could be activated by the patient himself when he desired to perform voluntary movements.

Many other possible applications could be explored including the treatment of anorexia nervosa by stimulation of the feeding centers of the lateral hypothalamus, the induction of sleep in cases of insomnia by excitation of the center median or of the caudate nucleus, the regulation of circulating ACFH by activation of the posterior hypothalamus, and the increase of patients' communication

196

for psychotherapeutic purposes by excitation of the temporal lobe.

A two-way radio communication system could be established between the brain of a subject and a computer. Certain types of neuronal activity related to behavioral disturbances such as anxiety, depression, or rage could be recognized in order to trigger stimulation of specific inhibitory structures. The delivery of brain stimulation on demand to correct cerebral dysfunctions represents a new approach to therapeutic feedback. While it is speculative, it is within the realm of possibility according to present knowledge and projected methodology.

Circumvention of Damaged Sensory Inputs

The miracle of giving light to the blind and sound to the deaf has been made possible by implantation of electrodes, demonstrating the technical possibility of circumventing damaged sensory receptors by direct electrical stimulation of the nervous system,

Brindley and I.ewin (24) have described the case of a 52-year old woman, totally blind after suffering bilateral glaucoma, in whom an array of eighty small receiving coils were implanted subcutaneously above the skull, terminating in eighty platinum electrodes encased in a sheet of silicone rubber placed in direct contact with the visual cortex of the right occipital lobe. Each receiving coil was tuned to a frequency of 6 or 9-5 megahertz and could be activated by pressing a transmitting coil against the scalp. With this type of transdermal stimulation, a visual sensation was perceived by the patient in the left half of her visual field as a very small spot of white light or sometimes as a duplet or a cluster of points. The effects produced by stimulation of contacts 2.4 millimeters apart were easily distinguished, and simultaneous excitation of several electrodes evoked the perception of predictable simple visual patterns. The investigators suppose that by implanting six hundred tiny electrodes it would be possible for blind patients to discriminate visual patterns; they could also achieve a normal reading speed by using electrical signals from an automatic page scanner.

Using a different approach, the Mexican investigator del Campo (26) has designed air instrument called an "amaroscope," consisting of photoelectric cells, to transform luminous images into electrical impulses which are modulated and fed through electrodes placed over the skin above the eyes to stimulate the supraorbital branches of the trigeminal nerve. Impulses are thus carried to the reticular system and the cerebral cortex. The instrument is not too sophisticated and its neurophysiological principles are controversial, but its experimental testing in more than too persons has proved that visual perceptions may be electrically produced in blind patients, even in some who have no eyes at all.

Auditory sensations have also been produced in a deaf person by electri-

MATRIX OF THE MIND

cal stimulation of the auditory nerve through permanently implanted electrodes. Simmons et al. (208) studied a 60-year-old male who had been totally deaf in his right ear for several years and nearly deaf in the left for several months. Under local anesthesia, a cluster of six electrodes was implanted on the right auditory nerve with a connector anchored to the skull just beneath the right ear. Two weeks after surgery, electrical stimuli were able to produce perception of different kinds of auditory sensations. Pitch varied with the point stimulated and also depended on the electrical parameters used. For example, 3 to 4 pulses per second were heard as "clicks," to per second as "telephone ringing," 30 per second as "bee buzz," and 100 to 300 per second could not be discriminated. Loudness was related to amplitude of stimulation and to pulse duration, and was less affected by its frequency.

To evaluate these studies we must understand that the refinement of the senses cannot be duplicated by electronic means because receptors are not passive transducers of energy but active modulators and discriminators of impulses. The reciprocal feedback between peripheral and central neurons and the processes of filtering and cross-correlation of information which takes place during afferent transmission of impulses are absent in the instrumental reception of inputs. It is doubtful that refined perceptions comparable to physiological ones can be provided by electronic means, but the perception of sensations - even if crude - when hope had been lost is certainly encouraging and demands the continuation of research efforts,

Brain Viability

The clinical distinction between life and death was not too difficult to establish in the past. When respiration and palpitations of the heart had ceased, a person was pronounced dead, and there was little that a doctor could do. It is true that in some extraordinary cases the signs of death were only apparent, and a few patients have revived spontaneously, creating quite a hock for their doctors, relatives, and for themselves, but these fantastic stories are the very rare exceptions.

A new situation has been created in recent years because medical technology has often taken the determination of human death away from natural causality. Respiratory arrest is no longer fatal, and many poliomyelitic victims have survived with the help of iron lungs; cardiac block does not necessarily signal the end of life because heart beats may be artificially controlled by pacemakers; kidney failure will not poison the patient if dialysis machines are available to clean his blood. To the growing collection of ingenious electromechanical instruments a new methodology has recently been added: the cross-circulation between a sick human being and a healthy baboon in order to clear the human blood. This procedure was first tested in December, 1967, by Dr. Hume at the Virginia Medical College Hospital to treat a woman patient in deep hepatic coma with jaundice and edema. A 35-pound baboon was anesthetized, cooled, and its blood completely washed out with Ringer solution and replaced with human blood matched to the patient's. Then a cross-circulation was established from the ape's leg to the patient's arm. In twelve hours the patient had excreted about 5 liters of fluid through the baboon's kidney and regained consciousness. Twenty-two days later the patient went home, and the baboon was alive and healthy. A similar procedure was successfully used later in other cases (21).

Today the lives of many patients do not depend completely on the well-being of their own organic functions but on the availability of apes, organ donors, the voltage of a battery, integrity of electronic circuits, proper management of pumps, and teamwork of doctors and technicians. In certain cases death can be delayed for weeks or months, and current technology has placed upon doctors the tremendous responsibility, the nearly deific power, of deciding the duration of patients' survival. A heated controversy, reaching the public and the British Parliament, was created by the recent disclosure that in London's Neasden Hospital the records of patients over sixty-five years of age and suffering from malignant rumors or other serious chronic diseases were marked "NTBR" ("not to be resuscitated") in case of cardiac arrest. Artificial prolongation of human life is time consuming and expensive in terms of instrumentation and personnel, and it imposes added stress on tire patients and their families. Because resources are limited, it is materially impossible to attempt to resuscitate all the patients who die every day, and it is necessary to select those who have the best chance of prolonged and useful survival. Why should life be maintained in unconscious patients with irreversible brain damage and no hope of recovery?

This dramatic decision between individual life and death illustrates both man's recently acquired power and the necessity to use it with intelligence and compassion. To make the situation even more complex, the recent development of organ transplantation is creating a literally "vital" conflict of interests because a person kept alive artificially owns many good working organs-including kidneys, pancreas, heart, and bones -that are needed by other dying patients.

Death, personality, and biological human rights must be redefined in view of these new scientific advances. Possessions to be disposed of after death include not only real estate, stocks, and furniture, but teeth, corneas, and hearts as well. This prospect involves many ethical and legal questions and sounds altogether gruesome and uncomfortable, but that is only because it is unfamiliar. Giving blood to be transfused, skin to be grafted, spermatozoas for artificial insemination, and kidneys to be transplanted are more acceptable practices because they do not depend on the death of the donor; but when death cannot be avoided, the idea of the transfer and survival of some organs should be consid-

MATRIX OF THE MIND

ered reasonable.

The possibility of piecemeal survival of functions and organs introduces the basic question of what part of the organism to identify with human personality. There is general agreement that the organ most fundamental to individual identity is not the stomach, the liver, or even the heart, but the brain. In the necessary redefinition of death it has been proposed that in difficult cases when circulation, digestion, metabolic exchange, and other functions are still active, the decisive information about whether a person should be considered alive-entailing the decision to continue or to withdraw artificial support for survival-must come from the viability of the brain. In some hospitals the ultimate arbiter of death is the EEG machine, and at the Massachussetts General Hospital, Dr. Robert Schwab has proposed that death should be determined by flat lines on all EEG leads for twenty minutes of continuous recordings and lack of response to sensory and mechanical stimuli. In the absence of EEG activity tested twenty-four and forty-eight hours later, death is presumed to have occurred even if (as happens in rare cases) the heart is still beating normally.

In the near future it will be necessary to examine this question in greater detail in order to determine the parts of the brain considered essential for the survival of human personality. We already know that portions of the brain may be destroyed or taken away with negligible or only moderate psychic changes. Destruction of the motor cortex produces paralysis; ablation o f the temporal lobe may affect recent memory; and destruction of the frontal lobes may modify foresight and affective reactions, but in all these cases the patient's behavior is recognized as human. Destruction of the hypothalamus or reticular formation, however, may induce permanent loss of consciousness, and in this case it is questionable whether personal identity persists. The possible piecemeal survival of psychological functions will make the definition of man more difficult and will perhaps increase the present problem of deciding what human life is. From the examination of these questions, however, a deeper understanding of the essential qualities of a human being - and of the direction of their evolution with intelligent purpose - will emerge.

Ethical Considerations

Placing electrodes inside of the brain, exploring the neuronal depth of personality, and influencing behavior by electrical stimulation have created a variety of problems, some of them shared with general medical ethics and others more specifically related to moral and philosophical issues of mental activity.

Clinical Use of New Procedures

One of the main objectives of animal research is the discovery of new prin-

MATRIX OF THE MIND

ciples and methods which can be applied for the benefit of man. Their potential advantages and risks cannot be ascertained until they have been extensively tested in human subjects, and preliminary trials must always be considered experimental. Evidence that penicillin or any other new drug may be therapeutically effective is obtained initially in vitro and then in different species of mammals, but the conclusive demonstration of its clinical safety and efficacy requires application to man. In spite of established safeguards, there is an inherent possibility that unforeseen, slowly developing side effects may have serious consequences. A thorium product used in the early thirties as a contrast medium for X-ray analysis of the liver was found to be radioactive and caused the slow death of hundreds of patients. A supposedly innocuous drug, the ill-famed thalidomide given as a sedative, had damaging effects on fetal development, creating the tragedy of children born with severe physical deformities. Accidents like these have promoted more stringent regulations, but the gap between animal and human biology is difficult to fill and in each case a compromise must be reached between reasonable precautions and possible risks.

The historical demonstration by Fulton and Jacobsen (81) that frustration and neurotic behavior in the chimpanzee could be abolished by destruction of the frontal lobes Was the starting point of lobotomy, which was widely used for treatment of several types of mental illness in human patients. This operation consisted of surgical disruption of the frontal lobe connections and demonstrated the important fact that psychic manifestations can be influenced by physical means as bold as the surgeon's knife. The Nobel Prize bestowed on the first neurosurgeon to perform human lobotomies, Egas Moniz, recognized the significance of the principle that the mind was not so unreachable as formerly believed, and that it could be the object of experimental investigation.

In spite of initial acclaim, lobotomy was soon severely criticized as a therapeutic procedure because it often produced concomitant undesirable alterations of personality, and more conservative treatments Were actively sought in order to provide a "less damaging, less sacrificial means of dealing with mental disorders than are lobotomy, leucotomy, gyrectomy, thalamotomy, and other intentional destructions of nervous structures" (145). Among these efforts, implantation of electrodes in the brain offered promising possibilities. In monkeys, stimulation or limited destruction of the caudate nucleus produced several of the symptoms of frontal lobotomy with more discrete behavioral changes (191). Implantation of electrodes in man permitted access to any cerebral structure for recording, stimulation, or destruction. Their potential clinical application raised controversial issues about risks, rationale, and medical efficacy, but there is general agreement that depth recordings may provide significant information which cannot be obtained by other means and is essential for the proper diagnosis and treatment of patients with some cerebral disturbances. Therapeutic use of electrodes in cases of mental illness has been more doubtful and must still be considered in an experimental phase.

Recordings and stimulations in a patient equipped with intracerebral leads provide basic information about neurophysiological mechanisms in man which may be of great value for the patient himself, for the welfare of other patients, and for the advance of science. In addition, they provide a unique opportunity to obtain important data about neuronal functions which may not be directly related to the patient's illness. In this case we are facing ethical issues of human research which must be carefully considered.

Human Experimentation

While medical practice has generally accepted guidelines based on the hippocratic oath - to do what "I consider best for my patients, and abstain from whatever is injurious" - research with human subjects has lacked traditional codes and has followed the investigator's personal criteria-which have not always been correct. According to Beecher (12), leading medical schools and renowned doctors have sometimes conducted unethical research. Extremely high doses of a drug have been administered, with resulting behavioral disturbances, in order to evaluate the toxicity of the product; placebos have been given instead of a well-known beneficial drug, with a resulting increase in the incidence and severity of illness; live cancer cells have been injected tinder the skin of twenty-two elderly patients wit or telling them what the shots were, at New York's well-respected Sloan-Kettering Institute. Beecher does not believe that these studies demonstrate a willful disregard of the patient's rights, but a thoughtlessness in experimental design.

Although no formal ethical code has been universally accepted for the performance of research in man I basic guidelines have been formulated by the American Psychological Association (43); by the judges of the Nuremberg war crime trials (218); by the World Medical Association (246); and by the Medical Research Council of Britain (153). A 1966 editorial in the New England Journal of Medicine (161) states that in medicine and in human investigations the welfare of the sick patient or the experimental subject has traditionally been of prime importance. "This implies clearly that therapeutic or theoretical experiments with significant risk of morbidity or mortality are undertaken only with a view to the immediate benefit of the patient; for the experimental subject to whom no benefit may accrue, the most meaningful possible informed and unforced consent must be secured." In the summer of i966, the United States Public Health Service issued regulations for their sponsored research involving humans, specifying the need for full consent by the participating subjects and careful review of the projects by an

MATRIX OF THE MIND

ad hoc committee. In a detailed discussion, Wolfensberger (245) clarified the meaning of informed consent: The experimental subject understands all the essential aspects of the study, the types and degrees of risks, the detrimental or beneficial consequences, if any, and the purpose of the research.

One of the main ethical issues is the conflict of interest between science, progress, and society, and the rights of the individual. The principles of personal dignity, privacy, and freedom are often waived - voluntarily or forcefully - in favor of the group. Firemen, policemen, and soldiers may risk or lose their lives for the benefit of the community. Civilized activities are full of regulations which limit behavioral freedom. We are obliged to reveal our income, to pay taxes, and to serve in the army. We cannot walk around naked, take flowers from public gardens, or leave our cars where we please. We are searched when crossing borders and put in jail if our conduct is considered antisocial by the law. Although respect for the individual is highly prized and accepted in theory, in practice it is often challenged and curtailed. The balance between social duties and individual rights is decided not by the individual but by customs and laws established by the group.

In the case of medical research, it is difficult to write an ethical code. As the Panel Of Privacy and Behavioral Research concluded in 1967, "legislation to assure appropriate recognition of the rights of human subjects is neither necessary nor desirable," and "because of its relative inflexibility, legislation cannot meet the challenge of the subtle and sensitive conflict of values under consideration." Ethical decisions in science require not only moral judgment but also factual information, technical knowledge, and experience, especially in the evaluation of risks and benefits. In order to decide to undergo open heart surgery, a patient must have a medical evaluation of his condition and of the state of the surgical art, a judgment which the doctor, but rarely the patient, is prepared to make. In medical research, consent is certainly essential, but the main responsibility still lies with the investigator and his institution. The request for consent from a patient-or from a student participating in a research project carries a heavy weight of moral authority and a degree of coercion, and granting of it does not relieve the director of full responsibility in the experimental design and consequences. The simple request to perform a dubious procedure must be considered unethical because it represents psychological stress for the patient. Children and adults with mental disturbances cannot give proper consent, and relatives must be consulted. Their decisions, however, are easily influenced by the picture presented by the attending physician, thus increasing his responsibility which preferably should be shared by a group of three or more professional consultants.

There is one aspect of human research which is usually overlooked: the existence of a moral and social duty to advance scientific knowledge and to improve the welfare of man. When important medical information can be obtained with negligible risk and without infringing on individual rights, the investigator has the duty to use his intelligence and skills for this purpose. Failure to do so represents the neglect of professional duties in some way similar to the negligence of a medical doctor who does not apply his full effort to the care of a patient. Subjects with implanted electrodes provide a good example, because the use of telemetry, and video tape recordings in them makes possible many studies concerning the sources of normal and abnormal activities, spectral analysis of electrical waves, conduction time, evoked potentials, and electrobehavioral correlations. This type of research may provide data of exceptional value-available only from man-without any risks or even demands on a patient's time or attention. Information can be obtained while the subject is engaged in spontaneous normal activities like reading a paper, watching television, or sleeping. Only the recording equipment and research team need to be alert and working. Methodology for the telemetric study of the brain is very new, and it will take some time before its potential and practicality are recognized and its use spreads to different hospitals. In my opinion this research is both ethical and desirable.

However, procedures which represent risk or discomfort for the patient should be ruled out. The implantation time of electrodes cannot be prolonged unnecessarily, and-administration of drugs, injections, or catheterizations for research purposes are not acceptable. Any contemplated exception to this rule should be very carefully evaluated and clearly explained to the experimental subject.

When a patient needs to have electrodes in his brain for a period of weeks or months, the medical doctors in charge face a dual responsibility, first not to do anything harmful or unpleasant for the sake of science, and second to do as much research as possible provided it is safe and comfortable for the patient.

The use of healthy volunteers in medical research is controversial, partly because they are usually recruited from prisons, the military services, universities, or other groups which are more or less bound to authority and therefore have a diminished capacity for free choice. One of the most famous experiments was a study of antimalarial drugs which had to be performed in man. In a well-planned research project 1,000 army volunteers in Australia were deliberately infected with malaria. This study was later continued in several federal penitentiaries in the United States. A most dramatic and successful mass experiment was the application of poliomyelitis vaccine to thousands of school children a few years ago, statistically demonstrating the effectiveness of a new vaccine. Decisions about experiments like these must be reached by careful consideration of the factors involved, with the basic ethical guidelines clearly in mind.

MATRIX OF THE MIND

Individual volunteers have greater freedom of choice, and I have received letters from many people offering themselves as "human guinea pigs" for implantation of electrodes in their brains. For both ethical and practical reasons their offers cannot be accepted, but it is interesting to note the varied motivations behind these proposals. They included pure scientific interest. hopes for monetary reward or fame, manifestations of psychotic disturbances, and also a most generous intent: Some people wished to donate their brains for study in the hope that information could be obtained leading to the cure of loved ones whose brain dysfunctions could not be cured by standard therapies. The most articulate expression of this wish to contribute one's own brain for scientific research was that of a most distinguished investigator, Dr. David Rioch, who at the close of a conference about the unanesthetized brain, held in Washington, D.C., in 1957, declared:

> When I come to retire ... I might quite reasonably approach an experimental neurosurgeon in whose work and scientific orientation I had confidence and say "Let us do an experiment together, as there are a number of things both you and I would like to find out." I would be considerably intrigued to know what "attitudes" and "sensations" a good experimenter could evoke electrically from my amygdala and even more intrigued to check personally on the sense of euphoria and the sense of disphoria (185).

Electrical Manipulation of the Psyche

The most alarming aspect of ESB is that psychological reactivity can be influenced by applying a few volts to a determined area of the brain. This fact has been interpreted by many people as a disturbing threat to human integrity. In the past, the individual could face risks and pressures with preservation of his own identity. His body could be tortured, his thoughts and desires could be environmental circumstances, but he always had the privilege of deciding his own fate, of dying for an ideal without changing his mind. Fidelity to our emotional and intellectual past gives each of us a feeling of transcendental stability-and perhaps of immortality-which is more precious than life itself.

MATRIX OF THE MIND

New neurological technology, however, has a refined efficiency. The individual is defenseless against direct manipulation of the brain because he is deprived of his most intimate mechanisms of biological reactivity. In experiments, electrical stimulation of appropriate intensity always prevailed over free will; and, for example, flexion of the hand evoked by stimulation of the motor cortex cannot be voluntarily avoided. Destruction of the frontal lobes produced changes in effectiveness which are beyond any personal control.

The possibility of scientific annihilation of personal identity, or even worse, its purposeful control, has sometimes been considered a future threat more awful than atomic holocaust. Even physicians have expressed doubts about the propriety of physical tampering with the psyche, maintaining that personal identity should be inviolable, that any attempt to modify individual behavior is unethical, and that method and related research -which can influence the human brain should be banned. The prospect of any degree of physical control of the mind provokes a variety of objections: theological objections because it affects free will, moral objections because it affects individual responsibility, ethical objections because it may block self-defense mechanisms, philosophical objections because it threatens personal identity.

These objections, however, are debatable. A prohibition of scientific advance is obviously naive and unrealistic. It could not be universally imposed, and, more important, it is not knowledge itself but its improper use which should be regulated. A knife is neither good nor bad; but it may be used by either a surgeon or an assassin. Science should be neutral, but scientists should take sides (242). The mind is not a static, inborn entity owned by the individual and self-sufficient, but the dynamic organization of sensory perceptions of the external world, correlated and reshaped through the internal anatomical and functional structure of the brain. Personality is not an intangible, immutable way of reacting, but a flexible process in continuous evolution, affected by its medium. Culture and education are meant to shape patterns of reaction which are not innate in the human organism; they are meant to impose limits on freedom of choice. Moral codes may vary completely from civilization to civilization. Polygamy was acceptable in biblical times, and it is still practiced among Moslems, but it is rejected by many other civilizations with strong social, legal, religious, and educational pressures to make behavior monogamous. Of course there is no physical impediment to the acquisition of half a dozen wives - at least until the law or the ladies catch up - but then we enter into a play of forces, into the dynamic equilibrium among all of the elements which determine behavioral choice. If there are very strong reasons to react in a particular way (for example, to have only one wife), the chance of living by a different custom is so slim as to be negligible.

This is precisely the role of electrical stimulation of the brain: to add a new factor to the constellation of behavioral determinants. The result as shown experimentally in animals is an algebraic summation, with cerebral stimulation usually prepotent over spontaneous react ions. It is accepted medical practice to try and modify the antisocial or abnormal reactions of mental patients. Psychoanalysis, the use of drugs such as energizers and tranquilizers, the application of insulin or electroshock, and other varieties of psychiatric treatment are all aimed at influencing the abnormal personality of the patient in order to change his undesirable mental characteristics. The possible use, therefore, of implanted electrodes in mental patients should not pose unusual ethical complications if the accepted medical rules are followed. Perhaps the limited efficiency of standard psychiatric procedures is one reason that they have not caused alarm among scientists or laymen. Psychoanalysis requires a long time, and a person can easily withdraw his cooperation and refuse to express intimate thoughts. Electroshock is a crude method of doubtful efficacy in normal people. Although electrical stimulation of the brain is still in the initial stage of Its development, it is in contrast far more selective and powerful; it may delay a heart beat, move a finger, bring a word to memory, or set a determined behavioral tone.

When medical indications are clear and the standard therapeutic procedures have failed, most patients and doctors are willing to test a new method, provided that the possibility of success outweighs the risk of worsening the situation. The crucial decision to start applying a new therapeutic method to human patients requires a combination of intelligent evaluation of data, knowledge of comparative neurophysiology, foresight, moral integrity, and Courage. Excessive aggressiveness in a doctor may cause irreparable damage, but too much caution may deprive patients of needed help. The surgical procedure of lobotomy was perhaps applied to many mental patients too quickly, before its dangers and limitations were understood; but pallidectomy and thalamotomy in the treatment of Parkinson's disease encountered formidable initial opposition before attaining their present recognition and respected status.

While pharmacological and surgical treatment of sufferers of mental illness is accepted as proper, people with other behavioral deviations pose a different type of ethical problem. They may be potentially dangerous to themselves and to society when their mental functions are maintained within normal limits and only one aspect of their personal conduct is socially unacceptable. The rights of an individual to obtain appropriate treatment must be weighed with a professional evaluation of his behavioral problems and their possible neurological basis-which necessitates a value judgment of the person's behavior in comparison with accepted norms. One example will illustrate these considerations.

In the early 1950s, a patient in a state mental hospital approached Dr. Hannibal Hamlin and me requesting help. She was an attractive 24-year-old woman of average intelligence and education who had a long record of arrests for disorderly conduct, She had been repeatedly involved in bar brawls in which she incited men to fight over her and had spent most of the preceding few years either in jail or in mental institutions. The patient expressed a strong desire as well as an inability to alter her conduct, and because psychiatric treatment had failed, she and her mother urgently requested that some kind of brain surgery be performed in order to control her disreputable, impulsive behavior. They asked specifically that electrodes be implanted to orient possible electrocoagulation of a limited cerebral area; and if that wasn't possible, they wanted lobotomy.

Medical knowledge and experience at that time could not ascertain whether ESB or the application of cerebral lesions could help to solve this patient's problem, and surgical intervention was therefore rejected. When this decision was explained, both the patient and her mother reacted with similar anxious comments, asking, "What is the future? Only jail or the hospital? Is there no hope?" This case revealed the limitations of therapy and the dilemma of possible behavioral control. Supposing that long-term stimulation of a determined brain structure could influence the tendencies of a patient to drink, flirt, and induce fights; would it be ethical to change her personal characteristics? People are changing their character by self-medication through hallucinogenic drugs, but do they have the right to demand that doctors administer treatment that will radically alter their behavior? What are the limits of individual rights and doctors' obligations?

As science seems to be approaching the possibility of controlling many aspects of behavior electronically and chemically, these questions must be answered. If, as in the case of this patient, the deviation of behavior conflicts with society so seriously as to deprive her of her personal freedom, medical intervention could be justified. The case of habitual criminal conduct is another example of this type of problem. Therapeutic decisions related to psychic manipulation require moral integrity and ethical education. Scientific training concentrates mainly in natural sciences and often neglects the study and assimilation of ethical codes, considering them beyond the realm of science. Perhaps it is often forgotten that the investigator needs a set of convictions and principles, not only to administrate grant money, to give proper credit to the work of others, and to be civilized with his colleagues, but especially to direct his life and his research, and to foresee the implications of his own discoveries.

A LIST OF ARTICLES FROM TECH PUBLICATIONS

Here we list articles from technology publications which show how these technologies are being marketed in commercial form, and have also been and are being used to harass covert weapons testing victims:

The reader is asked to remember that ANNOUNCED inventions with poten-

MATRIX OF THE MIND

tial for "national security" use are ALWAYS already in use covertly when announced. The SR-71 "Blackbird" surveillance aircraft was in use for many years before the public saw it.

Articles from technology publications show how these technologies are being used to harass covert weapons testing victims, and are now coming out in commercial form, or have been announced to the public:

1. Aviation Week & Space Technology, March 10, 1997 "Radar Warns Birds of Impending Aircraft"

This article by Bruce Nordwall (Washington bureau) describes research being carried on by the USAF Wright Laboratory at Dayton Ohio. The article describes the use of MODULATED radar signals to produce AUDIBLE SOUND within the brains of birds near airport runways to cause them to fly away and avoid collisions with landing aircraft.

Other references on work with animals or humans with "audible microwaves":

Science, vol. 181, 27 July 73, page 356 Nature, vol. 216, DEC 16 1967, page 1139 Nature, vol. 210, May 7 1966, page 636 Journal Acoustical Society of America, June 1982, page 1321 Bioelectromagnetics conference, 1992, 13:323-328 (pages 323-328)

This list was furnished by the lab at Wright- Patterson Air Force Base where this type of unclassified development is now in progress.

** The transmission via MODULATED microwave pulses carrying voices to selected weapons testing victims has been carried on for more than two decades, as reported by the victims. There has been little published about this phenomenon, and since direct-to-skull voice transmissions are consistently mis-interpreted by psychiatrists as 'schizophrenia', getting this information to the public needs concerted attention.

2. Electronic Business Today, February 1997 "Business Trends" section, page 20

Inventor Elwood Norris, and his small company, (American Technology Corp., Poway CA) have designed a market ready device called an "acoustical heterodyne".

This device sends out two sound signals in the ultrasonic (above-human-hearing) range which, when they impact a surface, which may be a living creature, then and only then produce a sound at a frequency equal to the DIFFERENCE ("heterodyne") of the two ultrasound frequencies.

** This technology has been used extensively by harassers who follow a

209

walking or driving victim and bounce raucous, unnatural bird calls and other strange sounds off surfaces near the victim. This type of sound is tape recordable.

ATC Corporate Headquarters 13114 Evening Creek Dr. S. San Diego, CA 92128 (800)41-RADIO (417-2346) (619)679-2114 (619)679-0545 FAX atc-info@atcsd.com http:/www.atcsd.com

3. New York Times, April 7, 1997, "Devices May Let Police Find Hidden Guns on Street" article

This article, with photos supplied by Millitech Corporation, describes recently unclassified "millimeter wave" cameras (and some other see- thru technologies less well developed.)

These units operate like camcorders, giving the user a real-time thru-clothing, thru- luggage image for detecting weapons and drugs.

Technology like this does not just pop out of nowhere overnight, and it probably has its roots in the 1960's classified microwave weapon "renaissance" - about the same time as the U.S. embassy staff in Moscow discovered they were being bathed in Soviet microwave signals.

OEM Magazine, February 1997, page 20 "Electronic Dipstick" article

This article describes "micropower impulse radar" or "MIR" radar, developed at Lawrence Livermore Lab in California, and licensed to several large companies for consumer products. Basically, this radar uses the highest radio frequencies and does not require the supporting hardware like rotary antennas which 'conventional' radar does.

Uses include vehicle blind-spot sensors, traffic control sensors, heart muscle response monitors, and ** see thru plaster ** stud finders.

** Thru the wall radar has been covertly used for a number of years on weapons testing victims. One common use has been to detect where the victim is standing or walking in their apartment, and 'follow' the victim's position by rapping floor, walls, or ceiling from an adjacent apt. This is designed to let the victim know he/she is under constant surveillance.

4. Defense Electronics, July 1993, page 17

MATRIX OF THE MIND

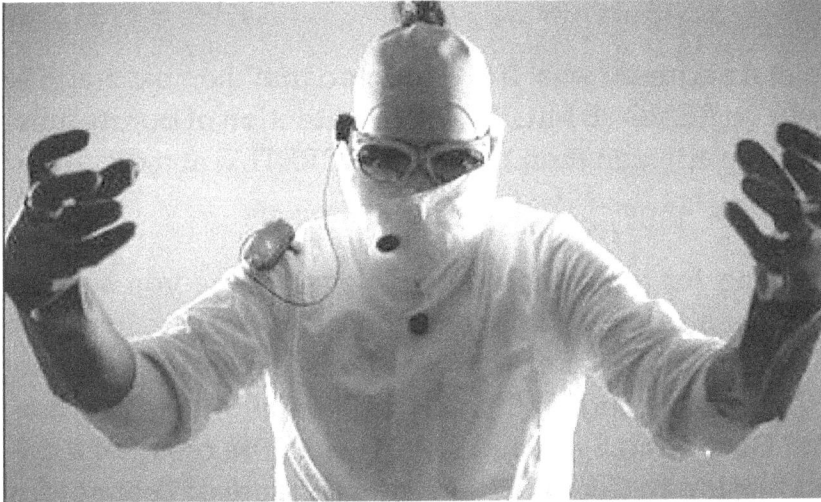

DOD, INTEL AGENCIES LOOK AT RUSSIAN MIND CONTROL CLAIMS

Federal law enforcement officials considered testing a Russian scientist's acoustic mind control device on cultist David Koresh a few weeks before the fiery conflagration that killed the Branch Davidian leader and 70 of his followers in Waco, Texas, DEFENSE ELECTRONICS has learned.

In a series of closed meetings beginning March 17 in suburban northern Virginia with Dr. Igor Smirnov of the Moscow Medical Academy, FBI officials were briefed on the Russian's decade- long research on a computerized acoustic device allegedly capable of implanting thoughts in a person's mind without that person being aware of the source of the thought.

His account of the meetings was confirmed by Psychotechnologies Corp., a Richmond, Virginia based firm that owns the American rights to the Russian technology.

[Not necessarily unclassified, but at least made known to a limited segment of the public]

5. Dan Rather's CBS Evening News, Dec. 9, 1997

Police helicopters were the topic, and one of the features soon to be added to police helicopters was "an electromagnetic ray gun which can stop speeding cars dead."

While this is primitive technology compared with that used to manipulate the minds and nervous systems of e-weapons victims of the 1990's, it does demonstrate quite clearly that government is putting substantial resources into electromagnetic weapons development.

6. Canadian version, Discovery Channel, "Invention" segment, Thursday December 25, 1997

During part of the show, it was stated that the current development of polygraphs (lie detectors) using massive computer-aided database comparisons was now a reality and these machines were making substantial progress towards near-

MATRIX OF THE MIND

perfect accuracy.

The final statement in that segment was: It is expected that the next stage in polygraph devel- opment will be REMOTE MICROWAVE detection of bodily functions, which will mean the polygraph can then be used SECRETLY, at a distance.

7. Associated Press: (Dec. 2, 1997)

TOKYO - Tired of reaching for the remote control every time you surf the channels? Help is on the way - at a price. A Japanese company plans to market a device that changes television channels and activates household appliances at the flicker of a brain wave. The price: roughly 600,000 yen ($4,800). The product, called the Mind Control Tool Operating System, or MCTOS, is the result of a collaboration between the Technos Japan Co. and the Himeji Institute of Technology in southwestern Japan.

Say you want to turn on the air conditioner. Simply focus on that icon on the MCTOS computer display menu while wearing a pair of beta-wave trapping goggles. Then, according to Technos spokesman Sadahiro U#ani, say something like "Ei!!" inside your head. Soon your air conditioner will be pumping cool air into the room.

MCTOS is scheduled to go on sale in April, 1998.

8. On Jan. 19 the Washington Post had an article about a device for remotely detecting heartbeats by detecting the electromagnetic pulses emitted by beating hearts.

URL: www.washingtonpost.com... 1998-01/19/0171-011998-idx.html

An excerpt:

"The pumping of the human heart is controlled by electrical signals, which doctors measure in electrocardiograms. The heart's activity generates an irregular, ultralow-frequency electric field that extends in a circle around the body.

"The field is faint, but it can pass through almost any physical barrier. The LifeGuard can pick up on the strongest part of the field, the heart, through barriers including concrete walls, heavy foliage and rocks. Company officials say the LifeGuard can detect a person in less than five seconds and can pinpoint his or her location with a high degree of accuracy."

The company is marketing the device for potentially locating people in need of rescue, or detecting where individuals are located inside a building.

-- submitted by: Allen L. Barker www.cs.virginia.edu...

Here is more info on this type of device:

MATRIX OF THE MIND

69. VSE - Life Assesment Detector System DATE 020597 93% (Nasdaq: VSEC) LIFE ASSESMENT DECTECTOR SYSTEM (LADS) Patent Pending The Life Assessment Detector System (LADS), a microwave Doppler movement measuring device, can detect human body surface motion, including heartbeat and respiration, at ranges up.. www.vsecorp.com... 3296 bytes, 08Feb97 --

9. Nature magazine, Vol 391, January 22, 1998, page 316, "Advances in neuroscience may threaten human rights" by Declan Butler

(PARIS - Pasteur Institute - Speech by Chairman of the French national bioethics committee Jean-Pierre Changeaux)

"But neuroscience also poses potential risks, arguing that advances in cerebral imaging make the scope for invasion of privacy immense.

"Although the equipment needed is still highly spec- ialized, it will become commonplace and capable of being used at a distance, he predicted. That will open the way for abuses such as invasion of personal liberty, control of behaviour, and brainwashing."

"These are far from being science-fiction concerns, said Changeaux, and constitute a serious risk to society."

Also in that article:

"Denis LeBihan, a researcher at the French Atomic Energy Commission, told the meeting that the use of imaging techniques has reached the stage where we can almost read people's thoughts."

NOTE: These scientists are speaking ONLY about the UNCLASSIFIED scientific arena. Classified technology can always be assumed well ahead of unclassified.

MATRIX OF THE MIND

MIND GAMES

New on the Internet: a community of people who believe the government is beaming voices into their minds. They may be crazy, but the Pentagon has pursued a weapon that can do just that.

By Sharon Weinberger

Sunday, January 14, 2007; Page W22

If Harlan Girard is crazy, he doesn't act the part. He is standing just where he said he would be, below the Philadelphia train station's World War II memorial -- a soaring statue of a winged angel embracing a fallen combatant, as if lifting him to heaven. Girard is wearing pressed khaki pants, expensive-looking leather loafers and a crisp blue button-down. He looks like a local businessman dressed for a casual Friday -- a local businessman with a wickedly dark sense of humor, which had become apparent when he said to look for him beneath "the angel sodomizing a dead soldier." At 70, he appears robust and healthy -- not the slightest bit disheveled or unusual-looking. He is also carrying a bag.

Girard's description of himself is matter-of-fact, until he explains what's in the bag: documents he believes prove that the government is attempting to control his mind. He carries that black, weathered bag everywhere he goes. "Every time I go out, I'm prepared to come home and find everything is stolen," he says.

The bag aside, Girard appears intelligent and coherent. At a table in front of Dunkin' Donuts inside the train station, Girard opens the bag and pulls out a thick stack of documents, carefully labeled and sorted with yellow sticky notes bearing neat block print. The documents are an authentic-looking mix of news stories, articles culled from military journals and even some declassified national security documents that do seem to show that the U.S. government has attempted to develop weapons that send voices into people's heads.

"It's undeniable that the technology exists," Girard says, "but if you go to the police and say, 'I'm hearing voices,' they're going to lock you up for psychiatric

214

MATRIX OF THE MIND

evaluation."

The thing that's missing from his bag -- the lack of which makes it hard to prove he isn't crazy -- is even a single document that would buttress the implausible notion that the government is currently targeting a large group of American citizens with mind-control technology. The only direct evidence for that, Girard admits, lies with alleged victims such as himself.

And of those, there are many.

It's 9:01 P.M. when the first person speaks during the Saturday conference call.

Unsure whether anyone else is on the line yet, the female caller throws out the first question: "You got gang stalking or V2K?" she asks no one in particular.

There's a short, uncomfortable pause.

"V2K, really bad. 24-7," a man replies.

"Gang stalking," another woman says.

"Oh, yeah, join the club," yet another man replies.

The members of this confessional "club" are not your usual victims. This isn't a group for alcoholics, drug addicts or survivors of childhood abuse; the people connecting on the call are self-described victims of mind control -- people who believe they have been targeted by a secret government program that tracks them around the clock, using technology to probe and control their minds.

The callers frequently refer to themselves as TIs, which is short for Targeted Individuals, and talk about V2K -- the official military abbreviation stands for "voice

to skull" and denotes weapons that beam voices or sounds into the head. In their esoteric lexicon, "gang stalking" refers to the belief that they are being followed and harassed: by neighbors, strangers or colleagues who are agents for the government.

A few more "hellos" are exchanged, interrupted by beeps signaling late arrivals: Bill from Columbus, Barbara from Philadelphia, Jim from California and a dozen or so others.

Derrick Robinson, the conference call moderator, calls order.

"It's five after 9," says Robinson, with the sweetly reasonable intonation of a late-night radio host. "Maybe we should go ahead and start."

The idea of a group of people convinced they are targeted by weapons that can invade their minds has become a cultural joke, shorthanded by the image of solitary lunatics wearing tinfoil hats to deflect invisible mind beams. "Tinfoil hat," says Wikipedia, has become "a popular stereotype and term of derision; the phrase serves as a byword for paranoia and is associated with conspiracy theorists."

In 2005, a group of MIT students conducted a formal study using aluminum foil and radio signals. Their surprising finding: Tinfoil hats may actually amplify radio frequency signals. Of course, the tech students meant the study as a joke.

But during the Saturday conference call, the subject of aluminum foil is deadly serious. The MIT study had prompted renewed debate; while a few TIs realized it was a joke at their expense, some saw the findings as an explanation for why tinfoil didn't seem to stop the voices. Others vouched for the material.

"Tinfoil helps tremendously," reports one conference call participant, who describes wrapping it around her body underneath her clothing.

"Where do you put the tinfoil?" a man asks.

"Anywhere, everywhere," she replies. "I even put it in a hat."

A TI in an online mind-control forum recommends a Web site called "Block EMF" (as in electromagnetic frequencies), which advertises a full line of clothing, including aluminum-lined boxer shorts described as a "sheer, comfortable undergarment you can wear over your regular one to shield yourself from power lines and computer electric fields, and microwave, radar, and TV radiation." Similarly, a tinfoil hat disguised as a regular baseball cap is "smart and subtle."

For all the scorn, the ranks of victims -- or people who believe they are victims -- are speaking up. In the course of the evening, there are as many as 40 clicks from people joining the call, and much larger numbers participate in the online forum, which has 143 members. A note there mentioning interest from a journalist prompted more than 200 e-mail responses.

Until recently, people who believe the government is beaming voices into their heads would have added social isolation to their catalogue of woes. But now, many have discovered hundreds, possibly thousands, of others just like them all over the world. Web sites dedicated to electronic harassment and gang stalking have popped up in India, China, Japan, South Korea, the United Kingdom, Russia and elsewhere. Victims have begun to host support meetings in major cities, including Washington. Favorite topics at the meetings include lessons on how to build shields (the proverbial tinfoil hats), media and PR training, and possible legal strategies for outlawing mind control.

The biggest hurdle for TIs is getting people to take their concerns seriously. A proposal made in 2001 by Rep. Dennis Kucinich (D-Ohio) to ban "psychotronic weapons" (another common term for mind-control technology) was hailed by TIs as a great step forward. But the bill was widely derided by bloggers and columnists and quickly dropped.

Doug Gordon, Kucinich's spokesman, would not discuss mind control other than to say the proposal was part of broader legislation outlawing weapons in space. The bill was later reintroduced, minus the mind control. "It was not the concentration of the legislation, which is why it was tightened up and redrafted," was all Gordon would say.

Unable to garner much support from their elected representatives, TIs have started their own PR campaign. And so, last spring, the Saturday conference calls centered on plans to hold a rally in Washington. A 2005 attempt at a rally drew a few dozen people and was ultimately rained out; the TIs were determined to make another go of it. Conversations focused around designing T-shirts, setting up congressional appointments, fundraising, creating a new Web site and formalizing a slogan. After some debate over whether to focus on gang stalking or mind control, the group came up with a compromise slogan that covered both: "Freedom From Covert Surveillance and Electronic Harassment."

Conference call moderator Robinson, who says his gang stalking began when he worked at the National Security Agency in the 1980s, offers his assessment of the group's prospects: Maybe this rally wouldn't produce much press, but it's a first step. "I see this as a movement," he says. "We're picking up people all the time."

Harlan Girard says his problems began in 1983, while he was a real estate developer in Los Angeles. The harassment was subtle at first: One day a woman pulled up in a car, wagged her finger at him, then sped away; he saw people running underneath his window at night; he noticed some of his neighbors seemed to be watching him; he heard someone moving in the crawl space under his apartment at night.

Girard sought advice from this then-girlfriend, a practicing psychologist, whom he declines to identify. He says she told him, "Nobody can become psychotic in their late 40s." She said he didn't seem to manifest other symptoms of psychotic behavior -- he dressed well, paid his bills -- and, besides his claims of surveillance, which sounded paranoid, he behaved normally. "People who are psychotic are socially isolated," he recalls her saying.

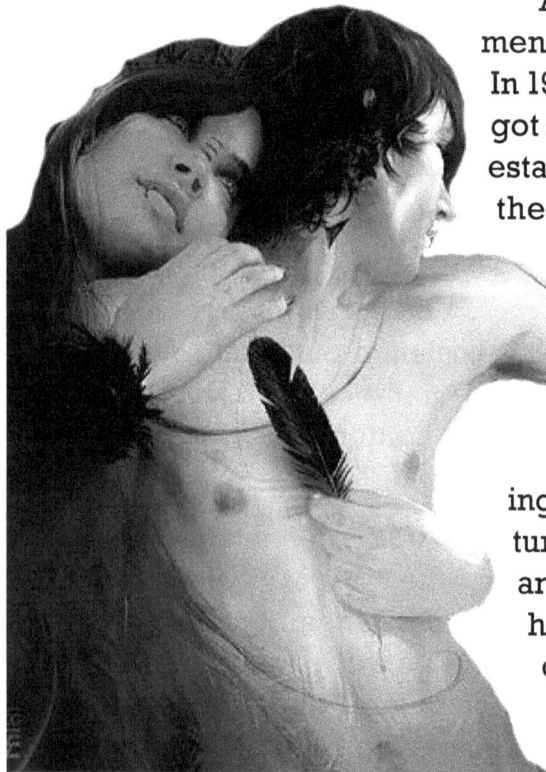

After a few months, Girard says, the harassment abruptly stopped. But the respite didn't last. In 1984, appropriately enough, things got seriously weird. He'd left his real estate career to return to school at the University of Pennsylvania, where he was study-

ing for a master's degree in landscape architecture. He harbored dreams of designing parks and public spaces. Then, he says, he began to hear voices. Girard could distinguish several different male voices, which came complete with a mental image of how the voices were being generated: from a recording studio, with "four slops sitting around a card table drinking beer," he says.

The voices were crass but also strangely courteous, addressing him as "Mr. Girard."

They taunted him. They asked him if he thought he was normal; they suggested he was going crazy. They insulted his classmates: When an overweight student showed up for a field trip in a white raincoat, they said, "Hey, Mr. Girard, doesn't she look like a refrigerator?"

Six months after the voices began, they had another question for him: "Mr. Girard, Mr. Girard. Why aren't you dead yet?" At first, he recalls, the voices would speak just two or three times a day, but it escalated into a near-constant cacophony, often accompanied by severe pain all over his body -- which Girard now attributes to directed-energy weapons that can shoot invisible beams.

The voices even suggested how he could figure out what was happening to him. He says they told him to go to the electrical engineering department to "tell them you're writing science fiction and you don't want to write anything inconsistent with physical reality. Then tell them exactly what has happened."

Girard went and got some rudimentary explanations of how technology could explain some of the things he was describing.

"Finally, I said: 'Look, I must come to the point, because I need answers. This is happening to me; it's not science fiction.'" They laughed.

He got the same response from friends, he says. "They regarded me as crazy, which is a humiliating experience."

When asked why he didn't consult a doctor about the voices and the pain, he says, "I don't dare start talking to people because of the potential stigma of it all. I don't want to be treated differently. Here I was in Philadelphia. Something was going on, I don't know any doctors . . . I know somebody's doing something to me."

It was a struggle to graduate, he says, but he was determined, and he persevered. In 1988, the same year he finished his degree, his father died, leaving Girard an inheritance large enough that he did not have to work.

So, instead of becoming a landscape architect, Girard began a full-time investigation of what was happening to him, often traveling to Washington in pursuit of government documents relating to mind control. He put an ad in a magazine seeking other victims. Only a few people responded. But over the years, as he met more and more people like himself, he grew convinced that he was part of what he calls an "electronic concentration camp."

What he was finding on his research trips also buttressed his belief: Girard learned that in the 1950s, the CIA had drugged unwitting victims with LSD as part of a rogue mind-control experiment called MK-ULTRA. He came across references to the CIA seeking to influence the mind with electromagnetic fields. Then he found references in an academic research book to work that military researchers at Walter Reed Army Institute of Research had done in the 1970s with pulsed microwaves to transmit words that a subject would hear in his head. Elsewhere, he came across references to attempts to use electromagnetic energy, sound waves or microwave beams to cause non-lethal pain to the body. For every symptom he experienced, he believed he found references to a weapon that could cause it.

How much of the research Girard cites checks out?

MATRIX OF THE MIND

Concerns about microwaves and mind control date to the 1960s, when the U.S. government discovered that its embassy in Moscow was being bombarded by low-level electromagnetic radiation. In 1965, according to declassified Defense Department documents, the Pentagon, at the behest of the White House, launched Project Pandora, top-secret research to explore the behavioral and biological effects of low-level microwaves. For approximately four years, the Pentagon conducted secret research: zapping monkeys; exposing unwitting sailors to microwave radiation; and conducting a host of other unusual experiments (a sub-project of Project Pandora was titled Project Bizarre). The results were mixed, and the program was plagued by disagreements and scientific squabbles. The "Moscow signal," as it was called, was eventually attributed to eavesdropping, not mind control, and Pandora ended in 1970. And with it, the military's research into so-called non-thermal microwave effects seemed to die out, at least in the unclassified realm.

But there are hints of ongoing research: An academic paper written for the Air Force in the mid-1990s mentions the idea of a weapon that would use sound waves to send words into a person's head. "The signal can be a 'message from God' that can warn the enemy of impending doom, or encourage the enemy to surrender," the author concluded.

In 2002, the Air Force Research Laboratory patented precisely such a technology: using microwaves to send words into someone's head. That work is frequently cited on mind-control Web sites. Rich Garcia, a spokesman for the research laboratory's directed energy directorate, declined to discuss that patent or current or related research in the field, citing the lab's policy not to comment on its microwave work.

In response to a Freedom of Information Act request filed for this article, the Air Force released unclassified documents surrounding that 2002 patent -- records that note that the patent was based on human experimentation in October 1994 at the Air Force lab, where scientists were able to transmit phrases into the heads of human subjects, albeit with marginal intelligibility. Research appeared to continue at least through 2002. Where this work has gone since is unclear -- the research laboratory, citing classification, refused to discuss it or release other materials.

The official U.S. Air Force position is that there are no non-thermal effects of microwaves. Yet Dennis Bushnell, chief scientist at NASA's Langley Research Center, tagged microwave attacks against the human brain as part of future warfare in a 2001 presentation to the National Defense Industrial Association about "Future Strategic Issues."

"That work is exceedingly sensitive" and unlikely to be reported in any unclassified documents, he says.

Meanwhile, the military's use of weapons that employ electromagnetic radiation to create pain is well-known, as are some of the limitations of such weapons. In 2001, the Pentagon declassified one element of this research: the Active Denial System, a weapon that uses electromagnetic radiation to heat skin and create an intense burning sensation. So, yes, there is technology designed to beam painful invisible rays at humans, but the weapon seems to fall far short of what could account for many of the TIs' symptoms. While its exact range is classified, Doug Beason, an expert in directed-energy weapons, puts it at about 700 meters, and the beam cannot penetrate a number of materials, such as aluminum. Considering the size of the full-scale weapon, which resembles a satellite dish, and its operational limitations, the ability of the government or anyone else to shoot beams at hundreds of people -- on city streets, into their homes and while they travel in cars and planes -- is beyond improbable.

But, given the history of America's clandestine research, it's reasonable to assume that if the defense establishment could develop mind-control or long-distance ray weapons, it almost certainly would. And, once developed, the possibility that they might be tested on innocent civilians could not be categorically dismissed.

Girard, for his part, believes these weapons were not only developed but were also tested on him more than 20 years ago.

What would the government gain by torturing him? Again, Girard found what he believed to be an explanation, or at least a precedent: During the Cold War, the government conducted radiation experiments on scores of unwitting victims, essentially using them as human guinea pigs. Girard came to believe that he, too, was a walking experiment.

Not that Girard thinks his selection was totally random: He believes he was targeted because of a disparaging remark he made to a Republican fundraiser about George H.W. Bush in the early 1980s. Later, Girard says, the voices confirmed his suspicion.

"One night I was going to bed; the usual drivel was going on," he says "The constant stream of drivel. I was just about to go to bed, and a voice says: 'Mr. Girard, do you know who was in our studio with us? That was George Bush, vice president of the United States.'"

Girard's story, however strange, reflects what TIs around the world report: a chance encounter with a government agency or official, followed by surveillance and gang stalking, and then, in many cases, voices, and pain similar to electric shocks. Some in the community have taken it upon themselves to document as

MATRIX OF THE MIND

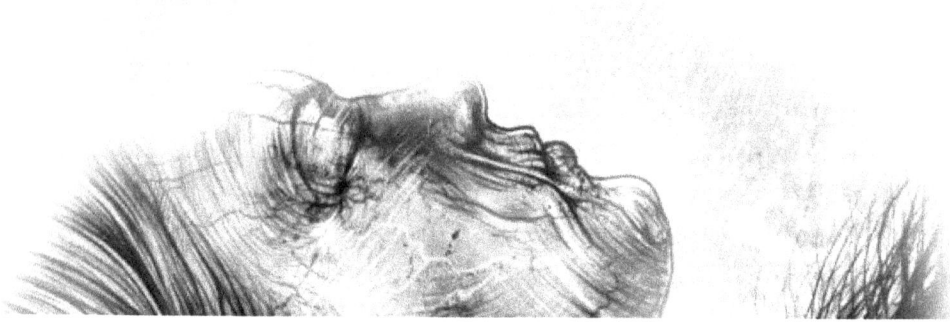

many cases as possible. One TI from California conducted about 50 interviews, narrowing the symptoms down to several major areas: "ringing in the ears," "manipulation of body parts," "hearing voices," "piercing sensation on skin," "sinus problems" and "sexual attacks." In fact, the TI continued, "many report the sensation of having their genitalia manipulated."

Both male and female TIs report a variety of "attacks" to their sexual organs. "My testicles became so sore I could barely walk," Girard says of his early experiences. Others, however, report the attacks in the form of sexual stimulation, including one TI who claims he dropped out of the seminary after constant sexual stimulation by directed-energy weapons. Susan Sayler, a TI in San Diego, says many women among the TIs suffer from attacks to their sexual organs but are often embarrassed to talk about it with outsiders.

"It's sporadic, you just never know when it will happen," she says. "A lot of the women say it's as soon as you lay down in bed -- that's when you would get hit the worst. It happened to me as I was driving, at odd times."

What made her think it was an electronic attack and not just in her head? "There was no sexual attraction to a man when it would happen. That's what was wrong. It did not feel like a muscle spasm or whatever," she says. "It's so . . . electronic."

Gloria Naylor, a renowned African American writer, seems to defy many of the stereotypes of someone who believes in mind control. A winner of the National Book Award, Naylor is best known for her acclaimed novel, The Women of Brewster Place, which described a group of women living in a poor urban neighborhood and was later made into a miniseries by Oprah Winfrey.

But in 2005, she published a lesser-known work, 1996, a semi-autobiographical book describing her experience as a TI. "I didn't want to tell this story. It's going to take courage. Perhaps more courage than I possess, but they've left me no alternatives," Naylor writes at the beginning of her book. "I am in a battle for my mind. If I stop now, they'll have won, and I will lose myself." The book is coherent, if hard to believe. It's also marked by disturbing passages describing how

MATRIX OF THE MIND

Jewish American agents were responsible for Naylor's surveillance. "Of the many cars that kept coming and going down my road, most were driven by Jews," she writes in the book. When asked about that passage in a recent interview, she defended her logic: Being from New York, she claimed, she can recognize Jews.

Naylor lives on a quiet street in Brooklyn in a majestic brownstone with an interior featuring intricate woodwork and tasteful decorations that attest to a successful literary career. She speaks about her situation calmly, occasionally laughing at her own predicament and her struggle with what she originally thought was mental illness. "I would observe myself," she explains. "I would lie in bed while the conversations were going on, and I'd ask: Maybe it is schizophrenia?

Like Girard, Naylor describes what she calls "street theater" -- incidents that might be dismissed by others as coincidental, but which Naylor believes were set up. She noticed suspicious cars driving by her isolated vacation home. On an airplane, fellow passengers mimicked her every movement -- like mimes on a street.

Voices similar to those in Girard's case followed -- taunting voices cursing her, telling her she was stupid, that she couldn't write. Expletive-laced language filled her head. Naylor sought help from a psychiatrist and received a prescription for an antipsychotic drug. But the medication failed to stop the voices, she says, which only added to her conviction that the harassment was real.

For almost four years, Naylor says, the voices prevented her from writing. In 2000, she says, around the time she discovered the mind-control forums, the voices stopped and the surveillance tapered off. It was then that she began writing 1996 as a "catharsis."

Colleagues urged Naylor not to publish the book, saying she would de-

MATRIX OF THE MIND

stroy her reputation. But she did publish, albeit with a small publishing house. The book was generally ignored by critics but embraced by TIs.

Naylor is not the first writer to describe such a personal descent. Evelyn Waugh, one of the great novelists of the 20th century, details similar experiences in The Ordeal of Gilbert Pinfold. Waugh's book, published in 1957, has eerie similarities to Naylor's.

Embarking on a recuperative cruise, Pinfold begins to hear voices on the ship that he believes are part of a wireless system capable of broadcasting into his head; he believes the instigator recruited fellow passengers to act as operatives; and he describes "performances" put on by passengers directed at him yet meant to look innocuous to others.

Waugh wrote his book several years after recovering from a similar episode and realizing that the voices and paranoia were the result of drug-induced hallucinations.

Naylor, who hasn't written a book since 1996, is now back at work on an historical novel she hopes will return her to the literary mainstream. She remains convinced that she was targeted by mind control. The many echoes of her ordeal she sees on the mind-control forums reassure her she's not crazy, she says.

Of course, some of the things she sees on the forum do strike her as crazy. "But who I am to say?" she says. "Maybe I sound crazy to somebody else."

Some TIs, such as Ed Moore, a young medical doctor, take a slightly more skeptical approach. He criticizes what he calls the "wacky claims" of TIs who blame various government agencies or groups of people without any proof. "I have yet to see a claim of who is behind this that has any data to support it," he writes.

Nonetheless, Moore still believes the voices in his head are the result of mind control and that the U.S. government is the most likely culprit. Moore started hearing voices in 2003, just as he completed his medical residency in anesthesiology; he was pulling an all-nighter studying for board exams when he heard voices coming from a nearby house commenting on him, on his abilities as a doctor, on his sanity. At first, he thought he was simply overhearing conversations through walls (much as Waugh's fictional alter ego first thought), but when no one else could hear the voices, he realized they were in his head. Moore went through a traumatic two years, including hospitalization for depression with auditory hallucinations.

"One tries to convince friends and family that you are being electronically harassed with voices that only you can hear," he writes in an e-mail. "You learn to stop doing that. They don't believe you, and they become sad and concerned,

MATRIX OF THE MIND

and it amplifies your own depression when you have voices screaming at you and your friends and family looking at you as a helpless, sick, mentally unbalanced wreck."

He says he grew frustrated with anti-psychotic medications meant to stop the voices, both because the treatments didn't work and because psychiatrists showed no interest in what the voices were telling him. He began to look for some other way to cope.

"In March of 2005, I started looking up support groups on the Internet," he wrote. "My wife would cry when she would see these sites, knowing I still heard voices, but I did not know what else to do." In 2006, he says, his wife, who had stood by him for three years, filed for divorce.

Moore, like other TIs, is cautious about sharing details of his life. He worries about looking foolish to friends and colleagues -- but he says that risk is ultimately worthwhile if he can bring attention to the issue.

With his father's financial help, Moore is now studying for an electrical engineering degree at the University of Texas at San Antonio, hoping to prove that V2K, the technology to send voices into people's heads, is real. Being in school, around other people, helps him cope, he writes, but the voices continue to taunt him.

Recently, he says, they told him: "We'll never stop [messing] with you."

A week before the TIs rally on the National Mall, John Alexander, one of the people whom Harlan Girard holds personally responsible for the voices in his head, is at a Chili's restaurant in Crystal City explaining over a Philly cheese steak and fries why the United States needs mind-control weapons.

A former Green Beret who served in Vietnam, Alexander went on to a number of national security jobs, and rubbed shoulders with prominent military and political leaders. Long known for taking an interest in exotic weapons, his 1980 article, "The New Mental Battlefield," published in the Army journal Military Review, is cited by self-described victims as proof of his complicity in mind control. Now retired from the government and living in Las Vegas, Alexander continues to advise the military. He is in the Washington area that day for an official meeting.

Beneath a shock of white hair is the mind of a self-styled military thinker. Alexander belongs to a particular set of Pentagon advisers who consider themselves defense intellectuals, focusing on big-picture issues, future threats and new capabilities. Alexander's career led him from work on sticky foam that would stop an enemy in his or her tracks to dalliances in paranormal studies and psychics, which he still defends as operationally useful.

MATRIX OF THE MIND

In an earlier phone conversation, Alexander said that in the 1990s, when he took part in briefings at the CIA, there was never any talk of "mind control, or mind-altering drugs or technologies, or anything like that."

According to Alexander, the military and intelligence agencies were still scared by the excesses of MK-ULTRA, the infamous CIA program that involved, in part, slipping LSD to unsuspecting victims. "Until recently, anything that smacked of [mind control] was extremely dangerous" because Congress would simply take the money away, he said.

Alexander acknowledged that "there were some abuses that took place," but added that, on the whole, "I would argue we threw the baby out with the bath water."

But September 11, 2001, changed the mood in Washington, and some in the national security community are again expressing interest in mind control, particularly a younger generation of officials who weren't around for MK-ULTRA. "It's interesting, that it's coming back," Alexander observed.

While Alexander scoffs at the notion that he is somehow part of an elaborate plot to control people's minds, he acknowledges support for learning how to tap into a potential enemy's brain. He gives as an example the possible use of functional magnetic resonance imaging, or fMRI, for lie detection. "Brain mapping" with fMRI theoretically could allow interrogators to know when someone is lying by watching for activity in particular parts of the brain. For interrogating terrorists, fMRI could come in handy, Alexander suggests. But any conceivable use of the technique would fall far short of the kind of mind-reading TIs complain about.

Alexander also is intrigued by the possibility of using electronic means to modify behavior. The dilemma of the war on terrorism, he notes, is that it never ends. So what do you do with enemies, such as those at Guantanamo: keep them there forever? That's impractical. Behavior modification could be an alternative, he says.

"Maybe I can fix you, or electronically neuter you, so it's safe to release you into society, so you won't come back and kill me," Alexander says. It's only a matter of time before technology allows that scenario to come true, he continues. "We're now getting to where we can do that." He pauses for a moment to take a bite of his sandwich. "Where does that fall in the ethics spectrum? That's a really tough question."

When Alexander encounters a query he doesn't want to answer, such as one about the ethics of mind control, he smiles and raises his hands level to his chest, as if balancing two imaginary weights. In one hand is mind control and the

MATRIX OF THE MIND

sanctity of free thought -- and in the other hand, a tad higher -- is the war on terrorism.

But none of this has anything to do with the TIs, he says. "Just because things are secret, people tend to extrapolate. Common sense does not prevail, and even when you point out huge leaps in logic that just cannot be true, they are not dissuaded."

What is it that brings someone, even an intelligent person, to ascribe the experience of hearing disembodied voices to government weapons?

In her book, Abducted, Harvard psychologist Susan Clancy examines a group that has striking parallels to the TIs: people who believe they've been kidnapped by aliens. The similarities are often uncanny: Would-be abductees describe strange pains, and feelings of being watched or targeted. And although the alleged abductees don't generally have auditory hallucinations, they do sometimes believe that their thoughts are controlled by aliens, or that they've been implanted with advanced technology.

(On the online forum, some TIs posted vociferous objections to the parallel, concerned that the public finds UFOs even weirder than mind control. "It will keep us all marginalized and discredited," one griped.)

Clancy argues that the main reason people believe they've been abducted by aliens is that it provides them with a compelling narrative to explain their perception that strange things have happened to them, such as marks on their bodies (marks others would simply dismiss as bruises), stimulation to their sexual organs (as the TIs describe) or feelings of paranoia. "It's not just an explanation for

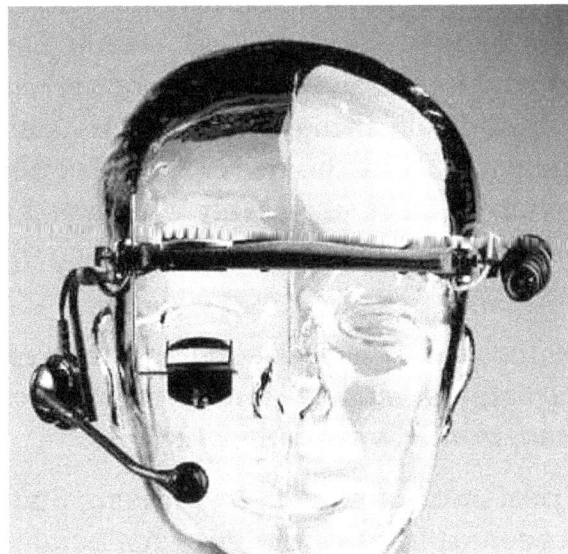

your problems; it's a source of meaning for your life," Clancy says.

In the case of TIs, mind-control weapons are an explanation for the voices they hear in their head. Socrates heard a voice and thought it was a demon; Joan of Arc heard voices from God. As one TI noted in an e-mail: "Each person undergoing this harassment is looking for the solution to the problem. Each person analyzes it through his or her own particular spectrum of beliefs. If you are a scientific-minded person, then you will probably analyze the situation from that perspective and conclude it must be done with some kind of electronic devices. If you are a religious person, you will see it as a struggle between the elements of whatever religion you believe in. If you are maybe, perhaps more eccentric, you may think that it is alien in nature."

Or, if you happen to live in the United States in the early 21st century, you may fear the growing power of the NSA, CIA and FBI.

Being a victim of government surveillance is also, arguably, better than being insane. In Waugh's novella based on his own painful experience, when Pinfold concludes that hidden technology is being used to infiltrate his brain, he "felt nothing but gratitude in his discovery." Why? "He might be unpopular; he might be ridiculous; but he was not mad."

Ralph Hoffman, a professor of psychiatry at Yale who has studied auditory hallucinations, regularly sees people who believe the voices are a part of government harassment (others believe they are God, dead relatives or even ex-girlfriends). Not all people who hear voices are schizophrenic, he says, noting that people can hear voices episodically in highly emotional states. What exactly causes these voices is still unknown, but one thing is certain: People who think the voices are caused by some external force are rarely dissuaded from their delusional belief, he says. "These are highly emotional and gripping experiences that are so compelling for them that ordinary reality seems bland."

Perhaps because the experience is so vivid, he says, even some of those who improve through treatment merely decide the medical regimen somehow helped protect their brain from government weapons.

Scott Temple, a professor of psychiatry at Penn State University who has been involved in two recent studies of auditory hallucinations, notes that those

who suffer such hallucinations frequently lack insight into their illness. Even among those who do understand they are sick, "that awareness comes and goes," he says. "People feel overwhelmed, and the delusional interpretations return."

Back at the Philadelphia train station, Girard seems more agitated. In a meeting the week before, his "handlers" had spoken to him only briefly -- they weren't in the right position to attack him, Girard surmises, based on the lack of voices. Today, his conversation jumps more rapidly from one subject to the next: victims of radiation experiments, his hatred of George H.W. Bush, MK-ULTRA, his personal experiences.

Asked about his studies at Penn, he replies by talking about his problems with reading: "I told you, everything I write they dictate to me," he says, referring again to the voices. "When I read, they're reading to me. My eyes go across; they're moving my eyes down the line. They're reading it to me. When I close the book, I can't remember a thing I read. That's why they do it."

The week before, Girard had pointed to only one person who appeared suspicious to him -- a young African American man reading a book; this time, however, he hears more voices, which leads him to believe the station is crawling with agents.

"Let's change our location," Girard says after a while. "I'm sure they have 40 or 50 people in here today. I escaped their surveillance last time -- they won't let that happen again."

Asked to explain the connection between mind control and the University of Pennsylvania, which Girard alleges is involved in the conspiracy, he begins to talk about defense contractors located near the Philadelphia campus: "General Electric was right next to the parking garage; General Electric Space Systems occupies a huge building right over there. From that building, you could see into the studio where I was doing my work most of the time. I asked somebody what they were doing there. You know, it had to do with computers. GE Space Systems. They were supposed to be tracking missile debris from this location . . . pardon me. What was your question again?"

Yet many parts of Girard's life seem to reflect that of any affluent 70-year-old bachelor. He travels frequently to France for extended vacations and takes part in French cultural activities in Philadelphia. He has set up a travel scholarship at the Cleveland Institute of Art in the name of his late mother, who attended school there (he changed his last name 27 years ago for "personal reasons"), and he travels to meet the students who benefit from the fund. And while the bulk of his time is spent on his research and writing about mind control, he has other interests. He follows politics and describes outings with friends and family members with whom

MATRIX OF THE MIND

he doesn't talk about mind control, knowing they would view it skeptically.

Girard acknowledges that some of his experiences mirror symptoms of schizophrenia, but asked if he ever worried that the voices might in fact be caused by mental illness, he answers sharply with one word: "No."

How, then, does he know the voices are real?

"How do you know you know anything?" Girard replies. "How do you know I exist? How do you know this isn't a dream you're having, from which you'll wake up in a few minutes? I suppose that analogy is the closest thing: You know when you have a dream. Sometimes it could be perfectly lucid, but you know it's a dream."

The very "realness" of the voices is the issue -- how do you disbelieve something you perceive as real? That's precisely what Hoffman, the Yale psychiatrist, points out: So lucid are the voices that the sufferers -- regardless of their educational level or self-awareness -- are unable to see them as anything but real. "One thing I can assure you," Hoffman says, "is that for them, it feels real."

It looks like almost any other small political rally in Washington. Posters adorn the gate on the southwest side of the Capitol Reflecting Pool, as attendees set up a table with press materials, while volunteers test a loudspeaker and set out coolers filled with bottled water. The sun is out, the weather is perfect, and an eclectic collection of people from across the country has gathered to protest mind control.

There is not a tinfoil hat to be seen. Only the posters and paraphernalia hint at the unusual. "Stop USA electronic harassment," urges one poster. "Directed Energy Assaults," reads another. Smaller signs in the shape of tombstones say, "RIP MKULTRA." The main display, set in front of the speaker's lectern has a more extended message: "HELP STOP HI-TECH ASSAULT PSYCHOTRONIC TORTURE."

About 35 TIs show up for the June rally, in addition to a few friends and family members. Speakers alternate between giving personal testimonials and descriptions of research into mind-control technology. Most of the gawkers at the rally are foreign tourists. A few hecklers snicker at the signs, but mostly people are either confused or indifferent. The articles on mind control at the table -- from mainstream news magazines -- go untouched.

"How can you expect people to get worked up over this if they don't care about eavesdropping or eminent domain?" one man challenges after stopping to flip through the literature. Mary Ann Stratton, who is manning the table, merely shrugs and smiles sadly. There is no answer: Everyone at the rally acknowledges it is an uphill battle.

MATRIX OF THE MIND

In general, the outlook for TIs is not good; many lose their jobs, houses and family. Depression is common. But for many at the rally, experiencing the community of mind-control victims seems to help. One TI, a man who had been a rescue swimmer in the Coast Guard before voices in his head sent him on a downward spiral, expressed the solace he found among fellow TIs in a long e-mail to another TI: "I think that the only people that can help are people going through the same thing. Everyone else will not believe you, or they are possibly involved."

In the end, though, nothing could help him enough. In August 2006, he would commit suicide.

But at least for the day, the rally is boosting TI spirits. Girard, in what for him is an ebullient mood, takes the microphone. A small crowd of tourists gathers at the sidelines, listening with casual interest. With the Capitol looming behind him, he reaches the crescendo of his speech, rallying the attendees to remember an important thing: They are part of a single community.

"I've heard it said, 'We can't get anywhere because everyone's story is different.' We are all the same," Girard booms. "You knew someone with the power to commit you to the electronic concentration camp system."

Several weeks after the rally, Girard shows up for a meeting with a reporter at the stately Mayflower Hotel in Washington, where he has stayed frequently over the two decades he has traveled to the capital to battle mind control. He walks in with a lit cigarette, which he apologetically puts out after a hotel employee tells him smoking isn't allowed anymore. He is half an hour late -- delayed, he says, by a meeting on Capitol Hill. Wearing a monogrammed dress shirt and tie, he looks, as always, serious and professional.

Girard declines to mention whom on Capitol Hill he'd met with, other than to say it was a congressional staffer. Embarrassment is likely a factor: Girard readily acknowledges that most people he meets with, ranging from scholars to politicians, ignore his entreaties or dismiss him as a lunatic.

Lately, his focus is on his Web site, which he sees as the culmination of nearly a quarter-century of research. When completed, it will contain more than 300 pages of documents. What next? Maybe he'll move to France (there are victims there, too), or maybe the U.S. government will finally just kill him, he says.

Meanwhile, he is always searching for absolute proof that the government has decoded the brain. His latest interest is LifeLog, a project once funded by the Pentagon that he read about in Wired News. The article described it this way: "The embryonic LifeLog program would dump everything an individual does into a giant database: every e-mail sent or received, every picture taken, every Web page surfed, every phone call made, every TV show watched, every magazine read. All of this -- and more -- would combine with information gleaned from a variety of sources: a GPS transmitter to keep tabs on where that person went, audiovisual sensors to capture what he or she sees or says, and biomedical monitors to keep track of the individual's health."

Girard suggests that the government, using similar technology, has "catalogued" his life over the past two years -- every sight and sound (Evelyn Waugh, in his mind-control book, writes about his character's similar fear that his harassers were creating a file of his entire life).

Girard thinks the government can control his movements, inject thoughts into his head, cause him pain day and night. He believes that he will die a victim of mind control.

Is there any reason for optimism?

Girard hesitates, then asks a rhetorical question.

"Why, despite all this, why am I the same person? Why am I Harlan Girard?"

For all his anguish, be it the result of mental illness or, as Girard contends, government mind control, the voices haven't managed to conquer the thing that makes him who he is: Call it his consciousness, his intellect or, perhaps, his soul.

"That's what they don't yet have," he says. After 22 years, "I'm still me."

MATRIX OF THE MIND

THE SECRET AGENDA OF MIND CONTROL

Please note: the letters and numbers after each paragraph denote the book and page number from which the information was taken.

BB—Bluebird

MC—Mind Controllers

NB—A Nation Betrayed.

A declassified CIA document dated 7 Jan 1953 [1] describes the experimental creation of multiple personality in two 19-year old girls. "These subjects have clearly demonstrated that they can pass from a fully awake state to a deep H [hypnotic] controlled state by telephone, by receiving written matter, or by the use of code, signal, or words, and that control of those hypnotized can be passed from one individual to another without great difficulty. It has also been shown by experimentation with these girls that they can act as unwilling couriers for information purposes." BB 32

Under the provisions of the National Security Act of 1947, the CIA was established. One of the main areas investigated by the CIA was mind control. The behavior control program was motivated by Soviet, Chinese, and North Korean use of mind control techniques. The CIA originated its first program in 1950 under

MATRIX OF THE MIND

the name BLUEBIRD. MKULTRA officially began in 1953. It was closed in 1964. In 1973, tipped off about forthcoming investigations, CIA Director Richard Helms ordered the destruction of any MKULTRA records. [2] MC 3, 10, 17

The Senate Intelligence Committee did find some records during its investigation in 1976. Senator Frank Church, who led the congressional investigations of the CIA's unlawful actions, said that the agency was "a rogue elephant" operating above the law as it plotted assassinations, illegally spied on thousands of Americans, and even drugged our own citizens in its effort to develop new weapons for its covert arsenal. [3] In 1977, through a Freedom of Information Act request, 16,000 pages of mind control documents were found, held as part of the Agency's financial history. That is how much of this information has been pieced together. MC 5, 18, NB xvi, 38

C.I.A. Data Show 14-Year Project
On Controlling Human Behavior

The Central Intelligence Agency conducted a 14-year program to find ways to "control human behavior" through the use of chemical, biological and radiological material, according to agency documents made public today by John Marks, a freelance journalist.

Mr. Marks, an associate of the Center for National Security Studies, asserted at a news conference that Adm. Stansfield Turner, Director of Central Intelligence, in a letter to the Senate Select Committee on Intelligence last week, "seriously distorted" what the C.I.A. research programs involved.

Mr. Marks said that, based on documents about the program he had received under the Freedom of Information Act, he had concluded that Admiral Turner "seems to be practicing what used to be called 'a modified limited hangout'" when he called the agency's activity "a program of experimentation with drugs."

"To be sure, drugs were part of it," he said, "but so were such other techniques as electric shock, radiation, ultrasonics, psychosurgery, psychology, and incapacitating agents, all of which were referred to in documents I have received."

The documents made public today and the disclosure by the C.I.A. last week that it had found another cache of previously undiscovered records suggested broader experimentation on unwitting humans by the intelligence agency or its paid researchers than had been publicly known before. Mr. Marks said he had obtained or read about 1,000 C.I.A. documents, many of which were never turned over to the Senate intelligence committee for its 1975 investigation of agency activities.

C.I.A. spokesmen declined comment on Mr. Marks's charges. However, Admiral Turner told newsmen after leaving a meeting with senators that the agency was moving swiftly to review the documents it had found.

Mr. Marks distributed 20 documents that described the following incidents, among others:

In 1956, the C.I.A. contracted with a private physician to test "bulbocapnine," a drug that can cause stupor or induce a catatonic state, on monkeys and "convicts incarcerated at" an unnamed state penitentiary. The agency wanted to known [sic] if the drug caused the "loss of speech in man," "loss of sensitivity to pain -- loss of memory, loss of will power."

A letter from an unnamed C.I.A. official in 1949 discussed ways of killing people without leaving a trace. "I believe that there are two chemical substances which would be most useful in that they would leave no characteristic pathological findings, and the quantities needed could be easily transported to places where they were to be used," the letter said. The letter also suggested exposure of an individual to X-rays or to an environment in which he would freeze to death. If these methods were too difficult, two methods needing no special equipment, the letter said, would be to "smother the victim with a pillow or to strangle him with a wide piece of cloth, such as a bath towel."

Aware of

Questionable Nature

In 1952, two Russian agents who were "suspected of being doubled" were interrogated using "narcohypnotic" methods. Under medical cover, the documents said the two men were given sodium pentothal and a stimulant. One interrogation produced a "remarkable" regression, the papers said, during which "the subject actually relived certain past activities of his

MATRIX OF THE MIND

life, some dating back 15 years while, in addition, the subject totally accepted Mr. [name deleted] as an old and trusted and beloved personal friend whom the subject had known in years past in Georgia, U.S.S.R."

A summary of a 1953 meeting reported a suggestion that the C.I.A. work with scientists of an unidentified foreign government, since "that country allowed experiments with anthrax," a disease contracted from infected cattle and sheep, and the United States did not.

The documents given to Mr. Marks were heavily edited, apparently for security reasons, but they showed that even while the C.I.A. was operating this program it was conscious of its questionable nature.

One 1950 memorandum, on finding psychiatrists to conduct experiments, noted that one applicant's "ethics might be such that he might not care to cooperate in certain more revolutionary phases of our project." But it said another candidate's "ethics are such that he would be completely cooperative in any phase of our program, regardless of how revolutionary it may be."

A 1963 inspector general's report that apparently resulted in a program being discontinued noted "the concepts involved in manipulating human behavior are found by many people both within and outside the agency to be distasteful and unethical."

According to Mr. Marks's documents and an earlier Senate investigation, the C.I.A. conducted secret medical experiments from 1949 through 1963 under the code names Bluebird, Artichoke, MK Ultra and MK Delta. The C.I.A. inspector general's report in 1963 described the program as the "research and development of chemical, biological and radiological materials capable of employment in clandestine operations to control human behavior."

5,000 New Documents

Last week, Admiral Turner announced that the agency had discovered some 5,000 documents pertaining to the program that were not available to the Senate intelligence committee in 1975. They are financial records of the various experiments and include the names of doctors and medical institutions that performed the tests.

Today, Admiral Turner gave the members a closed-door briefing on the new material. He will appear before a joint public hearing of the intelligence committee and Senator Edward M. Kennedy's health subcommittee on July 29 to more fully describe the new findings. The intelligence committee staff will begin studying the documents later this week.

Under the Freedom of Information Act, private citizens can obtain heretofore secret government documents, provided they do not endanger current national security matters or disclose matters that could invade the privacy of other individuals.

Mr. Marks charged that it had taken him nearly two years of legal pressure to dislodge the material he had received. He said he had been promised the additional 5,000 documents before the end of the month.

A Secret Agenda Leads to First Mind Control Programs

Please note: the letters and numbers after each paragraph denote the book and page from which the information given was taken. BB stands for Bluebird; MC for Mind Controllers; NB for A Nation Betrayed. To order these books, see our Resource List: www.WantToKnow.info/resources#mindcontrol

A declassified CIA document dated 7 January 1953 [1] with a section heading "Outline of Special H Cases" describes the experimental creation of multiple personality in two 19-year old girls by the CIA. "H" is used as shorthand for hypnotic, hypnotized, or hypnotism in these documents: "These subjects have clearly demonstrated that they can pass from a fully awake state to a deep H controlled state by telephone, by receiving written matter, or by the use of code, signal, or words, and that control of those hypnotized can be passed from one individual to another without great difficulty. It has also been shown by experimentation with these girls that they can act as unwilling couriers for information purposes." BB 32

After the end of World War II, German scientists were being held in a variety of detainment camps by the allies and Russians. In 1946, President Truman authorized Project Paperclip [2][3][4] to exploit German scientists for American research, and to deny these intellectual resources to the Soviet Union. Some reports bluntly pointed out that they were "ardent Nazis." They were considered so vital to the "Cold War" effort, that they would be brought into the US and Canada. Some of these experts were accused of participating in murderous medical experiments on human subjects at concentration camps. A 1999 report to the Senate and the House said that "between 1945 and 1955, 765 scientists, engineers, and technicians were brought to the US under Paperclip and similar programs." [5] BB 3, NB xi, xii

According to the Central Intelligence Agency's Fact Book, [6] the NSC (National Security Council) and the CIA were established under the provisions of the National Security Act of 1947. In December 1947, the NSC held its first meeting. James Forrestal, the Secretary of Defense, pushed for the CIA to begin a 'secret war' against the Soviets. Forrestal's initiative led to the execution of psychological warfare operations (psy-ops) in Europe. CIA personnel were not opposed to working with Nazi doctors who had proven to be proficient in breaking the mind

MATRIX OF THE MIND

and rebuilding it. In some cases military bases were used to hide these covert activities. It was decided that the communist threat was an issue that took priority over constitutional rights. MC 1, 3, 7, 8, NB xvii

The concept of running a secret 'black' project was no longer novel. In 1941, Roosevelt had decided, without consulting Congress, that the US should proceed with the utmost secrecy to develop an atomic bomb. Secrecy shrouded the Manhattan Project (the atomic bomb program) to the extent that Vice President Harry Truman knew nothing about it. [7] The project meant that by 1947, the US Government had already gained vast experience in the initiation of secret operations. The existence of 'black projects' funded by 'black budgets' was withheld not only from the public, but also from Congress for reasons of national security. MC 8-10

A declassified CIA document [8] "Hypnotic Experimentation and Research, 10 February 1954" describes a simulation of relevance to the creation of unsuspecting assassins: "Miss [whited out] was instructed (having previously expressed a fear of firearms in any fashion) that she would use every method at her disposal to awaken Miss [whited out] (now in a deep hypnotic sleep). Failing this, she would pick up a pistol nearby and fire it at Miss [whited out]. She was instructed that her rage would be so great that she would not hesitate to "kill" [whited out] for failing to awaken. Miss [whited out] carried out these suggestions to the letter including firing the (unloaded) gun at [whited out] and then proceeded to fall into a deep sleep. Both were awakened and expressed complete amnesia for the entire sequence. Miss [whited out] was again handed the gun, which she refused (in an awakened state) to pick up or accept from the operator. She expressed absolute denial that the foregoing sequence had happened." BB 36, 37

One of the areas to be investigated by the CIA was mind control. The CIA's human behavior control program was chiefly motivated by perceived Soviet, Chinese, and North Korean use of mind control techniques. Under the protection of 'national security,' many other branches of the government also took part in the study of this area. The CIA originated its first program in 1950 under the name BLUEBIRD, which in 1951, after Canada and Britain had been included, was changed to ARTICHOKE. MKULTRA officially began in 1953. Technically it was closed in 1964, but some of its programs remained active under MKSEARCH well into the 1970s. In 1973, tipped off about forthcoming investigations, CIA Director Richard Helms ordered the destruction of any MKULTRA records. [9] MC 10, 17

Diligent use of the Freedom of Information Act (FOIA) helps to cast light on the advances that have been made in controlling the way people think and act. In 1977, through an FOIA request, 16,000 pages of documents were found, held as part of the Agency's financial history. That is how much of this information has been pieced together. The FOIA allows the most humble citizen to demand the

238

disclosure of documents, although inevitably some will be heavily censored or not released at all. MC 5 NB, xvi, xvii

Inevitably, however, it is an incomplete picture. Most of the important details were conveniently destroyed under orders of CIA Director Helms to conceal wrongdoing. [10] What the mind controllers were and are doing may be only hinted at in a memo footnote or in the memoirs of a retired researcher. Nevertheless, there is more than enough here to show that secret new techniques are being exploited that are no longer in the realm of science fiction. We must all be aware of this threat, so that those who wish to take liberties with democracy, and with our freedom to think, are deterred. MC 6, NB xvii

The CIA Mind Control Projects

Project BLUEBIRD was approved by the director of the CIA on April 20, 1950. In a 1951 memo, [11] Bluebird states that practical research was to be conducted to include these specific problems:

* Can we create by post-H [hypnotic] control an action contrary to an individual's basic moral principles?

* Can we in a matter of an hour, two hours, one day, etc., induce an H condition in an unwilling subject to such an extent that he will perform an act for our benefit?

* Could we seize a subject and in the space of an hour or two by post-H control have him crash an airplane, wreck a train, etc.?

* Can we by H and SI [sleep inducing] techniques force a subject to travel long distances, commit specified acts and return to us or bring documents or materials?

* Can we guarantee total amnesia under any and all conditions?

* Can we "alter" a person's personality?

* Can we devise a system for making unwilling subjects into willing agents and then transfer that control to untrained agency agents in the field by use of codes or identifying signs?

* How can sodium A or P or any other sleep inducing agent be best concealed in a normal or commonplace item, such as candy, cigarettes, coffee, tea, beer, medicines? [12] NB 13, 14, BB 23

Officially, MKULTRA was established on 13 April 1953, at Richard Helms' suggestion as "ultra sensitive work." [13] The operational wing of MKULTRA, known as MKDELTA, had as its mission to find out how to use chemical and biological weapon ingredients to alter the human mind. Originally established as a supplementary funding mechanism to the ARTICHOKE project, MKULTRA quickly grew into a mammoth undertaking that outflanked earlier mind control initiatives. MC 69, NB 28

[1] CIA MORI ID 190684, pp. 1, 4. This is a declassified CIA document dealing with mind control. To verify the statement in the text, use the FOIA (Freedom of Information Act) request as described on our ten-page mind control summary at http://www.WantToKnow.info/mindcontrol10pg#ciadocs. You should receive the government mind control CDs within a month of your request. For free, unlimited access to these documents, go to the Black Vault Government Archive at http://www.theblackvault.com/modules.php?name=core&showPage=true&pageID=23.

[2] New York Times, Aug. 2, 1977, Mind-Control Studies Had Origins in Trial of Mindszenty. This engaging article includes a concise history of mind control projects. The U.S. Department of Energy Website also provides a highly revealing, detailed report of these mind control projects and the destruction of their records at http://hss.energy.gov/healthsafety/ohre/roadmap/achre/chap3_4.html.

[3] Final Report. Book 1, Foreign and Military Intelligence. Senate Select Committee to Study Government Operations with Respect to Intelligence Activities, 94th Congress, 2nd Session, 26 April 1976, Special Report No. 94-755 (Better known as the Church Committee Report). See Book 1, p. 406. For a related article on George Washington University's National Security Archive website, see http://www.gwu.edu/~nsarchiv/news/20000817.

[4] CIA MORI ID 190691, p. 1. This is a declassified CIA document dealing with mind control. To verify the statement in the text, use the FOIA (Freedom of Information Act) request as described on our ten-page mind control summary at http://www.WantToKnow.info/mindcontrol10pg#ciadocs. You should receive the government mind control CDs within a month of your request. Once you receive them, look up the MORI ID number listed. For free, unlimited access to these documents, go to the Black Vault Government Archive at http://www.theblackvault.com/modules.php?name=core&showPage=true&pageID=23.

[5] CIA MORI ID 140401, pp. 6, 7. This is actually a declassified CIA document dealing with mind control from Project BLUEBIRD, the immediate precursor to MKULTRA. Its official estimated publication date is 1/1/52. The nature of the BLUEBIRD research was very similar that of the MKULTRA project. To order this highly revealing document go to:

http://www.foia.cia.gov/sample_request_letter.asp, and follow the instructions.

MATRIX OF THE MIND

For reasons unknown, this document is not included in the mind control CDs.

[6] Estabrooks, G.H. Hypnosis comes of age. Science Digest, 44-50, April 1971.

[7] Delgado, J.M.R. Evaluation of permanent implantation of electrodes within the brain. Electroencephalography and Clinical Neurophysiology, 7, 637-644, 1955.

[8] Delgado, J.M.R. Social rank and radio-stimulated aggressiveness in monkeys. Journal of Nervous and Mental Disease, 144, 383-390, 1967.

[9] Delgado, J.M.R. Physical Control of the Mind. New York: Harper & Row, 1971 (paperback 1977).

[10] New York Times, May 17, 1965, front page, 'Matador' With a Radio Stops Wired Bull; Modified Behavior in Animals Subject of Brain Study. Instructions to purchase this article from the New York Times archives and our free copy of the article are available at http://www.WantToKnow.info/650517nytimes.

[11] Faden, R.R. Final Report. Advisory Committee on Human Radiation Experiments. Washington, DC: US Government Printing Office, 1995. The full, highly revealing report is available on the U.S. Department of Energy Website at: http://www.hss.energy.gov/healthsafety/ohre/roadmap/achre/index.html. For the two pages detailing Dr. Sweet's experiments: Chapter five page 4, and page 5.

[12] Mark, V.H., & Ervin, F.R. Violence and the Brain. New York: Harper & Row, 19

[13] Gillmor, D. I Swear By Apollo. Dr. Ewen Cameron and the CIA-Brainwashing Experiments. Montreal: Eden press, 1987.

[14] Scheflin, A.W., & Opton, E.M. The Mind manipulators. New York: Paddington Press, 1978.

[15] Thomas, G. Journey into Madness. The Secret Story of Secret CIA Mind Control and Medical Abuse. New York: Bantam, 1989 (paperback 1990).

[16] Weinstein, H. Psychiatry and the CIA: Victims of Mind Control. Washington, DC: American Psychiatric Press, 1990.

[17] Collins, A. In the Sleep Room. The Story of CIA Brainwashing Experiments in Canada. Toronto: Key Porter Books, 1988/1998.

MATRIX OF THE MIND

[18] Cameron, D.E. Production of differential amnesia as a factor in the treatment of schizophrenia. Comprehensive Psychiatry, 1, 26-34, 1960.

[19] Cameron, D.E., Levy, L. Rubenstein, L., & Malmo, R.B. Repetition of verbal signals: Behavioral and physiological changes. American Journal of Psychiatry, 115, 985-991, 1959.

[20] CIA MORI ID 17748, pp. 2, 4, 6-9. This is a declassified CIA document dealing with mind control. To verify the statement in the text, use the FOIA (Freedom of Information Act) request as described on our ten-page mind control summary at http://www.WantToKnow.info/mindcontrol10pg#ciadocs. You should receive the mind control CDs within a month of your request. For free, unlimited access to these documents, go to the Black Vault Government Archive at http://www.theblackvault.com/modules.php?name=core&showPage=true&pageID=23.

A memorandum from Richard Helms, [14] Acting Deputy Director to CIA Director Allen Dulles dated 3 April 1953 and entitled "Two Extremely Sensitive Research Programs" (MKULTRA and MKDELTA) includes the statement, "Even internally in CIA, as few individuals as possible should be aware of our interest in these fields and of the identity of those who are working for us. At present this results in ridiculous contracts which do not spell out the scope or intent of the work." BB 125

The memorandum below was written 10 years later to Helms, who by then had become CIA Director.

MATRIX OF THE MIND

**26 July 1963, MEMORANDUM FOR: Director
of Central Intelligence [15]
SUBJECT: Report of Inspection, MKULTRA**

It was deemed advisable to prepare the report of the MKULTRA program in one copy only, in view of its unusual sensitivity. Normal procedures for project approval, funding, and accounting were waived. The program requires the services of highly specialized authorities in many fields of natural science. The concepts involved in manipulating human behavior are found by many people both within and outside the Agency to be distasteful and unethical. Nevertheless, there have been major accomplishments both in research and operational employment.

Over the ten-year life of the program many additional avenues to the control of human behavior have been designated under the MKULTRA charter, including radiation, electro-shock, harassment substances, and paramilitary devices. Some MKULTRA activities raise questions of legality implicit in the original charter. A final phase of the testing of MKULTRA products places the rights and interests of US citizens in jeopardy. Public disclosure of some aspects of MKULTRA activity could induce serious adverse reaction in US public opinion.

TSD [Technical Services Division of CIA] initiated a program for covert testing of materials on unwitting US citizens in 1955. TSD has pursued a philosophy of minimum documentation in keeping with the high sensitivity of some of the projects. Some files contained little or no data at all. There are just two individuals in TSD who have full substantive knowledge of the program and most of that knowledge is unrecorded. In protecting the sensitive nature of the American intelligence capability to manipulate human behavior, they apply "need to know" doctrine to their professional associates to a maximum degree.

J.S. Earman, Inspector General [NB 108-113 and footnote [15]]

The Senate Intelligence Committee did find some records during its investigation in 1976. [16] However it noted that the practice of MKULTRA was "to maintain no records of the planning and approval of test programs." Miles Copeland, a former CIA officer, said, "The congressional sub-committee which went into this got only the barest glimpse." [17] Senator Frank Church, who led the congressional investigations of the CIA's unlawful actions, said that the agency was "a rogue elephant" operating above the law as it plotted assassinations, illegally spied on thousands of Americans, and even drugged our own citizens in its effort to develop new weapons for its covert arsenal." MC 13, 18, NB 38

The focal point of MKULTRA was the use of humans as unwitting subjects [without their knowledge or consent]. The CIA sponsored numerous experiments of this kind. Regardless of a report by the CIA's Inspector General in 1963 recommending the termination of testing on unwitting subjects, future CIA Director Richard Helms continued to advocate covert testing on the grounds that "we are less capable of staying up with the Soviet advances in this field." On the subject of moral issues, Helms commented, "we have no answer to the moral issue." [18] MC 18

The Experience of CIA Mind Control Victim Carol Rutz [19]

The CIA bought my services from my grandfather in 1952 starting at the tender age of four. [20] Over the next 12 years, I was tested, trained, and used in various ways. Electroshock, drugs, hypnosis, sensory deprivation, and other types of trauma were used to make me compliant and split my personality [create multiple personalities for specific tasks]. Each alter or personality was created to respond to a post-hypnotic trigger, then perform an act and not remember it later. This "Manchurian Candidate" program was just one of the operational uses of the mind control scenario by the CIA. Your hard-earned tax dollars supported this.

As a survivor of CIA programs Bluebird/Artichoke and MKULTRA, I began my intense search to document some of the mind control experiments that I was made part of. Through a series of FOIA requests to various departments of the government, 48 years after I was first experimented on, I found solid proof of my memories—proof that was in the government vaults of the nearly 18,000 pages of declassified documents from the Bluebird/Artichoke and MKULTRA programs.

One of the declassified documents [21] states, "Learning studies will be instituted in which the subject will be rewarded or punished for overall performance and reinforced in various ways—with electric shock, etc. In other cases, drugs and psychological tricks will be used to modify attitudes. The experimenters will be particularly interested in dissociative states [multiple personality]. An attempt will be made to induce a number of states of this kind, using hypnosis." The government had finally handed me the validation I had been searching for. NB xvii, xviii

The basic premise of the book The Manchurian Candidate [22] is that a group

MATRIX OF THE MIND

of American POWs in the Korean War is brainwashed while crossing through Manchuria to freedom. They arrive back in the US amnesic for the period of brainwashing. One of them is programmed to be an assassin. His target is a candidate for president of the US. His handlers control him with a hypnotically implanted trigger. BB 23

In an experiment described in a document entitled "SI and H experimentation [23] (25 September 1951)," two female subjects took part in an exercise involving the planting of a bomb. Both subjects performed perfectly and were fully amnesic for the exercise: "[Whited out] was instructed that upon awakening, she would proceed to [whited out] room where she would wait at the desk for a telephone call. Upon receiving the call, a person known as "Jim" would engage her in normal conversation. During the course of the conversation, this individual would mention a code word. When she heard this code word, she would pass into a SI trance state, but would not close her eyes and remain perfectly normal and continue the telephone conversation.

She was told that upon conclusion of the telephone conversation, she would carry out instructions: [Whited out] was shown an electric timing device. She was informed that this device was a bomb, and was then instructed how to attach and set the device. After [whited out] learned how to set and attach the device, she was told to take the timing device which was in a briefcase, and proceed to the ladies room. In the ladies room, she would be met by a girl whom she had never seen who would identify herself by the code word "New York." [whited out] was then to show this individual how to attach and set the timing device and further instructions would be given that the timing device was to be carried in the briefcase to [whited out] room, placed in the nearest empty electric-light plug and concealed in the bottom, left-hand drawer of [whited out] desk, with the device set for 82 seconds and turned on." BB 37, 38

The Mind Control Doctors

In the second half of the 20th century, mind control projects resulted in extensive political abuse of psychiatry in North America. Many thousands of prisoners and mental patients were subjected to unethical mind control experiments by leading psychiatrists and medical schools. Organized academic psychiatry has never acknowledged this history. The network of mind control doctors involved has done a great deal of harm to the field of psychiatry and to psychiatric patients. BB, pg. K

The work of the mind control doctors did not occur in a vacuum. The importation of Nazi doctors to the US through secret programs like PAPERCLIP is part of the context. Mind control experimentation was not only tolerated by medical professionals, but published in psychiatric and medical journals. [24] The climate

245

MATRIX OF THE MIND

was permissive, supportive, and approving of mind control experimentation. BB 1

Dr. William Sweet [25] participated in both brain electrode implant experiments and the injection of uranium into medical patients at Harvard University. The 925-page Final Report. Advisory Committee on Human Radiation Experiments [26] tells the story of radiation experiments, and their linkage to mind control. BB 1

Martin Orne is one of the leading experts on hypnosis of the 20th century. [27][28][29] For about 30 years, he was the editor of The International Journal of Clinical and Experimental Hypnosis. Dr. Orne is one of two psychiatrists professionally still active into the late 1990's who is a documented CIA mind control contractor (along with Dr. Louis Jolyon West). BB 121, 124

P. Janet asked a "deeply hypnotized female to commit several murders before a distinguished group of judges, stabbing some victims with rubber daggers and poisoning others with sugar tablets." The hypnotized subject did all these things without hesitation. [30] MC 160

Army doctors were actively involved in LSD testing at least until the late 1970's. Subjects of LSD experiments included children as young as five years old, and brain electrodes were implanted in children as young as 11 years of age. Four of the CIA's MKULTRA Subprojects were on children. The mind control doctors included presidents of the American Psychiatric Association and psychiatrists who received full-page obituaries in the American Journal of Psychiatry. Responsibility for the unethical experimentation lies first with the individual doctors, but also collectively with the medical profession, and with academia as a whole. BB 21

The MKULTRA contractor about whom the most has been written is Dr. Ewen Cameron. [31][32][33][34][35] At various times, Dr. Cameron was President of the American, Canadian, and World Psychiatric Associations. He was one of four co-founders of the World Psychiatric Association. Dr. Cameron began conducting unethical, unscientific, and inhumane brainwashing experiments in the 1930's. Schizophrenic patients were forced to lie naked in red light for eight hours a day for periods as long as eight months. Another experiment involved overheating patients in an electric cage until their body temperatures reached 102 degrees. BB 125-128

From January 1957 until September 1960, Dr. Cameron's project received $64,242.44 in CIA funds. [36] When the CIA stopped funding him, Cameron received $57,750 from the Canadian government to continue his research from 1961 to 1964. [37] The actual number of patients on whom Cameron tried varieties of his experimental techniques is reported as 332. [38] NB 52, 53

Linda MacDonald was a victim of Dr. Ewen Cameron's unethical, destructive mind control experiments in 1963. Dr. Cameron used a "treatment" which

MATRIX OF THE MIND

involved intensive application of three brainwashing techniques; drug disinhibition, prolonged sleep, and prolonged psychological isolation. These were combined with ECT [Electro Convulsive Therapy] treatments. [39][40][41] The amount of electricity introduced into Linda's brain exceeded by 76.5 times the maximum amount recommended in the ECT Guidelines of the American Psychiatric Association. Dr. Cameron's "depatterning" technique resulted in permanent and complete amnesia. Dr. Cameron proved that doctors skilled in the right procedures can erase a subject's memory. To this day, Linda MacDonald is unable to remember anything from her birth to 1963. As recorded by nurses in her chart, Linda was completely disoriented. She didn't know her name, age or where she was. She didn't recognize her children. She couldn't read, drive, cook, or use a toilet. Not only did she not know her husband, she didn't even know what a husband was. BB 181-183

Life changed for Linda when the Canadian Broadcasting Corporation program, The Fifth Estate, aired a segment on Dr. Cameron on January 17, 1984. A Vancouver newspaper ran a full-page story on Robert Loggie, a Vancouver man who had been experimented on by Dr. Cameron. Loggie was a plaintiff in the class action suit against the CIA for Dr. Cameron's MKULTRA experiments, which was settled out of court for $750,000, divided among the eight plaintiffs in 1988. [42] Eventually Linda got $100,000 plus legal fees from the Canadian government. BB 187, 188

J.G. Watkins "induced a soldier to strike an officer by suggesting that the officer was a Japanese soldier." [43] In another experiment, two subjects who were told to throw sulphuric acid at a laboratory assistant (protected by glass) complied with the hypnotist's commands. [44] MC 158

G.H. Estabrooks is the only mind control doctor who has publicly acknowledged the building of Manchurian Candidates.

In his book Spiritism, [45] Dr. Estabrooks describes experiments done to create multiple personality. [46][47] In his book Hypnotism, [48] Dr. Estabrooks states that the creation of experimental multiple personality for operational use in military subjects, whom he refers to as super spies, is ethical because of the demands of war. BB 159, 162

In a 1971 article in Science Digest, [49] Dr. Estabrooks claimed to have created hypnotic couriers and counterintelligence agents for operational use. "By the 1920's not only had [clinical hypnotists] learned to apply posthypnotic suggestion, but also to split certain complex individuals into multiple personalities like Jeckyl-Hydes. During World War II, I worked this technique with a vulnerable Marine lieutenant I'll call Jones. I split his personality into Jones A and Jones B. Jones A, once a 'normal' working Marine, became entirely different. He talked

247

MATRIX OF THE MIND

communist doctrine and meant it. He was welcomed enthusiastically by communist cells, and was deliberately given a dishonorable discharge by the Corps and became a card-carrying party member. Jones B was the deeper personality, knew all the thoughts of Jones A, was a loyal American and was 'imprinted' to say nothing during conscious phases. All I had to do was hypnotize the whole man, get in touch with Jones B, the loyal American, and I had a pipeline straight into the Communist camp. It worked beautifully." BB 167-169

Dr. Estabrooks did experiments on children. He corresponded with FBI Director J. Edgar Hoover about using hypnosis to interrogate juvenile delinquents. His experimentation raises the possibility that he or other investigators might have attempted to create Manchurian Candidates in children. Such a possibility might seem far-fetched until one considers the LSD, biological and radiation experiments conducted on children, [50][51][52] and the fact that four MKULTRA Subprojects were on children. The deliberate creation of multiple personality in children is an explicitly stated plan in the MKULTRA Subproject Proposal submitted for funding on May 30, 1961. BB 61, 176, 177

LSD Tests

From 1950 until the 1970s, the CIA collaborated closely with the US Army while conducting LSD and other chemical tests on humans. Experiments were conducted where none of the volunteers gave their 'informed consent' prior to receiving LSD. There was a deliberate attempt to deny the volunteers any information that would have permitted them to evaluate the dangers involved. Most of the related records have been destroyed. [53] MC 20, 21, 29, 32

A field test plan called for use of LSD on foreign nationals overseas. The Surgeon General "offered no medical objections to the field experimental plan." [54] Subjects for the proposed field test were to be non-volunteer, foreign nationals. It is clear that from the start to finish the project violated Department of Defense policies, as well as specific procedures set for chemical or medical research. MC 33-36

Frank Olson was a biological warfare expert. He committed suicide (or was murdered) after being given LSD hidden in liqueur by Dr. Sidney Gottlieb, Director of MKULTRA. Olson's family determined that he committed suicide subsequent to a bad LSD trip only after reading Nelson Rockefeller's 1975 report on the CIA, finally published 22 years after Olsen's death. They were given $750,000 in compensation by Congress. [55] BB 49

Electronic Implants

Jose Delgado's development of the Stimoceiver in the 1950s brought intelligence agencies' ultimate dream of controlling human behavior one step closer to

248

reality. The Stimoceiver—a miniature electrode capable of receiving and transmitting electronic signals by FM radio—could be placed within an individual's cranium. And once in place, an outside operator could manipulate the subject's responses. Delgado demonstrated the potential of his Stimoceivers by wiring a fully-grown bull. With the device in place, Delgado stepped into the ring with the bull. The animal charged towards the experimenter – and then suddenly stopped, just before it reached him. The powerful beast had been stopped with the simple action of pushing a button on a small box held in Delgado's hand. [56] MC 147

Dr. Delgado, a neurosurgeon and professor at Yale, [57][58][59][60][61][62] received funding for brain electrode research on children and adults. He did research in monkeys and cats, and in one paper describes the cats as "mechanical toys." He was able to control the movements of his animal and human subjects by pushing buttons on a remote transmitter box. In 1966, Delgado asserted that his experiments "support the distasteful conclusion that motion, emotion and behavior can be directed by electrical forces, and that humans can be controlled like robots by push buttons." [63] BB 88, 89, MC 147

An 11-year old boy underwent a partial change of identity upon remote stimulation of his brain electrode: "Electrical stimulation of the superior temporal convolution induced confusion about his sexual identity. These effects were specific, reliable, and statistically significant. For example, the patient said, 'I was thinking whether I was a boy or a girl,' and 'I'd like to be a girl.'" After one of the stimulations the patient suddenly began to discuss his desire to marry the male interviewer. Temporal-lobe stimulation produced in another patient open manifestations and declarations of pleasure, accompanied by giggles and joking with the therapist. In two adult female patients stimulation of the same region was followed by discussion of marriage and expression of a wish to marry the therapist. [64] BB 88, 89

Brain electrode research was also conducted independently at Harvard by Dr. Delgado's coauthors, Drs. Vernon Mark, Frank Ervin, and William Sweet. Mark and Ervin describe implanting brain electrodes in a large number of patients at Harvard hospitals. A patient named Jennie was 14 years old when they put electrodes in her brain. In their book Violence and the Brain, [65] photographs show 18-year old Julia smiling, angry, or pounding the wall depending on which button is being pushed on the transmitter box sending signals to her brain electrodes. The mind control doctors saw their patients as biological machines, a view which made them sub-human, and therefore easier to abuse in mind control experiments. BB 88-91

Dr. Robert G. Heath, [66][67][68] Chairman of the Department of Psychiatry and Neurology at Tulane University, placed brain electrodes in a young homosexual man and fitted him with a box. A button on the box could be used to electrically stimulate an electrode implanted in a pleasure center. During one three-hour period, the patient, referred to as B-19, stimulated himself 1,500 times. "During these sessions, B-19 stimulated himself to a point that he was experiencing an almost overwhelming euphoria and elation, and had to be disconnected, despite his vigorous protests." [69] BB 94

Dr. John Lilly describes the technique of electrode implantation. "Electrodes could be implanted in the brain without using anesthesia. Short lengths of hypodermic needle tubing equal in length to the thickness of the skull were quickly pounded through the scalp into the skull. These stainless steel guides furnished passageways for the insertion of electrodes into the brain to any desired distance and at any desired location. Because of the small size of the sleeve guides, the scalp quickly recovered from the small hole made in it, and the sleeve guide remained imbedded in the bone for months to years. At any time he desired, the investigator could palpate [rub] the scalp and find the location of each of the sleeve guides. Once one was found, he inserted a needle down through the bone. After withdrawing the needle, the investigator placed a small sharp electrode in the track made by the needle and pressed the electrode through the skull and down into the substance of the brain to any desired depth." [70] NB 62 For more, click here and here.

Non-Lethal Weapons

Non-lethal weapons is a broad category which includes devices for beaming various kinds of energy at human targets in order to temporarily incapacitate them, or to control or affect their behavior. Non-lethal weapons research has been conducted at universities on contract to the CIA, and has overlapped with research on hallucinogens and brain electrode implants. BB 103

In 1991, Janet Morris, one of the main proponents of non-lethal weapons, issued a number of papers. [71] According one paper, US Special Operations Command already had a portable microwave weapon. "US Special Forces can cook internal organs." [72] Another concept was 'Infrasound' using acoustic beams. Laboratories were developing a high power, very low frequency acoustic beam weapon projecting non-penetrating acoustic bullets. Already, some governments have used infrasound as a means of crowd control. Very low frequency (VLF) sound, or low frequency RF modulations can cause nausea, vomiting and abdominal pains. "Some very low frequency sound generators can cause the disruption of human organs and, at high power levels, can crumble masonry." [73] MC 176-179

Funding of these experiments began in MKULTRA. Subproject 62 documents "certain kinds of radio frequency energy have been found to effect reversible neurological changes in chimpanzees." [74] Subproject 54 was studying how to produce concussions from a distance using mechanical blast waves propagated through the air. Such a concussion "is always followed by amnesia for the actual moment of the accident." It also states: "The blast duration would be in the order of a tenth of a second. Masking of a noise of this duration should not be difficult. It would be advantageous to establish the effectiveness of both of the above methods as a tool in brain-wash therapy." BB 103-105

A confidential report prepared by the US Army as early as 1969 detailed the effect an infra-sonic system would have on humans. These effects range from disruption of nervous systems to death. [75] MC 199, 200

That such weapons have been used can be in little doubt. When the deployment of Cruise missiles at American bases in the UK was at its height, women peace campaigners staged a series of highly publicized peaceful protests outside the perimeter wires. In late 1985, the women in the peace camps at Greenham Common began to experience unusual patterns of illness, ranging from severe headaches, drowsiness, menstrual bleeding at abnormal times or after the onset of menopause, to bouts of temporary paralysis and faulty speech coordination. Electronics Today [76] magazine carried out a number of measurements, and in December 1985 published their report which concluded: "Readings taken with a wide range of signal strength meters showed marked increases in the background signal level near one of the women's camps at a time when they claimed to be experiencing ill effects." They noted that if the women created noise or a disturbance near the fence, the signals rose sharply. MC 201

The evidence in hand suggests that the technology to produce 'voices in the head' does exist. The Department of Defense has already acquired the technology to alter consciousness through various projects and programs. A patent discusses methods and system for altering consciousness. The abstract from one such program states: "Researchers have devised a variety of systems for stimulating the brain to exhibit specific brain wave rhythms and thereby alter the state of consciousness of the individual subject." [77] Silent subliminal messages [were] "used throughout Operation Desert Storm (Iraq) quite successfully." [78] MC 203, 204

A US State Department report suggested it was possible to induce a heart attack in a person from a distance with radar. [79] MC 172

By 1974, Stanford Research Institute had developed a computer system capable of reading a person's mind by correlating the brain waves of subjects on an electroencephalograph with specific commands. [80] The concept of mind-reading computers is no longer science fiction. Neither is their use by Big Brotherly governments. Major Edward Dames of Psi-Tech said in April 1995 on NBC's The Other Side program: "The US government has an electronic device which could

MATRIX OF THE MIND

implant thoughts in people." Dames would not comment any further. MC 172

The latest development in the technology of induced fear and mind control is the cloning of the human EEG or brain waves of any targeted victim, or indeed groups. With the use of powerful computers, segments of human emotions which include anger, anxiety, sadness, fear, embarrassment, jealousy, resentment, shame, and terror, have been identified and isolated within the EEG signals as 'emotion signature clusters.' Their relevant frequencies and amplitudes have been measured. Then the very frequency/amplitude cluster is synthesized and stored on another computer. Each one of these negative emotions is separately tagged. They are then placed on the Silent Sound carrier frequencies and could silently trigger the occurrence of the same basic emotion in another human being. MC 205

The entire non-lethal weapon concept is literally a Pandora's Box of unknown consequences.

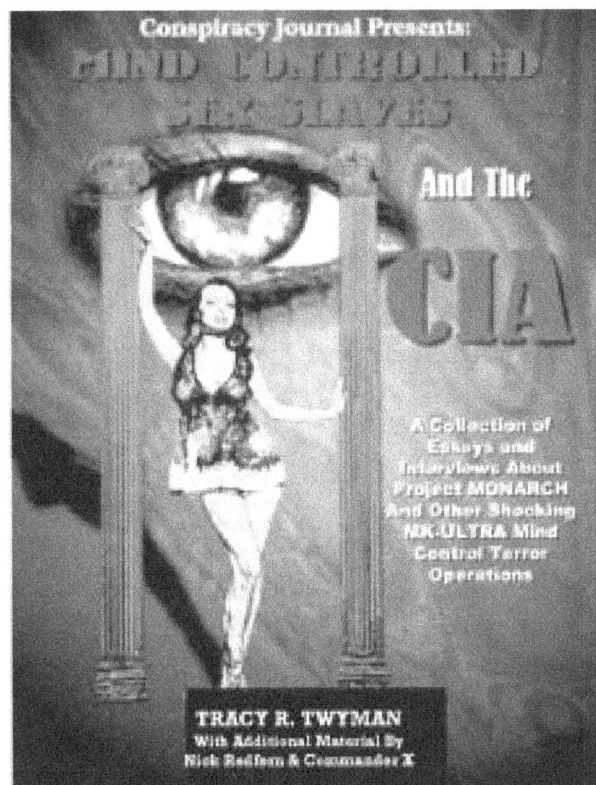

MIND CONTROL SEX SLAVES and the C. I. A.

PROJECT MONARCH— "In the months preceding Sept. 11, 2001, the airwaves of cable news channels were filled with the saga of Congressman Gary Condit, and the cover-up of his affair with intern Chandra Levy. Levy disappeared on April 30, 2001 — Walpurgisnacht — the most sacred witch holiday on the calendar. Condit's not very forthcoming statements on the matter, coupled with the fact that Chandra appeared to be on her way to visit him on the night she disappeared, led to speculation that he was somehow involved with her kidnapping and/or death.

This speculation reached a fevered pitch when bizarre details of Condit's sex life began to mount. 27 other women came forth claiming to have had sexual relations with the Congressman, including two woman (15 at the time), who claimed that he had volently raped them while still a State Assemblyman. Condit was described by one attorney involved in the case as "a serial predator of woman." One of the women, who met the leather-clad Condit at a biker convention, revealed that the Senator referred to his many ladies as his 'Sex Slaves.' She also said that he insisted on using code names with these women while talking on the phone, and refused to wear condoms, starting that "there's a cure for AIDS, anyway."

Following the Clinton-Lewinski sex scandal, and then the Condit-Levy affair, many people began to wonder why so many men in positions of power require lots of sex with a variety of people. And where do such men get this sense of entitlement, this attitude that they should be continually provided with a harem of sexual servants, often maintained at taxpayers' expense? Few, if any journalists brought up the amazing similarity between the story of Gary Condit's Sex Slaves and the stories of dozens of men and women who claim to have been forced into sexual slavery for the wealthy and powerful by none other than our own Central Intelligence Agency, through a program known as *Project MONARCH*."

UNIMAGINABLE RAPE, TORTURE AND BLOODY RITUALS. . . LEADING POLITICIANS INVOLVED IN CHILD ABUSE RINGS. . . U.S. PRESIDENTS AND VICE PRESIDENTS COMPLICIT. . . USE OF OCCULT AND 'SATANISM' AS TRAUMA BASE . . . ANTI-CHRISTIAN SERVICES AT CHRISTIAN CHURCHES.

Plus Exposing The Mind Controlled *"Stepford Whores,"* as well as Human Sacrifices at Bohemian Grove Retreat. But, what do Satanism, human trafficking, mind control experiments and child sex abuse have to do with the U.S. government? According to the testimony of experts and survivors, the CIA utilized all of these elements and more for their Top Secret Project Monarch, part of the MK-ULTRA mind control program. Dozens if not hundreds of people, many of them children, were allegedly subjected to unimaginable rape, torture, and bloody satanic rituals, with the aim of fracturing the human mind through trauma. This created multiple personalities that could then be programmed to perform specific tasks, including murder.

254

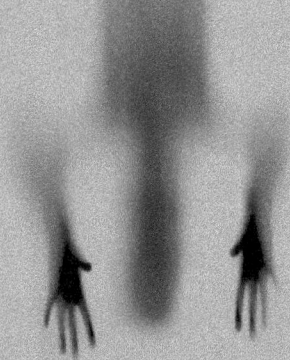

www.ingramcontent.com/pod-product-compliance
Lightning Source LLC
Chambersburg PA
CBHW081413270326
41931CB00015B/3263